College
Confidence
with ADD

College Confidence with ADD

The Ultimate Success Manual for ADD Students, from Applying to Academics, Preparation to Social Success, and Everything Else You Need to Know

MICHAEL SANDLER

SOURCEBOOKS, INC.®
NAPERVILLE, ILLINOIS

Published by Sourcebooks, Inc.
P.O. Box 4410, Naperville, Illinois 60567-4410
(630) 961-3900
Fax: (630) 961-2168
www.sourcebooks.com

Library of Congress Cataloging-in-Publication Data

Sandler, Michael.
  Conquering college with ADD / by Michael Sandler.
     p. cm.
  1. Attention-deficit disorder in adolescence. 2. Attention-deficit-disordered youth—Education (Higher) I. Title.

RJ506.H9S266 2007
618.92'8589—dc22
                    2007014397

Printed and bound in Canada.
TR 10 9 8 7 6 5 4 3 2 1

Dedication

There's a Japanese expression that says success takes more than talent, it also takes important encounters with people.

I know without such people in my life, I'd never have made it this far. No man is an island, especially me, and this project wouldn't have existed without so many people's incredible help and support. To each and every one of you, thank you. I dedicate this book to you.

In particular, I wish to dedicate this book to a few special people and their families and loved ones who've helped make this dream a reality.

Without Shinko Sakai and her entire family's support, love, encouragement and guidance, I'd have fallen just short of the goal. You've kept me going, and cheered me on.

The courage and lessons I learned from my Japanese running friends, who've given their all for country, company, family, and friends, have taught me that everything, no matter how difficult, happens for a reason, and to have patience, let go of the outcome, and accept life's twists, turns, and challenges for what they are: beautiful gifts.

To my sister, Elisa Share, whose voice has been my rope of hope and wisdom in trying times.

To Craig Harrison, without whose help I would never have made it cycling across the country.

To Nicki Cutean and the entire clan, without whose support and persistence I may have given up my creative endeavors or missed the mark in teaching this to others.

To Beverly Rohman (www.learningconnections.net), who helped start me down this helping path and who's stuck by me through many trying times. And Not-So-Crazy Bob, who doesn't think he has his act together, but teaches me so much, each and every day.

To Jack Burden, a friend, mentor, and guide; far wiser than an owl at the ever-younger age of eighty-six.

To Tom Masterson, who quietly lives by example, marathon-running mountains around the world, dancing to nature's tune with a constant smile, in his ever-younger seventies.

To Jonathan and Renee Knop (both of you, keep on healing!) for your courage, inspiration, guidance, and audiobook magic (see www.thecreativehealinginstitute.com)!

To my parents, without whose love, wisdom, insight, and unwavering support, I'd never have been diagnosed, gotten the help I needed, gone to college, or had this book published.

And to the memory of Kerri Korenko, whose trials and experiences taught me so much of what I now teach to others. You will be missed, but never forgotten, and your lessons will carry on.

And last, to my two guardian angels, confidants, and incredible four-legged companions Pumpkin and Sawa. You are my teachers, my guides, my support, and so much more. Without your unconditional love and unwavering joy for life, I probably wouldn't even be here, let alone writing this book.

To everyone, to the universe, to love, life, and nature itself, thank you and *arigatou*!

Contents

Acknowledgments

Rereading this book just weeks before it prints, I must admit I'm dumbfounded. I keep asking myself, "Who wrote this book?" Or, "How did 'I' write such a thing?" I put "I" in quotation marks because I'm not the person I was when I started this book five and a half years ago. I mean, I'm still me, but I'm not.

You see, the Michael Sandler who started this book died a year and a half ago. He hit the pavement while trying to avoid a toddler and his father when they inadvertently stepped out onto the bike path in front of him. I had an instant to decide to throw myself down rather than hit the little boy. In that moment, who I was ceased to be.

I am very thankful for that accident, and for all of the struggles and challenges to follow. And I'm incredibly thankful that the "new" me, the one who woke up to find someone else's blood being pumped into his veins, had the opportunity to rewrite much of this book.

You see, the book was originally a how-to guide for being the best square peg in a round hole. But when I came to, I realized that wouldn't do. I could no longer help students just fit in or get by. Life's too precious, too short, and we have far too much to offer. While good grades are great, I want to help students discover their inner talents, joy, and passion, so they may love, laugh, and achieve their dreams while living life to the fullest. I wanted to help them build castles in the sky.

I was fortunate enough to be given a second chance, both at life and with this book. Over the year and a half that followed, with the incredible patience and diligence of the great folks at Sourcebooks—and in particular Peter Lynch and Erin Nevius—I edited and rewrote the majority of this book. Even the title changed.

What you see is as much a part of their hearts and souls as it is mine.

And while I typed the words, I now know they came from some-place special. Whether you call it God, Nature, Source, the Universe, Spaciousness, or simply a "quiet mind," I know that while the words flowed through me, they didn't come from me. This energy is where

I give my true thanks, for this book, this world, and each moment of my existence.

I am thankful for everything, even, or especially, the frustration and delays experienced in finishing this book. While I was lying on the pavement, wiggling my fingers and toes, looking up at the uninjured boy and then at the sun, I began to smile. In that moment I knew everything in life happens for a reason. Without the delays, the new me could never have rewritten this book or had insight into the right layout and design.

For years I've talked about discovering creativity and inner passion. But not until I was crutching out into nature to heal and photographing the incredible beauty around me (see www.natureshealingspirit.com) did I truly begin to practice what I preach. Nor did I understand how we must each dance our own dance. Told I may never walk or run again, I stripped off my shoes and went barefoot to heal. Now I'm inexplicably running barefoot ten to twenty miles a day, always in awe and communing with nature; pen and camera at the ready. And I certainly hadn't discovered my "quiet mind" until I slowed down to see nature's beauty rewiring my brain, and began meditating my way back to total health.

Truly, everything in life happens for a reason.

With ADD it's so easy to lose one's self-confidence, esteem, and direction, and just give up. Now I know why there aren't more ADD books out there, despite the number of incredibly creative and talented individuals who could be writing them. It's a nightmare to organize, follow through, and hang in there. I want to thank so many wonderful souls who've helped me hang in there these five and a half years.

I especially want to thank those who stayed by my side after the accident. I cannot thank you enough for your warmth, kindness, energy, and guidance during these creative yet challenging times. And to those in the medical field who put me together again, I hope to pass along your courage and positive energy by doing my best to help others. I can't think of a better way to say thanks than by giving it all away.

Specific thanks to:

Dr. Ted Weston, Jr.; Ashley Klein; the entire Pauline Jensen SET clan (Sine, Liz, and Tasha); Dr. Wertz; Laurie Gille; Roger Boyd; Jodi; and everyone at Boulder Creek Apartments—you guys are the greatest! To Pablo Luna—thanks for keeping me rolling!

To Adolf and the entire Zoch family, Jennifer Zung, Rachael Osofsky, Naren Tayal (find your passion!), Linda Norman, Kenneth Mills, Xiang Zhou, Diane Saye (your son Oran lives on through your work), Donna Weaver, Trish Budd, and everyone with the IDL (www.gifteddifferentlearners.org) and the Howard County Maryland School System.

To everyone at ADDA (www.ADD.org), and especially Susan Caughman, Eve Gillman, and Rochelle Green; and everyone at *ADDitude* magazine.

To Rosemary and everyone at the Resources for Disabled Students Office at CSU; to Nick Skally and Rollerblade; and to Kris Brandriff at Smartwheels (www.smartwheelsinline.com). To Vladimir Ostromensky, Peter Doucet, Raina Denmark, Jody Goodwine, and everyone at the ADD support group in Greeley, Colorado (thanks for the inspiration!).

To Rabbi Zvi and everyone at Har Shalom. To Pam and Elijah Castillon (hang in there!) and everyone at Timberline. To Mike Reynolds (you can do it!).

To Professor John Hoxmeier, Professor Ann Gilley, Dr. Sanjay Ramchander, Dr. Cap Smith, Dr. Susan Athey, Dr. Daniel Turk, Dr. Charles Butler, Dr. John Plotnicki, Associate Professor Naomi Lederer, Dr. Alex Zedginidze, and Dr. Yung-Hai Chen.

To Devon Schiller, Aliya Sternstein, Yuka Sugiura, Andrew Lyman, Venkat Raj, and Renee Galvin. To Yoko, Lina, and Ken Takahashi for Nihongo assistance and support.

To Regina Cruz (never stop dancing!), Jessica McStravick (keep believing in yourself!), Joe, Rod, Pai-Lee, and everyone at the Boulder Rec. Centers.

Thanks to Dojna Shearer for her polishing at copyedit, Scott Miller for his beautiful design, and Christiaan Simmons for his hard work promoting the book.

And to anyone and everyone else I've missed but who's been in my life. You have been my teachers, my mentors, and my friends. I cannot thank you enough.

Honto-Ni Arigatou. Thank you.

With love and blessings always and forever more,
Michael

1

Introduction

"**Knowledge** of any kind…**brings about** a change **in awareness** from where it is **possible to** create **new realities**."

—**Deepak Chopra**

Congratulations on embarking down the road to college success. Whether you're already in school or just planning ahead, this can be one of the most exciting times of your life. Of course, it can also be a daunting challenge, which is why I developed this book.

Attention Deficit Disorder (ADD) is not well understood by the general population—it's not visible. It's a hidden challenge, which in some ways makes it more difficult to cope with in society than a visible one.

If someone's missing a leg, we immediately understand the problem and offer assistance and accommodations. If someone's missing the ability to focus, manage time, organize complex tasks, control impulsivity, or fit into a standardized learning program, we tend to tell him to shape up or ship out. Hype, popular culture, the media, and drug companies have all been accused of exaggerating both the severity of ADD and the number of people who suffer from it, but what we don't do is help people with this challenge.

Did you know that studies show an estimated 10 percent of all Americans have ADD? If you're in a classroom, that means two to three of your classmates are likely to have ADD as well. If you're a child with ADD, you have only a 5 percent chance of graduating from college (that is, if you don't have the tools you'll find in this book).

Sadly, ADD sufferers who become successful are rare birds. But like the founder of Kinko's or the CEO of Jet Blue, we credit our success to our ADD creativity and inability to follow the crowd. The same challenges that hinder us, when overcome, can be the very things that carry us to greatness. While they'll always be challenges, we can learn to make them work for us, not against us.

As someone with ADD, you have tremendous gifts and talents just waiting to be discovered. The trick is, we think differently than other people do...and that's a good thing. Would you want to trade in your sense of humor, creativity, or way of thinking just to be like everyone else? Who wants to be conventional?

Your gifts can be a huge benefit once you understand how to work with your ADD mind. Consider this book a how-to guide to using your ADD brilliance, or the owner's manual for your ADD mind. Throughout this book you'll find tips, strategies, secrets, and warnings that can help you overcome your challenges and bring out the talents we all have waiting inside of us. You'll begin to understand why you've had challenges; how, when, and where you work best (and why); and how to use your mind to potentially achieve at a level far beyond many non-ADDers.

Understanding ADD and its challenges is half the battle; once you master the second half, using your ADD to your advantage, success beyond your wildest dreams will come within your reach.

 One of my biggest challenges as an author with ADD was determining what to include in this book and where. Of course, my first inclination was to include everything under the sun. And of course, I wanted it all up front, because it's all important! Organization was never my strong suit, nor was prioritization. The final solution was a compromise...include as much as possible, and organize what I can chronologically.

I've often said that now is the best time in history to have ADD. Sure, there are challenges with the press— the perpetuation of ADD myths and stereotypes and the medication issues and debates— there really has never been a better time to have ADD. Why? One word: technology.

 Technology means we can finally harness the energy and speed of our ADD minds that have kept us stuck in the slow lanes even though we want to go fast. Think of us as astronauts without a spaceship. We look slow on the ground in our cumbersome space suits, but given the means to fly, the tools to use our supersonic brains, we can blast off.

Technology can help us free our minds to overcome challenges and utilize our full potential. Because of this, I've included Tech Tips throughout the book. If you read nothing else, check out these tips. They provide proven techniques to help you overcome significant hurdles throughout school, both in and out of the classroom, and will likely be a major factor in your lifelong success and happiness. They have been in mine!

Proficiency in using technology is essential for surviving college today and can help us achieve greatness later in life. If you're not in school yet, you may want to skim the book for the tech sections to see the tools available and to budget and plan for purchases before you arrive. They shouldn't be viewed as toys; devices such as PDAs and laptops can be essential to our survival, and cell phones and instant messengers can be the lifelines we need to survive away from home and our support network.

• • •

When I was first diagnosed with ADD, I had teachers tell my parents I was the worst student they'd ever had in their lives. I struggled in higher education, banging my head against the wall—literally and figuratively—out of frustration. I was bored, overwhelmed, dazed, and confused.

But then I researched everything I could about ADD and started implementing the ideas I discovered into my life and studies. I went from abysmally bombing quizzes and tests to getting A's. I went from crying in the middle of the night over not being able to keep up with my studies to having the time to work out, train, make friends…in short, the time to have a life. I successfully graduated and started helping others with ADD to do the same. I taught them the exact same tips and strategies that you'll be getting in this book, and armed with this information, they tapped into their gifts and found success.

And while they had my direct coaching available, you have even greater resources right at your fingertips. For almost any problem you face, you'll find a solution in this book. No matter the time of day or night, no matter the problem, it's here to help you through, get you on track, bring out your best, and help you succeed.

I know you can do it. Just the fact that you're reading this book speaks volumes about your commitment to overcoming your challenges and succeeding with ADD. Whether you're a struggling senior or have yet to apply to college, this book can turn things around and help you use your college experience to springboard you into a life filled with successes beyond your greatest expectations.

I wish you peace, happiness, and all green lights on your path to success through college and throughout life. And I'll be there with you, through this book, as we journey together toward your dreams. You are never alone in this; others have been through similar circumstances, surviving and thriving after overcoming these challenges. And remember: Sometimes laughter and a sense of humor are the most important things in getting us through the darkest of nights.

> "Creation is the greatest drug. When you create something, you get this little endorphin buzz. Why do you think Einstein looked like that?"
> —Robin Williams

Succeeding with ADD

> "**When a** defining moment **comes along,** you can do one **of two things.** Define **the moment, or let** the moment **define you**."
>
> —**Tin Cup**

I'm sure you've heard the expression "it's often darkest before the dawn." Perhaps nowhere is this truer than with us ADDers. Despite tremendous gifts, we often struggle in the shadows, fighting our own inner demons, people who don't believe in ADD, and a mind that's constantly shifting gears, tripping over itself, and getting stuck.

But there is hope. The great news is that we can get unstuck, overcome our challenges, and turn obstacles into our greatest teachers. We just can't allow ourselves to quit or stop pushing ahead, no matter what.

Inspiration: Think You Can't?

Thomas Edison was told he was unteachable; he was kicked out of three schools before being home schooled. His last headmaster said he'd never make it, that he was a screw up. But Edison never gave up. With his creative mind he devised and patented over ten thousand inventions, including the light bulb, the phonograph, and film.

Albert Einstein struggled in high school math. He wasn't a linear thinker and couldn't go from point A to point B the way his teachers wanted. Good thing he didn't, or we wouldn't have his incredible, far-reaching, and creative theory of relativity that's shaped modern physics. Do you like Disney World or Mickey Mouse? An editor once fired **Walt Disney** for a lack of good ideas.

Do you enjoy great novels? Russian author **Leo Tolstoy** flunked out of college!

Werner Von Braun, a visionary pioneer in rocket science, failed ninth grade algebra.

Winston Churchill, celebrated for pulling the United Kingdom through its darkest days during World War II and being instrumental in the Allied success, failed the eighth grade.

Ever struggled in chemistry? So did **Louis Pasteur**, a brilliant chemist and the creator of the pasteurization process. And apparently Einstein wasn't the only challenged physicist—**Sir Isaac Newton**, who discovered the laws of gravity, also struggled badly in grade school.

The next time you go to a department store, look around you at the clerks. There was once a twenty-one-year-old who wasn't allowed to talk to the customers because his bosses thought he lacked common sense. His name was **F. W. Woolworth**, and he went on to found Woolworth's, the basis for all modern department stores.

I was originally diagnosed with ADD in the second grade. We moved to a new town, with a school system that didn't dismiss ADD, and I was put on Ritalin and went from a straight F to a straight A student.

However, I still had major troubles with organization, time management, social skills, and impulsivity. Despite this, I muddled along until I was twelve. At that time my doctors, unsure of Ritalin's affect on boys in puberty (studies have since shown it to be one of the safest and most researched medicines on the market, but at that time this was still unproven), took me off Ritalin to be on the safe side.

I struggled through two junior highs and then two high schools, always trying to fit in and find a place for me and my ADD brain in the world. Over time I found I was good at drama and bicycling, both of which gave me confidence and greater self-esteem. Later on in high school I discovered a talent for writing and helped found and edit a new school newspaper. These successes were the body armor I needed to overcome the barrage of negativity from those around me, people who were certain I would never succeed.

After graduation I went to The Colorado College in Colorado Springs. This was great for me, because they were on the "block plan," which meant I only took one class at a time. Despite taking classes, my real major was bicycle racing. It calmed me down and helped me focus, and I dreamed of participating in the Tour de France. Unfortunately, it meant I didn't take my studies seriously. I earned a degree in political science not because I wanted to go into law or politics, but because it was easy enough to allow me to put my energies into biking.

After college I moved to Europe to chase my dream of becoming a Tour de France cyclist, but instead I was hit by a car while racing in the French Alps. After the three years I'd spent in Europe, my body was too injured to continue and I moved back to the States. At first I wallowed in feelings of failure and mediocrity, but eventually I found a job I enjoyed and became heavily involved in the business. My ADD gifts meant I was very creative, energetic, good with people, and able to see the "big picture," and I worked my way up the corporate ladder to become a high-level executive.

While I was great at ideas, I had immense difficulty with follow-through. And though I was highly productive and great at multi tasking, my poor sense of prioritizing meant I was always behind. My desk had a mountain of papers on it, and I had no idea how to sift through them. I also had trouble reading the social cues of my coworkers and employees.

In most people's eyes I was very successful, but I felt constantly on edge, as if failure (a piano-of-doom falling from the sky), or maybe a lynch mob, was right around the corner. I was constantly juggling too much and jumping from crisis to crisis, leaving myself with the sharp, nagging anxiety that things were about to plunge out of control.

Losing Focus

This unsettling, nagging feeling tore into my gut until I left my job, income, and semi-stability behind to chase my dreams and start my own company. I had a great idea and thought it'd be a tremendous success—and it might have been, had I followed through on it.

Without the stability of routine or accountability to anyone else, however, I couldn't get focused or remain on task. Without instantaneous success, riches, and accolades, I quickly tired of the new idea, switched gears, and started a second company, followed rapidly by a third. I was now flailing, bouncing from idea to idea without the foundation or direction I needed to stay on track and patiently wait to turn a profit.

Then I really jumped off the deep end. Having completed exactly one triathlon, I impulsively decided to leave business altogether and become a professional triathlete. I spent thousands of dollars to pack up all my belongings, put my house up for sale, and drive a U-Haul almost two thousand miles out to California. There with my two dogs, I lived out of my car, unable to rent even the most rundown of shacks with my spotty credit. Homeless, unemployed, without local friends, a support network, or savings, I finally saw I had made a terrible mistake. Frustrated and disheartened, after two weeks I came crying back to Colorado. I knew I had to stop bouncing from idea to idea.

After quite a bit of brainstorming and soul searching, I felt more education would help ground me and get my life back on track. Due to my love of business and people, I decided to pursue an MBA. In typical ADD style, I hyperfocused for two weeks to cram for the GMAT, barely sleeping and rooted to my computer. Though highly suspect and terrible on the body, my unorthodox study method worked. I scored well on the test and was accepted into Colorado State University's MBA program.

Going to school was a great idea, but what I did next was not. I was also interested in technology and computers, so I thought I'd pursue a computer degree after getting my MBA. However, a director at the school half-jokingly suggested that, instead of getting one degree and then the other, why didn't I get both at the same time? As a typical ADDer, I thought this was a great idea—if a little is good, then more is better! So I enrolled in both the accelerated MBA and computer information systems programs simultaneously.

When school started, I found out the hard way how ADD affected me as an adult student. School was completely overwhelming, and in particular, seven graduate-level classes at the same time was insane. I had been out of school for ten years, and had never even taken more than one class at a time! I didn't remember how to study, write papers, or concentrate in class. I couldn't keep track of what was due when, I was completely overwhelmed by the workload, and I would freeze up during my tests.

It was a miracle I survived my first two semesters. Everything was a struggle; I'd study until four in the morning, collapse, and then have to return to school at eight. In the midst of sleep-deprived tears and angst, I swung back and forth between thinking I'd flunk out of the programs and wanting to quit them. But I kept going and pushed through the nightmare, convinced it'd be beneficial in the long run. After the first year, however, I had had enough. I didn't want to quit, but I knew I had to do something. The second year was supposed to be much tougher than the first, and I had barely survived that.

I decided it was time to look into the symptoms and treatment of adult ADD. Until then I'd been trained and taught that "adult ADD" was just an excuse and not a reality. Psychiatric professionals who didn't believe in ADD had also pretty nearly convinced me that my problem was something else, and not as severe as I knew it to be. But what else could account for trying harder only to fall further behind, or knowing what to do but being unable to actually do it?

While I knew I was overextended, that didn't explain my freezing up, feelings of anxiety, poor juggling skills, disorganization, and lack of concentration. I had myself tested at the school for adult ADD, and the diagnosis was confirmed. I was prescribed Adderall, which helped me calm down, focus, and begin my ADD journey of self-exploration.

Rebuilding My Life

The medication worked like glasses—it helped me see things, like how much trou- ble I was in and the problems I was facing. I sought additional help for my ADD, trying to understand how it affected me and how to work with it effectively. I started reading everything: books, articles, research papers, anything I could get my hands on. Then I started to reevaluate every piece of my life as it related to ADD. I looked at where I placed my shoes in the morning, how and what I ate, when I slept, where, when, and how I studied…in short, everything.

I then rebuilt my life around ADD. In essence I had to write a new owner's manual for my brain. I had achieved success in many areas of my life in the past, so I looked at these areas to see how I had become successful and what techniques I had used. Then I applied these to my current experiences, both in and out of the classroom. It worked, and in the fall I went from struggling in class to achieving high marks. At the same time, I started racing bicycles again and won a cycling state championship. I owe all of these successes to rebuilding my life with an understanding of ADD.

Although I graduated with two master's degrees, the most important knowledge I gained wasn't the degrees themselves but the process of learning how to achieve at a high level with ADD. Now I write, coach, and speak on my experiences and what I gained from them to help others struggling with ADD, to aid them in succeeding without first having to bang their heads against the wall or make the kinds of mistakes I made.

Inspiration: Do You Recognize This Man?

- He failed as a business-man—as a storekeeper.
- He failed as a farmer—he despised this work.
- He failed in his first attempt to attain political office.
- After being elected to the legislature, he failed when he sought the office of Speaker.
- He failed in his first attempt to get elected to Congress.
- He failed when he sought the appointment to the United States Land Office.
- He failed when he ran for the United States Senate.
- He failed when friends sought for him the nomination for the vice presidency in 1856.
- In his entire life, this man only attended school for twelve months.
- He failed more times than many of us will even try.
- Yet he helped change the world and emancipated a population.

His name? **Abraham Lincoln**, freer of the slaves and arguably one of the best presidents to ever have served this country.

Source: www.nps.gov/pub_aff/pres/trivia.htm

You Are Not Alone

With ADD we often feel alone, isolated, and broken, as if something is wrong with us. With everything we've been through and heard and been told, we think we have moral failings or are stupid, defective, or just missing something that everyone else has. But there's nothing wrong with us, and we certainly didn't miss anything. On the contrary, we caught too much, concentrating on everything at once rather than the specific things we're supposed to. It earns us terrible, misinformed labels, and puts an amazing amount of negativity into our already skewed sense of self. We come to believe that we are lazy, crazy, or stupid after all.

The reality is that we all have potential greatness inside and can achieve beyond our wildest dreams. Success is about finding your gifts, aligning them with your passions, being creative, and letting yourself fly. With this book and others, we now have the advantage of knowing what we're up against and being certain of the special gifts inside each and every one of us. Our only limitation? Being too "realistic," not daring to dream high enough! We're the dream makers and achievers; therefore we must aim high.

What Can We Learn from This?

The lesson here is that you, like those mentioned above, can succeed far beyond your expectations. It doesn't matter that you think differently; creative minds always do. That's our biggest advantage! You are not what people say you are. You are a creator, a visionary, an inventor, a future leader, a living work of art who has the potential for tons of success. Look at the list of people below and envision yourself among them. You are capable of great things once you learn how to tap into your gifts.

Famous People Suspected of Displaying ADD Traits

- **ABRAHAM LINCOLN**
- Agatha Christie
- Albert Einstein
- Alexander Graham Bell
- Andrew Carnegie
- Anne Bancroft
- Ansel Adams
- Auguste Rodin
- **BABE RUTH**
- Beethoven
- Benjamin Franklin
- **BILL COSBY**
- Cher
- Danny Glover
- Dustin Hoffman
- Dwight D. Eisenhower
- Edgar Allan Poe
- Eleanor Roosevelt

- **ERNEST HEMINGWAY**
- F. Scott Fitzgerald
- Frank Lloyd Wright
- Carl Lewis
- Galileo Galilei
- George Frideric Handel
- George Bernard Shaw
- **GEORGE BURNS**
- Greg Louganis
- Hans Christian Anderson
- Harry Anderson
- Harry Belafonte
- Henry David Thoreau
- Henry Ford
- Henry Winkler
- Jimmy Stewart
- Jason Kidd
- **JIM CARREY**
- John D. Rockefeller
- John Denver
- **JOHN F. KENNEDY**
- John Lennon
- Jules Verne
- Kirk Douglas
- **LANCE ARMSTRONG**
- Leo Tolstoy
- Leonardo da Vinci
- Lewis Carroll
- Louis Pasteur
- Magic Johnson
- Malcolm Forbes
- Mariel Hemingway

- Meriwether Lewis
- **MICHAEL JORDAN**
- Muhammad Anwar el-Sadat
- Napoleon Bonaparte
- Nelson Rockefeller
- Nolan Ryan
- Nostradamus
- Orville Wright
- Ozzy Osbourne
- Pablo Picasso
- Pete Rose
- Prince Charles
- **ROBERT F. KENNEDY**
- Robin Williams
- Salvador Dali
- Sir Issac Newton
- Socrates
- Steven Spielberg
- **STEVIE WONDER**
- Sylvester Stallone
- Terry Bradshaw
- Thomas Edison
- Vincent van Gogh
- Walt Disney
- Whoopi Goldberg
- Wilbur Wright
- Will Smith
- William Butler Yeats
- **WINSTON CHURCHILL**
- Wolfgang Amadeus Mozart
- Woodrow Wilson

Inspiration: Remember This!

- Your creative mind is your ticket to greatness.
- Don't listen to the negativity.
- Don't believe what you know isn't true.
- You have a gift.
- Believe in yourself.
- Use the talent that lies within you.
- And no matter what, don't ever give up!!

"Anything is possible. You can be told that you have a 90 percent chance or a 50 percent chance or a 1 percent chance, but you have to believe, and you have to fight."

—Lance Armstrong

Succeeding with ADD

3

Understanding ADD

> "Not until we are **lost** do we begin to **understand ourselves**."
>
> —**Henry David Thoreau**

Chances are, if you're reading this chapter, you want to know more about ADD to see if:

- You have ADD.
- Your ADD is like everyone else's.
- You really are lazy, crazy, and stupid.˙

There's a reasonable explanation for your challenges, struggles, and inconsistencies. Let me begin by telling you this: You're not lazy, crazy, or stupid, and you are not alone. Many other people are facing the same challenges you are. But no two cases of ADD are ever alike. Let's start by looking at the symptoms.

Symptoms of ADD

> "Although the world is full of suffering, it is full also of the overcoming of it."—**Helen Keller**

All of our symptoms vary widely, and even vary within ourselves depending on our mood, moment, environment, and place in life.

Picture this: You set up twenty radios in your living room, tune them each to a different station, and blare them all at once. Can you concentrate? Can you focus? Do you know what to follow and what to tune out? That's what the ADD mind is often like.

Picture this: You slept through your alarm, you're late for class, and you can't find your keys. You drop everything to hunt for your keys. Finally you find them. But now you can't find your backpack. How in the world do you lose an overstuffed backpack the size of a small couch? Finally, you find your backpack, but now where are your blasted keys?!?!

Picture this: You're in school, but you don't know why. You're studying biology because you thought medicine might be cool. But the more you get into it, the less you like it. You want to change, but you've already gone through three majors. Every idea you get seems cool at the time, but soon loses its appeal. You feel lost, drifting, like a lonely piece of wood bobbing up and down with the tide.

ADD is unique; it comes in all flavors, shapes, and sizes. Many people without ADD think everyone has the same symptoms: distractibility, lack of focus, poor time-management skills. But who doesn't fit that description at one point or another? It's the severity of these symptoms and how much they affect daily life that determines whether someone has ADD or not. ADD is a spectrum of symptoms and disorders, and when they affect your life, your work, your health, and your happiness, they goes from being character traits to being symptoms.

What Are Some Common ADD Difficulties in College?

1. We have a hard time sustaining attention.
2. We experience difficulty paying attention to detail: we might be able to focus on the big picture but not its components.
3. We lose things often, particularly keys, supplies, important papers, this book, etc.
4. We're easily distracted, or lose our train of thought. (What was this list about again??)
5. We forget to do things.
6. We have difficulties with short-term memory.
7. We react impulsively or impatiently (blurting out "Pick me! Pick me!" shouting out answers, or not waiting our turns).
8. We have very poor planning and time-management skills.
9. Try as we might, we tend to make what are called "careless errors," particularly on math and science exams.
10. We have trouble with multiple step operations. Once we get the component pieces we're fine, but getting there is often a big challenge.
11. We often feel overwhelmed. At times like this our brains lock down, and we can't even remember our names.
12. Our physical environment is often a manifestation of our jumbled minds: if our brains feel scrambled, that's typically what our rooms will look like, too.
13. Though we're sharp as tacks, we often make terrible decisions—we're just far too impulsive. We often don't think things through or look at the ramifications. We wait until the last minute to get things done. Since our minds need stimulation in order to accomplish anything, we often don't function well until deadlines are frightfully close.
14. We appear thoughtless and unconcerned, which is just an indication that we're stuck thinking about something else.

What Are the ADD-vantages to Having ADD in College?

1. We tend to be very intelligent—we just have to find a way to harness our intelligence!
2. We're very energetic.
3. We're fast thinkers and quick on our feet.
4. We're extremely creative.
5. We're very intuitive and empathetic to what is going on with other people (though we may not have a clue as to what's going on with ourselves!).
6. We're always trying to help others, which can be a great advantage.
7. The more interesting the topic (to us), the more stimulated our brains become, the more we're able to focus and even hyper-focus.
8. We're capable of getting a lot of specific work done in a very short period of time.
9. We're often amazing multitaskers. Since our brains must be stimulated in order to focus, we often find it easier to do many things at once rather than one thing at a time.
10. We're highly perceptive and intuitive, as if we're better plugged-in, or directly connected to the world around us.

ADD Challenges: Creative Chemistry

As an ADDer, I had my butt kicked by advanced chemistry. I could understand the concepts quite easily and could even derive equations in my head, but I couldn't keep one equation straight from another. I would take steps one and two from one equation, three and four from another, and five and six from yet another...Sure, this was fantastic creativity, but I found myself answering chemistry questions on acids and bases with a theory about a parallel universe or a new form of slime mold. This might be great for my future as an inventor, but it sure didn't go over well with my chemistry professors!

How Do You Use the Positives and Negatives?

I'm sure you can see many of the positive and negative traits in yourself. Don't sweat the negatives—that's what this book is for. Besides, there really are no negatives, just challenges, and we'll work on capitalizing on them together. They can be overcome with the tools and techniques presented in the following chapters. The great news is that once you learn how to use these challenges and the knowledge you gain from them and manage your ADD in college, you're likely to become a tremendous success. It really is a gift in disguise, one for which you'll be grateful in the long run!

ADD Advantage: Do What You Love

Many symptoms of ADD go away when we are doing what we love. Our minds open up, allowing us to bring out the best that's within us. We can focus, concentrate, and see many steps ahead. Our intuition kicks in and it's as if we're in "the zone" and can do no wrong. We're energized, motivated, enthused, and brilliant. Don't let anyone dissuade you from a class, major, or career that captivates you; a boring subject is always work for an ADDer, but a fun subject is a joy and a privilege. It's hard to attend a boring class, but we're eager (and often early) for one that's fun. And as the expression goes, if you do what you love, the money will follow.

"Obstacles don't have to stop you. If you run into a wall, don't turnaround and give up. Figure out how to climb it, go through it, or work around it."—**Michael Jordan**

Medication

"Just a spoonful of sugar helps the medicine go down."—**Mary Poppins**

Medication is one piece of the puzzle of techniques and aids that can help you succeed and achieve with ADD.

Medication has been shown to be effective 90 to 95 percent of the time, and stimulant medication is one of the most studied medications ever: studies (short- and long-term) go all the way back to the 1930s.

The right medication at the right dosage can be highly effective in helping us focus and concentrate, but it is certainly not a "cure." Meds do not answer many of the how-to questions addressed in this book, nor do they answer the emotional issues. Giving someone a prescription and considering her ADD solved falls far short of the answer and may do more harm than good.

The biggest benefit of medication is in implementation and follow-through. We ADDers often know the solutions but still can't get the job done. That's one of the defining characteristics of ADD. Meds help us overcome this mental barrier by making it easier to start a task and see it through to completion. They stimulate the neurotransmitter activity in the brain for us.

I believe that over time, with diligent patience and trial and error, you can completely overcome the challenges of ADD using diet, exercise, homeopathic products, and meditation. But without first being on medication, you have no way to even see the problems, let alone formulate a plan for fixing them. If you don't want to be on meds for life, get on meds now (you won't get "hooked"; the right med in the right dose is not addictive), see the world clearly, and then start looking for other solutions. Finding the solution while the world is out of focus is almost impossible. Finding it when you can see both the problems and the potential solutions is a lot more likely to happen.

Many Students Tell Me They Don't Want to Try Meds

We can't help seeing the negative publicity about medication in the media today, and often our friends or family members are against it. Even great doctors who lack ADD experience often shy away from prescribing medication. And many students want to prove they can do it on their own, that they don't need medication, or that they've outgrown their childhood ADD.

Believe me, I understand this sentiment! But your ADD mind doesn't suddenly change at age eighteen. Think of ADD meds as the simplest path across a busy campus: When you first arrive at school and don't know exactly where you're going, this path is your safest bet to get you to and from class. Since you want to get on track- quickly without undue stress, this path can be the key to your success.

Now, once you are more familiar with campus, you might decide to head out and explore other routes. Perhaps there's one that's better suited to your needs or that you're more comfortable with. Perhaps there isn't. But at least you'll already know how to get to class and how long it should take. This allows you to judge the effectiveness of other routes, and keeps you from going too far off track. If you ever get lost, you can always go back to what you know works.

Taking Meds: Why Some Students Don't Take Meds

When ADD students go to college they sometimes blow off meds, saying they don't have ADD, don't want to use it as an excuse, or don't want to "cheat" by using meds to give themselves an unfair advantage. But before you take yourself off of your medication, here's my suggestion. Meds help you to focus, concentrate, and see the problems.

Stay on meds early in your college career, or get on them if you've been struggling. Once you've put the other pieces, such as diet, exercise, routine, study habits, etc., in place, then look at what you can use to replace the meds (meditation, herbal remedies, brain wave training, biofeedback, neutriceuticals, etc.). Once you have the foundation in place it's much easier to keep on track without the meds, and the experience with medication lets you know whether or not the alternatives are effective.

Medication Myth Buster #1: Youth Today Are Being Tranquilized

Most ADD medications are stimulants, like caffeine. Stimulants raise the neurotransmitter activity in the brain, allowing us to focus, not tranquilizing us. Even if a non-ADDer took ADD meds, he would be overstimulated, not drugged up.

Medication Myth Buster #2: ADD Meds Are Gateway Drugs

ADD meds help us focus and concentrate; they do not get us high. In the correct doses they're not addictive, and studies have shown that they actually decrease the desire to use drugs or self-medicate.

Medication Myth Buster #3: Meds Give You an Unfair Advantage

Medications aren't IQ boosters in a bottle. They help us to concentrate in ways the rest of the world already can. All they're doing is leveling the playing field, helping our brains to focus as much as anyone else's.

Taking Meds: Meds as a Last Resort

One of my greatest sources of frustration is the number of people today who think medication should be used as a last resort. I think that's like saying insulin for diabetics should be a last resort. Sure, there are many, many other things you can try, but ADD medications have been proven safe time after time after time and are effective in 90 to 95 percent of ADDers. Meds should be a starting point for people coping with ADD, certainly not the last thing they try.

When Do You Try Meds?

Since I'm not a doctor and since ADD manifests itself quite differently from individual to individual, it's hard to say when you should take it. It should always be a personal choice and never something forced on you. In my personal and professional experience, however, I've found the time to explore meds is when you're banging your head against the wall, frustrated that you're not making progress, or you know what to do to change things but you can't find a way to get it done. Exploring meds is never a bad option, but in the above situations, it's perhaps your best option. If you're struggling and nothing else seems to be working, give it a try.

Should You Stop Taking Meds over the Summer or While on Break?

Ever heard of taking a "medication vacation"? That term drives me batty. Is that like taking a break from your prescription glasses or your insulin? Our minds are fantastic machines when we have our focus under control, and I for one never want this taken away from me.

I think the idea that a break from meds is a good thing can hurt students. If you need meds and work best on them, why take a vacation from clarity and risk messing things up? Personally, I know my brain. I know I'm confused, overwhelmed, and flooded with information when I'm not on meds. I also know that in all the bike racing I've done, all of my serious accidents have happened when I was not on meds. If you don't have an alternate plan for keeping your ADD under control, I highly suggest keeping up with your prescription.

Taking Meds: ADD and Self-Medication

We self-medicate in many ways. Often, we're caffeine or nicotine addicts—or both. Caffeine and nicotine are stimulants that calm us in the same way that Adderall and Ritalin do. We're prone to addiction, particularly if we're not on medication. Illegal drugs, however, are much stronger than prescription drugs; they are not always made under safe conditions and don't always contain what dealers claim they do. Furthermore, they produce not only a high but the addiction that accompanies it. This leads to needing more and more to get that same feeling, and soon enough, the addiction is out of control.

Can ADD Meds Be Abused?

Sure. As with almost anything else, ADD meds can be abused. You could likely grind, snort, inject, inhale, or otherwise modify and consume your meds in a way that would produce a high. But why not save them for their real purpose—getting you through life? If that isn't important to you, I suggest leaving the privilege of this aid for someone who appreciates it.

While abuse is not rampant (from what I hear, it takes so much of it to have an affect that you'd run out far too quickly, and as a controlled substance you can't just stroll in for a daily or weekly refill), if you abuse these meds it brings down the whole ADD community. It places that much more of a stigma on ADD and on medicating for it, and makes it much less likely that another student gets the help he or she needs. Not to mention that if you're reading this book, you're most likely trying to make college a better experience for yourself—not a more challenging one.

What Are the Side Effects?

No medication is 100 percent safe; there are always risks—just check out any prescription drug commercial on TV—but the side effects for most tried-and-true ADD medications are typically minimal. They include difficulty falling asleep (particularly until you're used to the medication), dry mouth, and a decreased appetite (diet pills traditionally contain stimulants). Another possible side effect (and I don't even know if docs would call it this) is "rebound" or an icky feeling you experience after the meds wear off. I've felt this one. If I don't time my meds right, don't have the right dose, or haven't eaten enough, and the meds wear off midday, I feel a bit like I'm spinning and unhappy. Nevertheless, the right med in the right dose, combined with a consistent eating schedule, greatly reduces the likelihood of rebound effects.

What's a Good Way to Remember to Take Your Meds?

Forget to take your meds when you should? Have you tried positioning them where you can't miss them (beside your bed, rubber banded to your toothbrush, in your shoes in the morning)? Still miss 'em? How about getting an electronic pill minder, such as the e-pill minder? You can carry it in your backpack or purse, and when it beeps, just pull a pill out of the device, and you're good to go. Don't want to spend the money or schlep anything else around? Set a daily alarm on your PDA, cell phone, or laptop.

The key to remembering your pills is accessibility. Consider keeping them right next to your alarm clock. When the alarm goes off in the morning, take your pill, swig some water, and roll over...your brain will shortly wake up, painlessly, and then you will, too. Sure beats fighting the snooze alarm for an hour or two.

Keep a spare pill bottle in your purse, backpack, or glove box (or multiple locations) so that when you forget—notice I didn't say "if"—it's there when you remember.

What's the Difference between Generic and Brand Name Meds?
I'm told there are subtle differences between generic and brand name meds, and that in things like antibiotics, this may not make a big difference. But our brains may be more sensitive to subtle changes in a medication or its ingredients. For me, the switch from brand name Adderall to generic was a big challenge. My insurance wouldn't cover the brand name version anymore. For weeks after I switched to the generic I couldn't sleep! And I couldn't figure out why...then I heard about the differences between generic and brand name. But I still couldn't go back to the brand name. The best I could do was try generics made by different manufacturers until I found one that allowed me to sleep. I did, and for me, it was the Adderall equivalent made by Barr. All the others kept me awake. The take-home message? Understand the challenges of generics for the brain and stick with the brand name if you can. And if you change your medication, pay close attention to any side effects so you can figure out what's working or not working (and then make changes accordingly). Yes, it is work to do this, but you'll be happy once you get it figured out.

I Have to Take a Pill Two or Three Times a Day, and It's Hard to Remember. Are There Any Other Options?
Yes! There are several good choices now. If you struggle with taking meds multiple times a day, or if you feel the medication wearing off during the day, there are longer-acting medications. These typically last from eight to twelve hours, with some even lasting all day. Personally, I take an extended-release Adderall in the morning and then a small dose of short-acting Adderall in the afternoon. One really

cool idea I've heard about is new patches you wear that give you medication. The advantage? The medication releases steadily so you don't feel it wearing off and don't miss a midday dose.

Ask your doctor about these or other long-acting medicines. These medications will get you the majority of the way through the day. Make sure, however, that they're prescribed by an ADD specialist. These medications do not all wear off at the same rate, and you may need a second pill later in the day for studying or after classes. Only someone with significant experience with these medications will know how to handle that.

If you want information on specific meds, check out the latest ADD books or get a copy of *Delivered from Distraction* by Dr. Ned Hallowell. It has very thorough and up-to-date information on available medications, presented in a way that is useful and informative.

Alternatives to Medicine

There are many alternatives to medication today, including substances you ingest (such as homeopathic remedies, supplements, "nutraceuticals," and vitamins), meditation, brain exercises, physical exercises, spirituality, and much, much more. I'm sure there are merits to the vast majority of them, but how do you figure out what works for you? This takes patience and time—lots of time.

I hesitate to tell people what I take in addition to meds because I don't want to unfairly favor one product over another. And frankly, I haven't tried everything out there, and since ADD's so individual, I have no idea if what works for me will work for you. That said, here's what I take, what I do, and what I've heard. I'm not claiming it'll work for you, but I believe it's helping me. I also wouldn't try to do each of these things yourself —at least not all at once. Do what works for you. There are only twenty-four hours in a day; trying to do everything I recommend here or throughout the book would take up too many of them!

- **Organic foods.** I've gone 90 percent organic. I shoot for 100 percent, but it doesn't always work out. I try to avoid anything with preservatives, pesticides, artificial ingredients, and things I can't identify or pronounce. I've also cut out all meats. (Except for the occasional piece of sushi—I need my sushi!) I just don't know what the antibiotics, additives, and low-grade feed they put into animals will do to me. (As an added benefit, since going organic I no longer get the colds, flu, bronchitis, and sinus infections that used to plague me!)

- **Juice.** This may surprise you, but I don't drink any juice. And I'm very careful about eating fruit. I want to make sure I'm keeping close tabs on my blood sugar, and fruit sugars (particularly in juice) tend to spike it and drop it. As a general rule, I always try to have protein when I have fruit so that I've got something slow-burning to go along with the instant energy.

- **Soft drinks and sugar.** Out. I'm a recovering sugara-holic. It was a form of self-medication for me. But the more sugar I had, the more spiky things got and the more moody I was. I don't add sugar to my cereal, eat candy (peanut M&M's excepted), or have any drinks (even Gatorade) with sugar in them. My only vice here? Newman's Own organic chocolate cookies. Okay, I'm still a chocoholic, but they do use organic sugar!

- **Eggs and milk.** Out for the same reasons as meat.

- **Fast food.** Completely out because of all of the above.

- **Medication.** While there are subtle changes over the course of a year, at present I take a long-acting Adderall when I get up each morning. It doesn't make it all the way through the day, so I add a shorter-acting Adderall after it wears off. I've also added a concentrated berry drink product in the afternoons that's touted to help with focus and concentration. It's Ageless Xtra from Oasis (www.oasislifesciences.com).

- **Other dietary supplements.** My cabinets are full of other supplements, a few of which I take on a regular basis. The one I believe works the best of the bunch is flax seed oil or fish oil.

- **Meditation.** Meditation has worked wonders for me and is as important as medication in calming the mind and giving me greater focus throughout the day. I try to meditate for twenty minutes when I get up and again before I go to bed.

- **Exercise.** I'm a fanatic when it comes to a morning and evening walk, hike, or run, preferably in nature. I feel it sets my body clock (which helps me to wake, concentrate, and then sleep), relaxes my mind for the day, keeps me in touch with the "big picture," and gives me a sense of calm and tranquility to weather the day's storms.

- **Sleep.** The key here has been regularity. Though it's often a challenge, going to bed at the same time and waking up at the same time every day is essential. I often have to set an alarm to make sure I go to bed at the same time. Then I keep my curtains wide open to help my body wake *before* my alarm, according to the sun. This helps my body set its clock to the sun, waking me up after a more natural period of sleep rather than harmfully during deep sleep.

- **Regular schedule/routine.** It's been hard, but I keep trying to fine-tune or balance my day and routine to keep from being overextended. The slower my day, the more downtime I build into it (to let the mind unwind), the calmer, more focused, and more productive I am throughout the day. It turns out the more I try to cram in, the less I can get done!

- **Watching my input—books, movies, music, and news.** Think of your mind as a computer, constantly processing what's being put in, making new neural connections, and rewiring based on software. I find certain music, movies, and news to be triggers for negativity, unhappiness, and even an inability to sleep. I have only so much mental energy, so I want to keep it on the positives.

- **Feeding the mind.** Listening to audio books helps me stay on track, remember what's important, and learn cool life stuff rather than just the classroom stuff. This is a great life habit, not just for college, and can be a great way to keep your mind where you want it to be! For me, listening to a spiritual book in the morning helps me keep my eye on the ball (so to speak) throughout the day, giving me greater patience and compassion for others, and a better ability to laugh at the day's challenges, no matter how ugly they may be!

- **Music.** Just like a good steady beat can help you work out and pound out a sweat, I've found other kinds of music to be incredibly beneficial. The right music at the right time can calm you down, help you relax and focus, or get you going.

- **Background noise.** I tend to have a fountain and/or nature sounds (birds chirping and the like) going in my room. It helps ground me to nature; the water or rain sounds are incredibly relaxing, and I feel better in general.

- **Uncluttered environment.** Every object has an energy, and having things strewn all over the place makes our thoughts jumbled accordingly. A clean desk and work-space is essential for me to get work done.

- **Social outlet.** ADDers are social animals, and regular social interaction helps us reconnect with the world around us. It's recharging, energizing, and healing.

- **Creative outlet.** ADDers are wired for creativity. And I think we go bonkers if we don't stretch our creative muscles or have a creative outlet. I try to do creative writing or photography daily to keep these muscles in shape. It helps me feel productive and relaxed, which spills over into everything else!

- **Self-care.** Massage or self-massage, acupuncture, and proper hygiene help you feel more confident, more relaxed, and better about yourself. I try to take care of myself each day because how I look on the outside is often a reflection of how I feel (or want to feel) on the inside.

Use alarms, your calendar software, PDA, cell phone, or a pill minder device (such as e-pill minder) that allows you to keep your pills in little slots *in* the device. Set alarms to remind you to take your meds. Worried about embarrassment? Have your pop-up say something that only you'd understand. In my case it used to be "take time." That was enough. It'd pop up, I'd head for the bathroom, take my meds, and *voilà*, job done!

Be sure to keep your meds in several locations; that way you can take them when you remember. Do you drive to school? Keep a spare bottle in your glove box. Carry a backpack? Keep a spare bottle in your backpack.

"What you are is what you have been, and what you will be is what you do now."

—Buddha

Medication

4

Taking Advantage of Technology

"The **opportunities of man** are limited only by his **imagination**. But so few have **imagination** that there are **ten thousand fiddlers to one composer.**"

—Charles F. Kettering

Now is a cool time to have ADD. Technology in the twenty-first century is here to help us use our minds to the fullest. Before these breakthroughs, it was as though we had supercomputer brains with no successful means for input or output. Today's technology changes all that. Anything's possible with the pairing of today's technology and our creative minds; there truly are no limits to what we can do anymore!

Understanding Technology Before Choosing a School

This section of the book is strategically positioned here, before you have even packed for college, to ensure that you look at what technology you may want to bring along. Some of it's very inexpensive; some of it's even free. Other technology, such as laptops or tablet PCs, costs quite a bit. And there are other things you'll want to be sure that the school can provide. Unless the technology is super-simple, you'll want to play with it before you get to school or make time to get training to overcome the learning curve. So it's essential to look over the basics before you get to school, perhaps even before you choose a school.

Choosing Your Technology

There are a whole slew of products out there that can help you in college—how do you even begin to choose those that will prove most useful?

- **The first, most important question to ask yourself is what gadgets you'll need the most.** For instance, a PDA and/or laptop or tablet PC should be very high on the list.

- **What's the most difficult subject for you, or which causes the most stress and anxiety?** Once you know where you struggle the most (or what might cause the most difficulties in college), it's much easier to find the specific software to help you.

- **Get the dirt.** When shopping for technology, I like to begin by finding product reviews, comparisons, buyer's guides, and magazines at places like cnet.com. You can also check out sites like enablemart.com or shopzilla.com for comparisons, or throw the type of product into a search engine (my favorite's dogpile.com, a metasearch browser that checks Google along with a half dozen or so other search engines). If you see someone using a product you're interested in, ask him about it, and consider asking your school (or new school's Resources for Disabled Students (RDS) Office) for their thoughts on it as well.

- **Picture yourself using the product.** Is it still realistic? Is it too heavy to lug all over a college campus? Walk yourself through the basics of using it. For instance, would you really talk into a microphone while writing papers?

- **Try it out.** Test the keyboards—how do they feel? Can you write on a PDA that small? Do you like the layout or interface of the software or device?

- **Does it have what you need?** Make sure whatever you buy has the functions and tools necessary to perform your most crucial tasks—it doesn't matter if has twenty or thirty cool features you'll never use for school. Its primary purpose it to do the thing or things you need it to do really well. If not, the other features don't matter; in fact, they may just get in the way or confuse you.

- **Is it fun to use?** If it's not fun, you won't use it, no matter what it is. Check it out carefully and make sure you enjoy working with the product before you invest.
- **Check for support.** Make sure there is support and/or training available, either online, one-on-one, or through your school. Get training when you get the product and make sure more is available (especially technical support) in case you need it.
- **Go with your gut.** More than anything else, trust your intuition on this one. If you're not comfortable with something, don't try to convince yourself you'll like it later on just because it has the most features. Technology is a big investment; always choose the tool you will be most comfortable using for a long time.
- **Make sure its returnable.** This could be of particular importance if you buy something on the Internet. Be sure there is a return policy on any software you buy as well.

Tech Tip: The Gadget Rule—Keep It Simple

 You've all heard of the golden rule. Well, this is the gadget rule: keep it simple. Simplicity is golden because it means you actually can and will use the product.

No matter how much a gadget, software package, or computer can do, if you're not comfortable with it, if it doesn't feel right, if it confuses you, or if it's not reliable because it does too much, then you're not going to use it—or at least you're not going to be able to use it reliably. It's much better to have something simple that's fun and easy to use and that performs amazingly well one function, a function that you can't live without.

If you want something more complex or have to learn something that's not simple (such as software that types for you), hire a trainer or tutor and pay to have someone teach you how to use it. It's unlikely you have the time or energy to overcome the learning curve on your own, and if you don't get comfortable with it quickly, you're likely to give up. Make sure that if you're investing in something expensive or complex, you budget for the cost of training, tutoring, or assistance.

What Technology Should You Consider?

There are many technological tools and gadgets that can help immeasurably in college. Here's a list of some of the amazing devices and software you may want to consider.

1. **PDA.** A PDA lets you know where you need to be when, and lets you track deadlines and schedules. It could be the number one device for saving ADD students.

2. **Laptop.** Though I'm sure they're still out there, I personally don't know of any institution where you can't bring your computer to class nowadays. Having your laptop handy means better organization, research, note-taking, assignment-tracking, reading, math, and so much more.

3. **Digital voice recorder.** If you're an auditory learner or just have some tough classes, the ability to record lectures and play them back later is a must. You can use a PDA with a built-in recorder or a digital voice recorder; both will allow you to download and save your lectures onto your computer to go back later and easily find exactly what you're looking for.

4. **Speech recognition software (Text-to-Speech).** If you're dyslexic, if you struggle to write, or if you find it easier to talk your way through a paper or project than to write it, this software is a miracle worker. Once you know how to use it, you can simply talk into a microphone, and the computer types

up your words. You can even talk into your voice recorder and have the software type up your words later. The more sophisticated software (such as Dragon NaturallySpeaking (at nuance.com) lets you do all your editing and corrections right from the microphone, turning your computer into your own personal transcriber.

5. **Digital pen.** Simply write on a notepad with the pen, and it will record your notes into its memory. Then plug the pen into your computer later and download your data; many computers will even type up what you've written. Now you can have organized, outlined notes right on your computer, simply from doodling in your notebook!

6. **Tablet PC.** A bit smaller and more convenient than a laptop, a tablet PC takes note-taking, portability, text-to-speech software, and college computer usage itself to a whole new level. The tablet has a touch-sensitive screen that allows you to write on it with a special pen, so you're basically writing and typing your notes at the same time. Best of all, you can now take notes of charts, diagrams, drawings, and math and science problems and save them on the computer (something that's painful or impossible with a traditional laptop). Tablet PCs have built-in speech recognition software and many more features designed to help you organize your work and get things done on the go.

7. **Mind-mapping software.** This software helps visual learners draw or "map" their ideas. It's great for the ADD mind, which is often befuddled by lists and outlines. Mind-mapping software allows you to visually plot your notes, papers, projects, thoughts, and more.

8. **Digital camera or camera phone.** If your professor is okay with it, you can snap shots of the chalkboard or slides that are used in class. This is especially important for us ADDers, as it can be too distracting to copy down complex

formulas, problems, and/or concepts while listening to the professor at the same time.

9. **High-speed Internet connection.** Many teachers and professors have class information, notes, group discussion, slides, and downloads online. Download slides the night before class for extra preparation. Then bring your laptop or tablet PC to class and use the slides as an outline for fill-in-the-blank, pre-organized notes.

10. **Scanning pen.** Simply drag a scanning pen across text like a highlighter and it can read it, translate it, check spelling and grammar, and even download material to play back on your computer. These are great for research and surviving foreign language classes, and can be lifesavers if you have dyslexia— you can just plug in your headphones and let the pen read books out loud for you in the library.

11. **Reading software.** This software uses a synthesized voice to do the reading for you. Simply scan your books into the computer and it will read, highlight, color-code, and even help you organize the material. You can read back notes, books, and homework assignments, surf the Web, and more with this software.

12. **Scanner.** If you'll be using reading software, make sure you've got a scanner handy—you'll need it to scan in any books or reading material you can't find already converted to audio.

13. **Audio books.** You can get audio versions of many of your textbooks, read by experts who even explain all the charts and graphs with easy-to-understand description and detail. However, you need to order these well before a class begins. A great resource for audio textbooks is Recording for the Blind and Dyslexic (www.rfbd.org).

14. **Audiobook player.** Most audiobooks can be played on your iPod or favorite MP3 player, but unfortunately, audio textbooks (with their encryption) can't be played on such devices yet. Perhaps by the time you read this they can be, and if not,

soon enough they will. But for now, you'll either need an audiobook player (a fancy version of a CD player) or special software. These players and software allow you easy navigation of the audiobooks so you can jump around, bookmark places to go back to, do keyword searches (like looking in the index of a traditional book), and quickly move back, forward, or even paragraph by paragraph.

15. **iPod or MP3 player.** These are not just for music anymore. They can store notes or files (like a flash drive, another must-have for the student) and even play back videos. Many of them also double as sophisticated voice recorders!

16. **Keyfinder keychain.** This little twenty-dollar device is my most valuable commodity. It prevents hours of heartache and stress when it comes time to leave, and you can't find your wallet or keys. Simply press a button on the locator, and whatever you've placed the receiver on—keys, wallet, PDA, etc.—will beep.

17. **Cell phones.** The latest cell phones are basically minicomputers in their own right. Many have advanced PDA functionality, voice recorders, phone and video, and removable memory cards. Choose wisely and this one device could eliminate the need for half a dozen others. Just make sure there's a voice or data plan that's not going to blow your budget into the stratosphere.

18. **Proximity alert device.** If you've invested in an expensive PDA, voice recorder, or cell phone, you may want to get a proximity alert like the TagAlert. Stick a tag on the back of your device, and you'll be alerted if you leave it behind (it warns you if you're separated from your device by more than twenty or fifty feet). This keeps you from donating your devices to other college students.

19. **Electronic timers.** There are many types of timers available, from keychains to watches to timers you park on your desk or run on your computer. A timer is essential to helping you track time, get things done, switch gears, and stay on track.

My favorite is Time Timer Software, which is highly visual and helps me see time passing without having to think about it.

20. **External hard drive.** Get a one-touch external hard drive to back up your important documents or set up a button to back up files instantly or even automatically each night. You simply plug it in, click the mouse a few times, and the device will take care of the rest, day after day, no matter what.

Technological Assistance

Obviously, amazing gadgets and programs will not make you successful in college if you don't put in the necessary work to master the material. They can, however, be a great aid in keeping you focused on approaching deadlines and schedules and making sure your work is organized and on time. Identify a few of these devices that you think you may need and look into them before you choose or leave for college. They can be your greatest ally!

> "Some people worry that artificial intelligence will make us feel inferior, but then, anybody in his right mind should have an inferiority complex every time he looks at a flower."
>
> **—Alan C. Kay**

5

Choosing the College That's Right for You

> "**The direction** in which **education starts** a **man** will determine **his future life**."
>
> —**Plato**

While choosing a college isn't necessarily life-or-death, your decision is very important to your future success. College is the platform that springboards you into your future. And the importance of choosing the right school as an ADD student cannot be overstated. A proper fit will ensure a smoother transition and greater success, and help build a momentum to carry you through the college years and beyond.

One school, no matter how great, is not right for everyone. Which college to attend is an individual decision based on your interests, needs, and comfort. So in this chapter we'll look at four steps to choosing a school.

Step One: Who Are You?

Do you know what subject you'd like to study or what field you're headed for? Few high school students do. But we ADDers more than anyone need to understand and narrow our interests: we lose motivation if we can't find courses that excite us. Consider taking a skills or interest assessment exam so you can focus on applying to the kinds of schools that will fan your passions. Your guidance counselor may be able to administer an assessment. If you can't determine an academic focus, stick to liberal arts schools with broad ranges of programs, courses, and activities to sample from until you find one that holds your attention.

As well as academic programs, you should also determine what size, location, atmosphere, scholastic and extracurricular activities, etc. would suit you best. And, of course, there's the matter of the school's resources for ADD students.

Finding Fun

What is fun for you? If you could wave a magic wand and be anywhere you want to be in five or ten years, where would you be, and what would you be doing? Would you be acting in Hollywood? Designing computer games for the latest PlayStation? Perhaps you'd be writing for the *Chicago Tribune*, or traveling the world in search of stories for *National Geographic*? Would you be working for Greenpeace, your favorite religious organization, or another nonprofit?

College is your chance to make any of these dreams a reality. Starting college is like being born all over again. Who you are, what you want to do, and where you want to go with your life is completely up to you. If you focus (and here's where this book can help!), work hard, and believe in yourself, college is the beginning of accomplishing everything you want in life. There's only one trick: you have to figure out exactly what it is you want, and then you can work on how you want to get there.

What's required of you in college is doing what's fun and what you love with an eye on parlaying your hobby into your career. Have you ever noticed how doing what you love allows your mind to expand, your focus to grow, and you to do your best work? Whether it's playing Nintendo, soccer, or the tuba, or studying science or literature, doing what you love helps you stay focused and achieve greatness. With this in mind, you can see the importance of choosing a school with courses or programs that excite you.

As ADDers, we have a habit of letting adrenaline drive our choices for the future. This initial excitement can wear off quickly and leave you with the frustrating reality of a new class, job, car, or relationship that just isn't right for you. Think about your school choices ahead of time and try to think past the initial excitement. What will things look like a month, a year, or even three years from now? Do they offer enough courses or types of courses to keep you interested? Will the winter cold crush you? How about the stifling summer heat? Get past the initial rush of enthusiasm—what's left behind after it passes?

Info: The Critical Criteria

 While there is no one type of school that's right for all of us, there are many criteria you can use to make an informed decision. And let's face it, making big decisions is often difficult for us—we're impulsive and prone to changing our minds, and if the process is complex, we often give up in frustration.

So here's where you begin. Ask yourself these critical questions and be honest in your responses.

1. How much of a struggle has ADD been, and how much have others helped me to overcome my challenges?

2. How mature am I in dealing with my ADD, and how willing am I to seek help?

3. Where do I want to go in life—what do I enjoy studying and doing? What do I love to do and find interesting, exciting, or stimulating?

4. Where do I see myself in five, ten, or twenty years?

5. What are my best skills?

6. How independent am I?

These questions can give you a good grasp on how much aid a potential school needs to have in place to help you manage your ADD, what kinds of classes to focus on, and possible careers to work toward.

Info: The Critical Criteria

Knowing Your Strengths

In addition to knowing what you love to do and find exciting, you need to ask yourself what your particular skills are. Are you a fantastic writer or speaker? Are you great with your hands? Do numbers make instant sense to you? How about science? Or are you compulsively organized? Figure out what you're good at—when you're good at something, opportunities automatically appear before you.

We are often highly intuitive when it comes to others, but downright perplexed when it comes to understanding ourselves. Unsure what you like or what you're good at? Ask others, and take an assessment exam privately or through your guidance counselor's office to help you determine your strengths, personality type, and skills. While these tests aren't the gospel when it comes to determining your future, they can help point you in the right direction and suggest degrees or career paths to consider. Perhaps you didn't realize that a desk job would never be in your future or that being a firefighter or emergency room nurse was right up your alley. Maybe you didn't know that you prefer to work in an environment where you can problem-solve quietly, perhaps as an investigative accountant, X-ray technician, or experimental scientist. These tests can open a world of possibilities to you.

How Independent and Self-Motivated Are You?

- **Did you need support and structure in high school?** Chances are you'll still need them in college.

- **Do you routinely need help from others to keep you motivated and focused?** If so, you'll want smaller classes, greater professor input, more heavily armed resources for disabled students, or even a school with extra services for ADD students

- **Do you thrive on individual attention from teachers?** If this makes a significant difference in the quality of your work, focus on small schools with low student to teacher ratios.

- **Do you prefer to immerse yourself in a subject?** Think about schools that divide the year into quarters rather than semesters. When a school runs on a quarterly schedule, courses are shorter and more intense, and you take fewer at a time. If, however, it takes a while for you to settle in, opt for a school with a semester system.

- **Do you need a high-energy environment?** Many ADDers need the excitement of a bustling campus to stay motivated. If you're such a student, consider a mid-sized or large college that offers several extracurricular activities you can't wait to join. If you're heavily involved right now in a hobby, sport, or extracurricular activity that gives you great joy or sense of self or is very calming, choose a school that offers the activity you're doing.

- **Do you have trouble falling asleep?** Look for schools that offer single rooms or quiet hallways as accommodations for students with ADD, ADHD, or learning disorders. Having a private room eliminates roommate distractions and conflicts that can disrupt your studies.

ADD Challenges: Nothing But the Truth

In choosing a college, you must be brutally honest with yourself. If left to your own devices, how far off the deep end could you go? Could the overwhelming freedom coupled with a flood of work overload you and bring you to your knees? If so, you'll need to consider schools with more structure, accountability, or assistance. Be honest, then choose your college accordingly.

Many students rebel against ADD when they get to college. They want to prove to the world that they can make it on their own, that they're not responsible to anyone, and above all, that they do not have ADD. There's nothing wrong with feeling this way, but it can lead to overcorrecting for any assistance you've already gotten. Many students who were treated and assisted with their ADD in high school acknowledge neither the existence of ADD in college nor the fact that they have it; instead, they convince themselves it disappears after high school. Unfortunately, this is not the case.

This can develop into a huge problem if the student decides he or she won't need help ahead of time, when considering schools. The student could choose a program or school that offers absolutely no support or assistance for ADD students, or even put herself into the craziest of party schools just to prove she does not have ADD. This desire to feel complete, as if you're not defective and can stand on your own feet, is totally understandable. But remember: just because you suffer from ADD does not mean you are incomplete or defective in any way, so don't set yourself up for failure to prove an invalid point. If you're going to rail against ADD or the idea of getting assistance, at least give yourself the opportunity to someday change your mind. Just because you believe that your strength is so great you can make it on your own, don't throw away the safety net.

Step Two: Hunting for Colleges

Now that you've discovered a bit about yourself, we can move on to the next step in choosing a college. Head to your local library or bookstore and check out the college guides. (I've named several below, but when in doubt, ask your local librarian.)

Info

There are some great guides that can help you make an informed decision. There are two good books available that provide specific information for students with ADD and learning disabilities. These are *Peterson's Colleges with Programs for Students with Learning Disabilities or ADD* and the *K&W Guide to Colleges for Students with Learning Disabilities*. If you're specifically interested in a smaller, hands-on school, be sure to also check out *Colleges That Change Lives: 40 Schools You Should Know About Even If You're Not a Straight-A Student*. Not all of the schools listed in this book will have good programs or accommodations for students with disabilities, so you'll want to do a thorough check. That said, a lot of these schools may be more than worth the investigation, and a smaller environment can be very helpful for the ADD student.

Next, take your books, info, bookmarked pages, printouts, and anything else you have and head to your high school guidance counselor. Let him know you have ADD, the particular traits you're worried about control-

ling, and then pick his brains and see what schools he would recommend and why. If he's had experience with ADD students, he may have worthwhile advice. However, if he only muddies the waters further, consider seeking a college placement professional (who need not be local) to help you wade through the quagmire. Don't be afraid to spend time or even money on choosing a school. Sound insane to spend money to find a place where you'll spend even more money? Well (Mom and Dad, listen closely), wouldn't you be willing to spend a few hundred dollars to make sure this investment of up to or over one hundred thousand dollars is the right one? Only makes sense, doesn't it?

In this step of researching colleges, don't be afraid to put down ten, twenty, or even more schools on your list. Even if there's only an outside chance now, the more you look into things, the more some schools will eliminate themselves, while others may appear more and more worthy.

Info: For Parents

 While parents are often quick to spend thousands of dollars on placement exam preparation courses, less time and money is given to choosing schools or in helping the student to navigate the college application process. But this is often equally, if not more, important than the entrance exam grades themselves. A proper fit can make the difference between an immensely successful college career and your child returning home, taking a year off to "find himself" because the school beat the heck out of his confidence, esteem, motivation, and drive. Be sure to help your child by offering to get outside assistance if she needs it. (Typically I don't recommend helping them directly, as this can backfire, build resentment, and/or influence the child to go to the school that you want rather than the one that's the best fit for her.)

Put the time and effort into this all-important part of the process, and you (and your wallet) will breathe a much greater sigh of relief in the long run. And just think—time and money now could eliminate many harrowing, sleepless nights for you and your spouse in the very near future. Now isn't that worth it?

Step Three: The Process of Elimination

Now that you have a list of potential colleges, it's time to start narrowing it down to determine your top choices. A good way to start is by looking at the services each school has to offer for its ADD students. Make sure they have more services or assistance available than you think you'll need, because even the most brilliant and independent of ADD students will likely need some help during her college career. By law, schools are only required to offer "reasonable" accommodations, and what's reasonable at one school may not be reasonable at another. So to find out the real story, you'll need to call and talk with someone involved with or responsible for special services and assistance for students with disabilities.

ADD Advantage: Disabled Students' Office

When I first needed assistance at school, I had to figure out where to turn for help. It turns out I needed to go to the RDS office. I did not want to do this. I wasn't disabled and hated the label. But unfortunately, that's usually where the help for ADD students is housed. And the "disability" label is necessary for us to get accommodations and funding from the federal government. So, misnomer aside, you'll probably need to call the RDS office. Just try to keep in mind how lucky it is for you that they have services and accommodations available for ADD students at all. It makes life easier, levels the playing field, and gives you a greater chance for success.

Determine Their ADD Awareness

Look on each school's website to find out who's in charge of disabled student services, and when you call, speak to that person first. Try to get an idea from her if there's someone really there for ADD students in particular or if you're lumped in with everyone else. ADD students have very different needs from those of other students with disabilities. If the department is familiar with and well trained in helping ADD students, then they'll know how to help; if not, they may become increasingly frustrated with your inability to follow through, making you much less likely to come back and ask for the help you need.

Digging in and Comparing Services

- **Are there additional costs for ADD services?** While all schools must provide a minimum of services, many offer additional services that are more hands-on but that come with an additional cost. One of the best programs out there is the SALT program at the U of A. Unfortunately, it's at a very big school, but the services offer great guidance each step of the way and can keep students from the feeling of being overwhelmed that can come from attending a large institution. These services are also good for students who are undone by the mundane details of college life—such as arranging housing, choosing a meal plan, and renewing financial aid.

- **What accommodations can be made?** Get a breakdown of what's available as a regular service and what you can get at an additional cost. If you received any accommodations in high school, make sure that at least the equivalent is available to you in college, even if it was just help from your folks with signing up for classes, breaking down projects into smaller pieces, establishing due dates, etc.

- **What technology is available?** Ask if the school provides any software, computer training, or anything else in the way of technology to help the ADD student. As we'll see throughout this book, technology can make all the difference in the world. If a school or its disabilities office uses specific software and can help you with it, this can give you a distinct advantage.

- **What kind of professional assistance is available on campus?** Is there a learning specialist with training in working with ADD students? The more specialized help is available, the better. How long does it take to get help? If you need to plan well in advance when you might need assistance, this could be a problem. (Hey, we have ADD, how do we know if there will be a problem in advance?) So the more accessible the office is, the better.

- **How flexible is the program?** ADD students have a hard time planning ahead and frequently don't seek help until there's a crisis. How quickly you can get attention is a good indicator of how well the office understands and accommodates the ADD student.

- **What's their demeanor like?** This one is often hard to judge over the phone and is best evaluated in person. Try to get a feel for whether you'd be comfortable or feel encouraged to seek help from these professionals or this office. All the help in the world won't do you any good if you don't feel comfortable seeking and accepting it.

- **What documentation is needed?** If one school requires a much greater amount of documentation on your condition before you can get help than another school does, and you know you don't have that documentation ready, it may be one of many factors you use in your decision.

- **Do you know what you plan on studying?** If you're still unsure about special needs accommodations and you're not ready to visit, dial up the department of whatever discipline you think you might major in. See if you can talk to their chair about your disability. Try to get a feel for how much they accommodate students like you. It could be a stab in the dark, but it may also give you a strong impression, particularly if the chair starts mentioning specific cases and how he handled them.

 Now that you've asked the schools about the major criteria, sit back and review your list. Step away from it for a few hours or days, and let things roll around in your head.

Then go back to the list and chop it down to your top three to five schools. You can always add more, but remember: if it's hard to recall what you did yesterday, it may be impossible to keep ten or twenty school visits straight in your head.

Info: Find the Right Advisor

Make sure there's an ADD-experienced advisor available to help with your big decisions: classes, majors, and career direction. As an undergraduate, I ended up keeping the same advisor for all four years of school because I didn't like change or the hassle involved. This meant I had a geology professor advising me for my classes and major, which ended up being political science. He didn't know much about the major or about ADD and my special needs. It was a mismatch at best, and I ended up taking courses toward a degree that didn't get me where I wanted to go. Make sure there's a way to work with your RDS office to get an advisor with ADD experience who can help guide you through the process and onto the career path you'd like to follow.

Step Four: School Visits

Now that you have your short list, it's time for the most important step: the visit. Call each school on your list and schedule an overnight visit, with specific plans to speak with both admissions and the RDS office. You'll never know what school will work for you without trying it first. No one school is right for everyone, and a good fit is a must. This is very subjective; how you feel there is critical to how comfortable you'll be there.

Hang out with a student, preferably one with ADD. Attend classes and try to get a real feel for what attending the school is like. Eat in their food court, visit their bookstore, hang in the dorms, and check out the nightlife. This isn't a chance to let loose and party but rather an opportunity to try on the school for fit and flavor. It'll give you a much better idea about the reality of the place than taking a formal tour or interviewing faculty will. Time away from the administration and with the students, both in and out of the classroom, is really the best way to get to know the place.

Things to Consider on Your Visits

- **Atmosphere:** What are the students like? Are people open and friendly? Are they in their own worlds? Do they dress up for class or wear pajamas and flip flops? Spend at least one night on campus with a current student, preferably one with ADD. What was it like? Would you fit in?
- **Campus:** Walk the campus. Would you feel comfortable here? What part of town is the school located in? Is it surrounded by bookstores and cafés or bars and liquor stores? Read the flyers. Are they all for parties and beer or academic clubs and endeavors? What's the student center like? Do you see a place where you can picture yourself studying?
- **Disabilities office:** Go to the disabilities office. Is the staff friendly and welcoming? Can you picture working with them?
- **Current ADD students:** Can the disabilities office give you a few references for ADD students you can talk with about their experiences?
- **Potential departments:** If you know your field of interest, visit the department, meet the staff, and talk with a professor or the department chair. Be bold: mention you have ADD, and see what they say. If you get the chance, talk with the department's secretary—he or she can usually give you a very good idea of the reception you'll receive, and it's a great idea to make friends with the secretary in case you come back.

While choosing schools can be intimidating and overwhelming, it can also be a lot of fun. Just take it one step at a time, and trust your gut at every turn. Choose a school that excites you and that fits, one that offers an atmosphere, culture, courses, and student life that's comfortable and motivating, and that meets your needs.

An Alternate Solution

While attending college, I was also trying to make it as a professional bicycle racer. But an accident cut my training short, and I wasn't ready to go back to school. Instead of returning to The Colorado College to get more classes out of the way, I stayed home to recuperate and checked out the local community college. I must admit, the community college experience was fantastic, and nothing like I'd expected.

- Students at community colleges are very serious about their studies, possibly even more serious than traditional four-year students at a university. Why? Well, first, this is their stepping stone to getting into another institution or in some cases, their only chance to get a higher education. Second, many are nontraditional students, meaning older students or those with families and jobs. They don't have time to mess around.

- I thought the education would be subpar, and this, too, was far from the truth. Just as with any institu- tion, you have your good professors and your not-so-good ones.

- It is quite painless to get in and register. The community college didn't need my SAT scores, only my high school transcript (or college in this case) and what level courses I had taken (for placement purposes). The rest of the admission process I did online, and I could register up until the first day of classes!

- The RDS office was very accessible and friendly.

> "Tell me and I'll forget; show me and I may remember; involve me and I'll understand"
>
> **—Chinese proverb**

6

Applying to Schools

"**There is no passion** to be found playing **small—in** settling for a life that **is less than** the one **you are capable** of living."

—Nelson Mandela

After you've visited schools and know where you want to go, it's time for the dreaded college application process to begin. Don't let yourself be overwhelmed by the sheer size of the task involved or your desire to be a perfectionist; yes, the application is very important, but focusing on that can freeze you dead in your tracks. You need to remember to relax, have fun with it, and let your enthusiasm and passion—rather than your desire for perfectionism—shine through.

Info: When to Apply

It's best to apply to schools the summer before your senior year. This gives you plenty of time to write your essay and lets you concentrate on one last push for the SATs, getting good grades, and enjoying your senior year. Find a coach, mentor, teacher, guidance counselor, or some other professional who's enthusiastic about helping you and keeping you on track. Having someone to guide you through the process and make sure you follow through can be very beneficial, even crucial.

What is the Schedule?

The college application process can be confusing. It's made up of a lot of components, and it can be very easy to miss a step or two without realizing it until it's too late. Below is a list of what to do when—consider copying it and posting it in a conspicuous place in your home, such as the refrigerator. Being in such a public place will constantly remind you (and your parents) what needs to be done. You could also plug the dates into your cell phone, PDA, or computer for alerts of upcoming events and deadlines.

- **Freshman Year**

  Sign up for the more challenging courses—this will demonstrate your desire to learn. Also get involved in activities both in and out of school, such as sports, theater, or volunteer work. Don't specifically worry about how they'll look on a transcript; try different things until you find something you're passionate about.

- **Sophomore Year**

  Take the PSATs; it's a bit early, but if you struggle, it gives you plenty of time to work on improvement. Over the summer, you may want to try out college courses at your community college or in a summer program. These not only look good on transcripts but also can be amazing experiences that breed passion, excitement, and self-confidence.

- **Junior Year**

  Junior year is arguably the most important year of high school—it's the year when your grades matter most, and it's also when you take the daunting standardized tests. Here's a more detailed breakdown of this crucial year:

Fall	<ul><li>**Consider signing up for some AP courses this year.** These advanced level courses can give you a leg up on getting into college as well as earning you college credit. If there's a course that interests you, see if you can get in, even if you haven't been a stellar student in the past, and be politely insistent.</li><li>**Take the PSAT.**</li></ul>

Spring	• **Take the SAT and/or ACT.** (For info on registering for the SAT, visit www.collegeboard.com.) • **Attend college fairs.** These help you figure out what you're looking for in a school and get you started on putting together a list of potential schools to visit.
Summer	• **Finish your school visits.** Try to visit when summer classes are in session to get a feel for what it will be like during the school year. • **Take an SAT prep course.** Summer is the best time to do this—it won't interfere with your school work or your college applications. • **Start your essays.** Starting now leaves you plenty of time to brainstorm, modify, and let your creativity shine. Essays are often more important than SAT scores for the ADD student, so consider asking for help from a parent, teacher, or professional.

• **Senior Year**

This is it—the end is in sight. You should have your list of potential schools nearly completed and be almost ready to sit down and start whipping out those applications. Here are the final, crucial steps. As this is crunch time, there's quite a bit more to do.

September	• **Last chance for school visits.** Finish up before your fall really heats up to leave enough time to think about your choices and make wise, unhurried decisions. • **Get recommendations and transcripts.** • **More SAT prep.** Sign up for a fall SAT prep course if you're planning on retaking the test. It can make a huge difference in your score, which in turn can determine where you'll spend the next four years of your life. • **Start filling out applications.** Send these in as soon as you've finished them, but only after they've been thoroughly proofread by someone else. • **Fill out financial aid forms.** It takes a long time to pull this all together; make sure your parents have all the forms and information they need early on. • **Attend more college fairs.** Talk with representatives from the schools you're applying to—they may give you great tips about their programs and how to get into them.

October	• **Complete your applications.** Yes, this is very early; however, as an ADDer, you may miss something or need to make revisions at the last minute. Better to build this time into the plan than be surprised at the end of the process and miss the deadline. • **Proofread and submit your applications.** Have someone else look over your applications to make sure you've completed everything, then send them in. • **Financial needs analysis.** Start working on this with your guidance counselor. • **Contact residence halls.** Contact residence life and find out if you need a separate application for the dorms and when it needs to be submitted. This often has to be done before you've been accepted.
November	• **Retake the SATs and/or ACT.** Make sure you know which schools you'd like the results sent to and bring this list with you to the test.
December	• **Submit supporting materials.** Submit any letters, additional grades, additional financial information, additional resident information, citizenship information, testing information, or other documents requested by the colleges you're applying to, including financial forms (unless you're required to wait until the year's end, then submit first thing in January—just watch for deadlines!).
January– February	• **Send any additional information.** If you received requests for additional information, send it in now—that's why you applied early! Also, send in your fall transcripts as soon as they're available. • **Submit your housing forms.**
March– April	• **Decide where to attend.** If you're having a hard time deciding, do some serious soul searching (meditate, take long walks) and seek help from counselors, advisors, friends, or family members. Revisit a school if possible and remember that it's your opinion above all others that matters most. • **Submit your acceptance.** It's not uncommon for an ADD student to be accepted and miss the acceptance deadline. Don't let this happen to you—once you decide where you're going, let them know right away.

March– April (continued)	• **Decline invitations.** You also need to inform the schools that you won't be attending of your decision. • **Financial aid negotiations.** When you receive your financial needs analysis or award letter, make sure you follow the directions to keep the process going. Don't be afraid to negotiate and ask for a better aid package!
April– May	• **Get in touch with the RDS office.** Find out what substantiating materials the office needs for you to register with them and submit these materials. • **Check fall deadlines.** Use the RDS office for help keeping on top of deadlines for housing, financial aid, student employment, and class registration. • **Choose your fall classes early.** The RDS office can help you choose and register for classes and set up a successful fall schedule. If you're still unsure, get a good, qualified ADD coach. • **Contact your future roommate.** The earlier you do this and the more enthusiasm you put into it, the greater your chance for a positive roommate experience in the fall.
May– June	• **Send your final high school transcript.** When you receive your final high school transcripts in May or June, make sure you send them right away to the school you'll be attending. • **Make sure everything is in.** There may be something additional you need to get in, so call the disabled students office, check, and get it in.

Minding the Details

Here's a list of odds and ends that will help ease the application process outlined above. I know you're not always thinking about the details!

• Get your disabilities information together, such as your 504 plan, your IEP, and/or any testing records you have.

• Buy envelopes, labels, and postage for each application.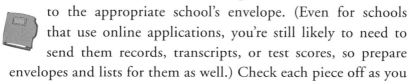

• Make a checklist for each school. Tape each checklist to the appropriate school's envelope. (Even for schools that use online applications, you're still likely to need to send them records, transcripts, or test scores, so prepare envelopes and lists for them as well.) Check each piece off as you add it to the envelope, then have someone else double-check the lists before you mail the envelopes.

- Make an assembly line. Try doing the same step for each application one after the other, then go on and do the next step. For example, start by filling out your basic info on each application. Then go back and do each of the short essays on each application. Then go back and do the long essays, then put together your recommendation letters, then transcripts, etc. This also allows you to use similar answers or reuse parts of the same essay for multiple applications.
- Take baby steps. Break the process down into the smallest pieces possible so it's less complicated and less daunting.

Info: Judging a Book by Its Cover

If you have terrible handwriting and need to do paper applications, recruit someone with neat penmanship to fill them out for you. Or, even better, type your responses on the application... It's very important to make a strong impression, and even if your application is mature and thoughtful, it won't matter if it's not legible or if it looks childish. Make a rough draft, and then have someone fill in the actual form and make it look polished. Don't be afraid to ask for help—just make sure you ask early rather than right before something's due!

How Do You Write Your College Essay?

While parents and students spend countless dollars and hours preparing for standardized tests, one of the most important parts of the application process, the essay, is often neglected until it's too late. Don't make this mistake.

The essay is often more important than anything else in the application. Stellar GPAs and standardized test scores rarely set you apart from the pack, while a great essay can immediately garner attention. ADD students can often write creatively about their struggles with classes and testing, compensating for them by proving their intelligence and originality.

Tips for Writing a Great College Essay

1. Grab a couple of books on great college essays (such as *50 Successful Harvard Application Essays* by the staff of the *Harvard Crimson*) and skim some of the essays. This will give you ideas on standing apart from the pack and showing your strengths.

2. Be original! We excel at this but are often afraid to show our true colors. Don't be afraid to stand out on your essay, despite what others say. Think about this: The person who reads your essay may have read ninety-nine others already that day and have two hundred more to go before Monday. They all start to blend together after a while. Give them something fun and unique to read, and they'll remember you for it.

4. Map out your key points before you start writing.

5. Write a first draft. Don't be afraid to just get things on paper. You can clean them up later; for now, simply get your ideas down.

6. Have someone you trust look it over. Ask him what parts he liked best and where there is room for improvement.

7. Revise and rewrite.

Set Yourself Apart from the Pack

Maybe the most important ingredient for your essay is originality. Ask yourself: How am I unique? What sets me apart from everyone else? What do I have to offer?

Personalize your essay for each individual school. Schools want to know you have a burning passion or desire to attend their institution, and why. So do your homework, point out to them specific things you like about their school, or even mention something you saw during the tour or read about that stood out to you. This shows you care. And by all means, if you're excited about a program they have, or anything else, mention it!

Also, don't be afraid to talk about how well you've done at something, and don't be at all concerned with sounding boastful or self-centered. As ADDers, we typically have self-esteem that's taken a bit of a beating. It's likely that are you're not giving yourself enough credit or doing justice to who you are and what you have to offer. Make yourself look as good as you know you are—now is not the time to be bashful or let ADD negativity get in the way.

ADD Challenges: Documenting Your ADD

Many ADD students lack documentation to present to their RDS office. They can't help you if you can't help them—they need proof of your ADD in order to get the ball rolling. Typically, you'll need to show them medical/psychiatric/educational test results from the last two, no more than three, years. You might also be asked to show them a 504 plan or IEP, or other supporting documentation.

Start pulling these together during the application process and have them ready to send in as soon as you're accepted. This way, the office can be helping you get everything set up for school and may even allow you to register for classes before the general population. The last thing you want is to be unable to register with the disabled student's office. You'll be ineligible for even the most basic accommodations, and this could be the difference between sinking and swimming.

E ver heard of the half-million dollar demo? I was given this concept by a friend of mine recently who was helping me to overcome my own challenges and put out a few audio books. I was stuck, unable to get going because I wanted things to be perfect. That's often what happens when we're applying to schools: we needlessly shoot ourselves down, becoming intimidated by the sheer scale and size of the task.

The half-million dollar demo is the typical musician's demo tape. He's so determined to make it perfect that he never finishes it. There are continual improvements, polishing, and changes, followed by procrastinating, self-intimidation, and loads of self-induced torture, until he ends up spending a half-million dollars of his own money, countless hours of his own time on a demo. Trouble is, even if these demos are the best thing in the world, they never get listened to, and it may be that the recording studio that would *love* it would be happy to polish things for the musician, if he'd only submit the thing so they could hear it.

The same goes for applying to school. You're a much more valuable commodity than you give yourself credit for. You're far too unique, creative, and intelligent to sit there on the sidelines, or to shoot opportunities down before giving yourself a chance. So instead, get help, break things down, dream big, and apply wherever your heart desires. Go for it in studying, in the tests, on the essays, in the applications, and everywhere you can. Believe in yourself and have faith. You can do this!

MY STORY

Applying to Schools

"I've missed more than 9,000 shots in my career. I've lost almost 300 games. Twenty-six times, I've been trusted to take the game-winning shot and missed. I've failed over and over again in my life. And that is why I succeed."

—**Michael Jordan**

7

Planning before You Arrive

> "**So many** fail because they don't **get started**—they don't go. **They don't overcome** inertia. **They don't** begin."
>
> **—W. Clement Stone**

Okay, here's the ugly truth, plain and simple. Despite our desire to fly free from the nest, leave our ADD or challenged minds behind, and completely reinvent ourselves in college, chances are, we're still going to need assistance.

To overcome the challenges you'll be facing, plan on asking for help and getting potential accommodations and assistance in place (or at least get the ball rolling) *before* you get to school. In this section, we'll look at where and how you can ask for help, and how to get things (such as your course schedule) set up in advance so that you're on target for success from day one.

Asking for Help

> "Refusing to ask for help when you need it is refusing someone the chance to be helpful." **—Ric Ocasek**

Want the secret to success in college? It's a four-letter word: help.

To succeed in college we need to ask for help, and we need to ask early. Self-advocacy—asking for help—can be one of the hardest things to do. When we were in grade school and high school, there were always people looking out for us and making sure we got the help we needed. It was often our parents, but our guidance counselors, teachers, and anyone else who saw us struggling would also step in. In college, this safety net doesn't exist. If we don't ask for assistance, it's not going to magically appear. So we must chuck our egos aside and ask for the help we need, even if it's a bit of an uncomfortable or humbling experience.

But self-advocacy is more than just asking for help when we need it. It's about being proactive, asking not only for the help we need now but also for the help we may need in the future. This is a big challenge. It means we must have the self-knowledge and awareness to anticipate future problems and ensure that we have a system in place to handle them when they arise.

ADD Advantage: Intuit It!

Throughout the book I've mentioned that we tend to have a stronger sense of intuition than the general population. If you take the time to listen to your inner voice, picture yourself going through classes, and visualize yourself writing papers and taking tests, you'll know when and where to get help. The realization that you need help may come to you in the form of a vision...but more likely you'll get this twisting feeling in your gut—the dreaded feeling that something's not right or that you don't even want to think that far ahead. This is a sign to get help NOW. Intuit it: use your intuition to guide you to get the help you need, before you need it; it's never too early.

Whom Do You Ask?

The Resources for Disabled Students Office

When you meet with a counselor or specialist here, let him or her know what your challenges have been in the past, what accommodations you've received, and any potential challenges that you think may arise. You need to be very honest; now's not the time to be quiet or to make yourself sound better than you really are. Believe me, I understand the desire to say "I don't know why I'm here…I really don't need any help at all." But the more open you can be, the more likely you'll be able to receive the help and assistance you need.

Potential Professors

While your RDS office can help you choose classes and find professors familiar with the particular challenges of teaching ADD students, it is still always a good idea to meet your professors before your classes begin. You can find out if they'll be a good fit for you and your learning style and troubleshoot any potential problems. Professors are a great place to turn for assistance; chances are, they've seen it all before, and there's a good chance they'll also want to help. It may be challenging, but you'll want to share a bit about your learning disability (you don't even need to say it's ADD—just describe your challenges in classes), ask for suggestions, and see what their thoughts are. You'll be able to tell rather quickly whether or not this is someone you'd enjoy taking a class from.

Asking for Help

Info: Current Professors

Already in class and struggling? Head for your professor's office ASAP. Don't think about it, don't procrastinate, just start walking. The sooner you talk with your professor about what your difficulties, the more accommodating she can be.

It may be as simple as getting extra time for an assignment or test, or even a bit of organizational help for a paper or test preparation.

The majority of professors are more than willing to help out as long as you are:

A. **Forthright.** Even if you completely messed up, tell them what happened. They're human, and they'll usually understand. But hiding the truth or lying will often just keep people from wanting to help you.

B. **Timely.** Don't come to them the day before a test or assignment due date complaining that you don't understand the material. They have little sympathy for procrastinators.

C. **Hardworking.** Show them what you've been doing and where your struggles lie. Telling them you can't do it, you're stuck, or you don't understand doesn't do much to build their confidence in your efforts. But showing them how and where you're stuck, and what you've tried to do, helps build an ally.

Classmates and Friends

Talk about a lifeline! Your classmates are in the trenches with you and may save you a thousand times over the course of your college career. They can help you study, help you understand why you're having trouble in a class or failing tests, show you how to do better on your papers, and much, much more. Just make sure you offer as often as you ask…better yet, always offer assistance; it'll come back tenfold!

Registrar's Office

Though your RDS office—and later in your college career, your advisor—should be your primary ally in registering for classes, sooner or later you'll need the registrar's help, too. Treat him well and explain your difficulties, and he'll more than likely help you out of a bind. Sign up for the wrong class? Drop the wrong class? Miss a deadline? Unsure about prerequisites? Need a copy of your transcript? These are all things you'll need the registrar's office to take care of for you.

Financial Aid Office

Your first meeting or visit with this office will probably take place before you've started school, perhaps even before you've accepted an offer. Treat them well—not only can they help you out in a jam, but they can save you a bunch of money, too! First off, always try to negotiate a better financial aid package, and even if you (or your parents) don't believe you'll be entitled to any financial aid, make sure you still apply for it. You never know what you might be eligible for.

Parents

While we all want to flee the nest and make it on our own, sooner or later we may have to turn to our folks for help. Try to keep the lines of communication open, and be as honest as you can about your progress—and especially the lack thereof. Now believe me, I understand about parents trying to take over your life. I know you may want to stay quiet, but if you have a problem they can help with, do your best to talk with them earlier rather than later. This gives them enough time to figure out how to help you or, if they can't, how to find someone who can.

Finances, medical issues, ADD/psychiatry issues, medical and financial records, money for tutoring, and perhaps most importantly, serious disciplinary or legal situations call for parental help and guidance. Don't think you can go these situations alone, particularly if there's to be any sort of a disciplinary or legal hearing. At these times you'll likely need the best help money can buy, and that means talking to mom and dad.

Coach

Getting an ADD coach is one of the best things you can do to help your college career. He has likely helped many students through situations similar to yours, and he'll guide you through your challenges without placing judgment. He can help you build a schedule and a routine, come up with a study strategy, figure out how to keep yourself from flunking out, or even get through a nightmarish roommate situation.

Counselor

Struggling with emotional issues? Before you start beating your head against the wall or sabotaging yourself, consider seeing a school counselor or psychologist. They're free or inexpensive for students, and just being able to talk and share with an unbiased listener can make a world of difference. Just one word of caution: find someone with ADD experience. A counselor without ADD experience can do more harm than good.

Tutor

If you're struggling in a class or there's a particularly ugly test or assignment looming on the horizon, consider seeing a tutor. Your professor may be able to suggest someone that's right for you (a tutor who has experience working with ADD students is ideal), or you can try your RDS office. Your "disability" may even entitle you to free tutoring.

Tutors can help you understand material, decipher undecipherable textbook reading, help you grasp whatever's taken place in class, and walk you through problem sets, writing papers, math formulas, and more. Regular meetings with a tutor help keep you accountable and on track with your homework and reading, and help you prepare for tests. They're also a great gauge for whether you're ready for a test or not. Tutors can help you spend less time studying to get better results.

Psychiatrist

Know the solutions but still can't get things done? Can't concentrate in class? Temper raging out of control? Anxious? *Anxious??* ANXIOUS??? Running out of meds? There are typically one or more psychiatrists on staff at your student health center, and they can help you with these problems and others. Try to find one with ADD experience. As with a counselor or psychologist, be honest with your psychiatrist—don't downplay the severity of your challenges or she won't be able to help you.

Doctor/Student Health Center

Sometimes students have to be near death before they'll drag themselves to the student health center. Far too many of us lose a semester at school (or worse) because they pushed their health far beyond its limits. If you're trying to get healthy or your health is spiraling downward, drag your carcass in—*now*. They'll likely have you better in no time—and before you've flunked out of school.

If you're running into a birth-control problem— hopefully *before*, but even after something's occurred— health centers are an amazing and totally confidential resource. Make an error in judgment? Do something irresponsible while under the influence the night before? Forget to take a pill or have a condom break? Or perhaps something terrible happened to you and you don't know where to turn. Whatever it is, get yourself to your student health center this minute. Put this book down and go, now.

Sibling

Did an older brother or sister go to the same school or perhaps even have the same professors? If so, you're in luck. He or she may be a great resource for guidance and direction. In fact, older siblings (though you might not think so when you're growing up) can be great confidants even if they attended a different school.

Family Friend

Need to talk to an elder but feel as though you can't turn directly to your family? Extended family members or family friends may be the answer. Often they'll help you work through problems and communicate with your family if necessary, and they may even be a valuable financial resource or emergency hospice in time of need.

Favorite Professor/Faculty Member/Mentor

Do you have a favorite professor, advisor, or mentor on campus? These people can be valuable resources when the going gets tough. There's a good chance they've helped other students through similar situations. They're confidential and they know the system. Personally, when I've found myself in really challenging situations, these are the people I've turned to first, and they've never let me down!

Info: When in Doubt, Seek Help!

As you can see, there's a long list of people you can turn to and places you can go for assistance. The challenges in surviving and thriving in college with ADD are almost always surmountable, if you're willing to seek help. Though it's often hard to believe, there's rarely a problem that's too big, or that can't be turned into a positive experience, when you have the right person guiding you through it (believe me, I've seen some doozies!). So take it from me, the original "I am an island" type of guy: let down your guard, put down your ego, be humble, and ask for help. If you've made it as far as college, don't let something as silly as your pride stop you from achieving your goals. And don't worry about being a burden—once you're doing better and are successful during or after college, you can always return the favor!

Choosing Courses and Creating a Schedule

 Choosing courses is often one of the last things students want to think about. But it can also be the greatest gift you give yourself. Whether you're just starting freshman year or about to graduate, you have the ability to make this your best semester ever.

> "Don't wait until everything is just right. It will never be perfect. There will always be challenges, obstacles, and less than perfect conditions. So what. Get started now. With each step you take, you will grow stronger and stronger, more and more skilled, more and more self-confident, and more and more skillful."—**Mark Victor Hansen**

Set yourself up for success…by building a winning college schedule.

The right course schedule makes college enjoyable, exciting, and maybe even a breeze. It's momentum-building, karma-cleansing, and helps you discover your passion and move forward with gusto.

You worked so hard to get into college and make it this far. This is not the time to martyr yourself or set yourself up for the slaughter. Instead, build a cool schedule for this fall, spring, or summer semester and make it the best of your life.

Is it really that simple?

Let's look at the facts:

1. We tend to listen to what others tell us, signing up for what the registrar or advisor recommends, rather than considering what's right for us.

2. We dread thinking about choosing courses (we don't want to make the wrong decision or even to think about it at all), so we wait far too long, and then either choose poorly or get stuck with the leftovers.

3. Think of course selection like playing chess: you need to know what move to make when. Do this and you're well on your way; play passively, without any forethought, and it's checkmate before you know it.

4. As undergraduates, many students choose courses based on whims. Some may register for the easiest courses available or register too late and get stuck with a few poor choices unrelated to their major. They may not give much thought to the timing of courses: students often place tougher classes back to back just to get them out of the way, or they cram all their classes into one or two days to get an

extended weekend. Even worse, students rarely examine their strengths and weaknesses and assess what they're capable of before choosing their classes.

Every semester you're given the opportunity to either make your life easier or make it a living hell. Strategizing, planning ahead, and understanding your strengths, weaknesses, and needs are essential to setting yourself up for success. In this section you'll learn how to choose classes that will set you up for a productive and successful semester.

Info

 A good semester, even with an "easy" schedule, builds momentum. And it is this momentum, not your grades or your knowledge, but the courage and esteem you gain from your success, that will carry you forth, up and over the inevitable hurdles that will come your way.

How Do You Develop a Class Schedule?

Choosing courses wisely is more essential to your success than it is for traditional students. Every detail, from what time a class begins, where it is located on campus, what the room is like, what the professor is like, how the course is taught, and what other classes you schedule on the same day can all affect your success.

Choosing college courses is quite complicated, and unlike high school, if you don't do it yourself and do it on time, you could end up without courses altogether. (This doesn't sound so bad at first, does it?).

In addition to making sure you sign up on time, there are a number of other pitfalls to navigate. Typically, you have to set up your online account in advance just to have access to the registration process. Then you have to make sure you sign up for the right class on the right day at the right time with the right professor and the right adjunct *and*…get the picture? There are almost an infinite number of variables and opportunities to make a simple mistake that could lead to a nightmarish semester or even an additional year at school, waiting for a required course that's only offered once a year to come around again.

How Do You Register for Classes?

1. **Get help.** Don't try to do it alone. Whether it's your first or last time, you might as well make it easy on yourself. Even for the most experienced student, a simple oversight can wreak havoc on your schedule.

2. **Ask for early registration.** Get in touch with the RDS office. If you haven't started college yet, do this as soon as you send back your acceptance. Find out what's necessary for you to be able to register for classes early. This is a common accommodation for ADD students. It allows you to get the most advantageous schedule for success (best professors, best time slots, most staggered schedule, etc.) before all the best classes fill.

3. **Follow your RSD's advice.** She'll help you jump through any necessary hoops to ensure you can register before the horde.

4. **Meet with an advisor or RSD counselor.** In addition to getting advice for early registration (or at the same time), meet with a counselor (preferably at the RDS office) to go over potential majors or tracks and to discuss class options. Schedule this meeting as early in the process as possible and make sure you attend.

5. **Talk with the department you're interested in.** If you and your counselor discuss a major that you're particularly interested in, you may want to speak with a professor, advisor, or secretary in that department to find out more about it. Do so before your registration date so you have more information to base your class choices on.

6. **Prepare your calendar and alarms.** Post a calendar or set numerous alarms to ensure you register on the first available day. If you can, schedule a meeting with a

counselor or specialist at your RDS office for that day so they can walk you through online registration. If that's not a possibility, seek outside help from a coach or mentor who understands the registration process.

7. **Do research in advance.** Discuss potential classes with the RDS office, a coach, a mentor, a friendly professor, or someone else you trust. Come up with a mock schedule and backup choices for classes that fit the time frame, locations, and difficulty level you have compiled. Take this mock schedule and list of backups with you when it's time to register.

8. **Get firsthand student advice.** Find students who have gone through your potential professor's classes to find out what they're like. Many schools even have a link on their website to student reviews of professors. You want to know how tough they are, the workload involved in the class, and if they're ADD friendly or not.

9. **Interview potential professors!** Be bold and visit professors before registering, if possible, or after if there's no other way. This falls into the category of self-advocacy (see the beginning of this chapter). Talk to them about your ADD and see what they have to say. Often, it's pretty easy to see whether you can work with this professor or if you need to run for your life!

10. **Prepare to register.** Now that you've done your homework, get ready to register. Make sure that you have your mock schedule and list of backups and that you're working with an experienced student or someone from the RDS office. Even if you think signing up for classes is very straightforward and easy, having someone else double-check your registration never hurts.

Info: Questions to Consider

Who? What? When? Where? and How? These are all crucial questions to be answered before you can compose a successful schedule.

1. Am I a morning person or a night person? Signing up for early morning classes if you're a night person will be a disaster; same goes for night classes if you're one of those rare morning people.

2. How do I avoid scheduling difficult classes on the same day, or how do I put as much time in between them as possible? Don't put difficult classes on the same day or near the same time—try to keep them on different days so you can devote equal study time for both.

3. Would it be better for me to stagger my classes through the day or week or put them back-to-back to get them out of the way? Typically, spacing them out as far as possible (either on a given day or over the course of the week) is the best way to do it, giving you the most study time and keeping you from sacrificing studies in one class over another. Do I want to schedule a light day in the middle of the week to recharge, or should I build a schedule that starts the weekend a little early?

4. Have I looked at the length of the classes I'm considering? Consider the length of the classes—putting several long classes on the same day or near each other can be a major challenge to your focus.

5. Can I start school with a reduced course load or at least put off some of the prerequisites until later on?

Additional Tips and Hints

Know How You Like to Work

> "If you know the enemy and know yourself you need not fear the results of a hundred battles." —**Sun Tzu**

Ask yourself how, when, where, why, and what helps you work best. This helps you take control of your schedule and set the ship's course for where you want it to go.

- If you need a break before you can switch gears and get going again, make sure you build in time between classes. On the other hand, if you have an easy time going from class to class but trouble getting to the first one of the day, then putting a few classes in close proximity to one another may not be a bad idea. There are positives and negatives to each strategy; you need to know which will best suit your style.

- Having classes back-to-back is great for getting them out of the way for the day. Problems arise when assignments are due in both classes on the same day or when there are tests in both classes on the same day. If this is how your schedule looks, eventually you'll end up having to cram for two tests or complete two assignments for the same day.

- Having a lot of time between classes gives you the chance to review your notes and do homework immediately after class ends, before switching gears for lunch or another class. You can work on new assignments while the professor or your classmates are still around and get their input. You also eliminate the transition time you would normally need. And that transition time typically eats into your study and homework time; opening books and getting into the material always takes longer than you think it will.

Avoid Night Classes If Possible

Sometimes a course you need is only offered as a night class with continuing education students. These courses have the advantage of meeting fewer times during the week, but the class period can be very lengthy—if you lose concentration easily during an hour-long class, you could be setting yourself up for disaster by taking a three- or four-hour night class. Additionally, if you tend to get tired after five o'clock this is not the best time for you to be stuck in class; the tiredness will just make you lose focus faster.

Avoid Lunchtime Classes or a Schedule that Leaves You Little Time to Eat

Make sure you aren't going to die of hunger pangs in the middle of class. If you like to eat at noon, don't schedule a class then. If your schedule requires back-to-back classes near the lunchtime hour, beware: you could be setting yourself up for failure. It's very hard to pay attention when you're famished.

Keep Your Fridays Light

This isn't always possible, but I've found it to be a great stress reliever. By Friday, my brain is fried from the rest of the week, and I'm thinking more about the weekend than I am about school during the day. So I try to put an easier class on Friday mornings and try to avoid classes in the afternoon altogether.

Schedule Your Hardest Class for Monday

Not early Monday morning—remember, this isn't supposed to be a recipe for disaster! Scheduling your hardest class on Monday gives you the maximum time to study, prepare, or do coursework; if you need to, you can devote almost the entire weekend to this single class.

Tech Tip: What Do I Do Next?

PDAs and Calendar Software to the Rescue!
There are oodles and oodles of software out there to help you organize your schedule (see scheduling section on how to use these most effectively). If you

have Microsoft Windows, there's a good chance you already have a great scheduling program: Microsoft Outlook should be on your computer. Another good option is the ADD Planner (www.addplanner.com); it's simpler than Microsoft Outlook with design features for ADDers, so it's well worth a look.

Computer calendars are a great tool to help you organize your life. You can easily block out time for recurring events, schedule time for a special test, and leave yourself reminders. I know many people whose computers tell them what to do, when. A message will pop up on the screen letting them know it's time to go to class, take their meds, or start study-ing? Computer calendars offer special features, including sound, color, and sometimes even ani-mation. Depending on how you set it up, a reminder will pop up on your screen and may even require a response before you go back to the task at hand.

If you have a Palm Pilot or other PDA, it has similar calendar software built in. This software synchronizes with your computer's calendar (such as Outlook) to give you alerts and alarms, keep track of your to-do list, and help you remember what you need to do and where you need to be next.

If you struggle to remember assignments, deliver-ables, projects, papers, or test dates, keep a PDA with you at all times. It's like having a portable coach with you, and can be the ultimate lifesaver!

"I also remember the moment my life changed, the moment I finally said, 'I've had it! I know I'm much more than I'm demonstrating mentally, emotionally, and physically in my life.' I made a decision in that moment which was to alter my life forever. I decided to change virtually every aspect of my life. I decided I would never again settle for less than I can be."

—**Tony Robbins**

8

Know Your Student Rights

"It makes no sense to worry about things you **have no control** over because there's nothing you can do about them, and why worry about things you do control? The activity of **worrying keeps you immobilized**"

—**Dr. Wayne Dyer**

No More Fighting for Your Rights

Fighting for assistance is a contradiction. Ever heard the expression "What you resist persists"? Mother Teresa knew this concept. To quote her: "I was once asked why I don't participate in anti-war demonstrations. I said that I will never do that, but as soon as you have a pro-peace rally, I'll be there." Fighting against something never works.

Whether in requesting accommodations or anything else, strive for teamwork. No matter how difficult, always ask, "How can I help *you*?" even if it almost kills you. Chances are, others will be shocked by the question, perhaps seldom having heard it before. This one question can turn them from your adversary into your strongest ally.

Understand this concept and you'll learn communication and negotiation skills that will serve you well, far beyond the artificial confines of academia. In short, it all comes down to the art of listening and allowing others to feel heard. Let them feel you're truly taking their needs, struggles, and challenges into account, and they'll become your most loyal advocates, even—or especially—when it comes to your rights.

How Do You Get Accommodations?

Go to your resources for RDS office to find out what accommodations are available for ADD students before your classes begin—in fact, it's something you should look into before you even agree to attend the school. They'll ask you what your particular difficulties are, and it's important to be completely honest with them. Don't sell yourself short or think that you're a wimp or a failure for admitting what's hard for you—that's what they're there for. Then see what they have to offer that will address your specific needs.

Commonly Available Accommodations

The help available to an ADD student varies from school to school and student to student depending on the severity of the symptoms. Schools also require you to have been tested for ADD within the last two to three years before you're eligible for accommodations.

ADD Advantage: Level the Playing Field

Don't think of accommodations as cop-outs or as taking advantage of the system. Personally, I wouldn't have survived graduate school without them. These accommodations help you level the playing field with the other students, making it easier for you to study, take notes, take tests, and complete many other tasks crucial to college success. Taking advantage of these aids means that you're smart—you're doing what you need to in order to overcome your ADD challenges.

If you received any accommodations in high school that aren't listed below but that you think you may need in college, check with your school and see what they can do for you. In addition, make sure you bring your IEP or 504 plan to your RDS office well in advance of your first semester.

Common accommodations include the following:

- Early registration and assistance registering for classes
- Prerequisites waived or modified
- Core curriculum requirements such as math those for or foreign languages waived or modified
- Waived or modified placement exams, such as those for math or languages; additional time to take them or additional time before you have to take them (such as an extra semester, etc.)
- Option to take a class again or even an entire semester again without it hurting your GPA if you've hit a wall due to your disability
- Extra time for exams
- Option to take exams in your chosen environment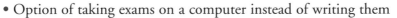
- Extra paper to work through problems on exams
- Option of taking exams on a computer instead of writing them
- Access to and use of text-to-speech software for tests and exams
- Access to and use of a spell-checker on exams
- Substituting oral exams for written exams
- A calculator for exams when necessary
- Extra time on assignments
- Extra time to meet with the professor
- Assistance with putting together large papers or projects
- Free tutoring
- Free notetaker in class
- Additional writing assistance (beyond what's available for the general student population)
- Option to turn in assignments in multiple pieces or segments
- Use of a laptop in class (most schools/classes allow this now anyway)
- Option of buying audio versions of textbooks
- Use of a computer center with software for LD and ADD students (such as reading software or text-to-speech software)
- Eating in class to keep blood sugar up
- Being able to stand or pace in the back of the classroom
- Housing accommodations, such as a single for students who need the quiet to study

Know Your Student Rights

Working with Your Professors

Visit with your professor at the first sign of trouble in a class. Don't go empty-handed—show them what you've been working on and, more importantly, that you've been working on it. Then ask for help. Make a study outline for a test or come with your research for an upcoming paper. They may point out what will be on the test and what won't be, which can save you valuable study time, or show you what areas of a paper you'll need to develop more thoroughly.

If you're struggling in a class but show the professor that you've been working hard on it, they'll usually be happy to give you accommodations such as extra time or rescheduling of tests or deadlines, and they'll just be more reasonable in general. There are exceptions to this rule—some professors may be unwilling to help no matter what—but the majority will go out of their way to help. Just don't break this cardinal rule: asking for extensions and accommodations at the time of a test or deadline is highly frowned upon. Make sure you ask before deadlines, or you probably won't get anywhere. So if you're in trouble, even if you think there's a slight chance that trouble's lurking around the corner, visit your professor before it's too late. Go and ask questions and get the help you need.

MY STORY

Be Proactive and Prepared

I almost failed out of my computer master's degree program because of the last test on the last day—had I not asked for accommodations, I definitely would have failed. It wouldn't have been a failure just on the test but of the entire program, because I needed that class to graduate. Without that class there would've been nothing I could do; I couldn't even go back and retake it.

It was a Java Algorithms programming class that required taking many small pieces of code or programming and piecing them all together like a puzzle to create a program. I had a great deal of difficulty with this, and I had learned to ask for accommodations in advance even though I had to go to the RDS office and say, "I'm a student with a disability," which was no fun. I also hated feeling like I was taking advantage of the system, almost cheating, by asking for extra time or accommodations on a test. Of course I wasn't; these aids are there to help level the playing field for us ADDers.

I had worked with my classmates to assemble a complicated project, and one day my professor asked me to tell him more about it. Though I had done all the work, unless I laid out all of the pieces and studied them, I had no idea how they fit together. The professor asked if I had done the work on my own—the fact was, nobody had done it all on his own: we had all worked on it as a giant group project, since this was more complex than any of us (ADD or not) could handle—but here I was, trapped. In college, as in life, honesty really is the best policy, and I told him the truth.

The professor appreciated my honesty, but told me, "If you do well on the final, you get a great grade in the class and you pass. But if not, if you show me that you don't know the material by failing it, you cannot retake this class and it's a requirement for your degree."

I studied like there was no tomorrow! My entire degree came down to this one test. My academic career was on the line, and the pressure made my brain turn into a quivering blubber of misfiring synapses and neurons during the test. Halfway through the time allotted I stood up, walked to the front of the class, and with tears in my eyes approached my professor. I pointed to some problems and couldn't even find the words to describe to him what was going on. At that point, I couldn't remember my name; my brain was in complete lockdown.

The professor looked at my work and said, "Michael, I am so disappointed in you. If you don't know this simple concept, it proves you don't know a single thing about this class, and you should not pass." That smack in the face brought me back to reality and my adrenaline kicked into high gear. I found the words I needed to say, "I need extra time on the exam."

The professor said, "No. It looks like you've answered everything—you don't need extra time." I responded, "Yes, but I requested accommodations before the test and you signed the form allowing extra time if necessary." The professor didn't want to give in but eventually conceded.

After the regulation time was over, I went into a quiet room with an hour to complete the exam. For the first half hour I just sat in the room and did nothing. I didn't write anything, I just stared at the ceiling, trying to think about other things. And then, eureka! Just as the name you'd been searching for appears in your head when you stop trying to find it, clarity struck. I could see exactly what I was doing wrong. It was so clear. It was so simple. And my answers so far were completely incorrect! No wonder he wanted to flunk me! In the next half hour I went through and rewrote the majority of the exam. He then graded it right in front of me. Almost a perfect score! The professor was so proud of me.

If I hadn't asked for accommodations, because of pride or because I thought I wouldn't need them, I wouldn't have made it through. So make sure you ask for help and have extra resources at the ready, because you never know!

Info: Find a Mentor

One of the keys to success in college is a finding a helping hand to guide you through. This mentor can often be an experienced professor who befriends you. She can offer great advice and help you get through tough times. Remember, chances are you aren't the first student she's counseled through a crisis. No challenge is new to them, even the challenges that come with learning disabilities. In my case it was Dr. Ted Weston who saved my hide a time or two at CSU. (Thank you, Dr. Weston!) A professor/mentor can give you school direction, career direction, and at times even life direction.

Should You Pay for Extra Services?

While all schools offer some degree of assistance for students with ADD, the level of assistance varies widely. It's not uncommon for public institutions—which receive greater financial assistance than private colleges—to offer a higher level of assistance and accommodations. It's also not uncommon for schools to offer tiered levels of service: while the basic tier is available to all students, you must pay extra or sign up for a special program to receive the most hands-on accommodations.

These programs offer much greater assistance and go above and beyond any institution's call of duty. They also cost the institution more money, which is why you may have to pay for them. There are activities, events, workshops, additional guidance, and much more offered. While you have to pay more, if you're at a larger institution or you received a good deal of hands-on assistance in high school, this is for you! These paid assistance programs help guide you through the details of college, leaving you free to focus on classes, studying, and life rather than on how to register, fill out paperwork, figure out housing, and all the other details you need to take care of.

In Conclusion

Understanding your needs and potential challenges is essential for college success. Ask yourself about services you've had in the past and what you could need in the future. Making sure the accommodations that you need are in place is essential in choosing the right college.

Remember: If you needed assistance to get through high school, you may need more assistance than you initially think in college. And if there's even a slim chance you may need an accommodation, make sure it's available. I made it through most of college without accommodations. However, had they not been there in the end, I would never have graduated. Make sure they're there in case you need them!

Better safe than sorry is *surely* the name of the game when it comes to accommodations and your rights!

> ### Tech Tip: Entitled to Tech Support
>
> Technically, there's nothing that says you're *required* to have assistive technology as an accommodation. Nevertheless, if you can't write with a pen but are highly proficient on a keyboard (or with dictation software), then use of a laptop may be a "reasonable accommodation." Work with your RDS and if you *know* you'll need tech assistance, ask about these things *before* you choose your school!

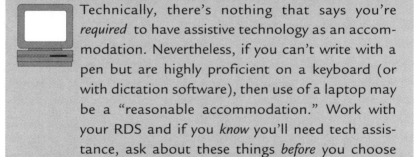

"It's easy to grin, when your ship has come in, and you've got the stock market beat. But the man worthwhile, is the man who can smile, when his shorts are too tight in the seat"

—*Caddyshack*

Taking Care of Yourself

9

> **"To keep the body** in good health is a duty...otherwise we shall not be able to **keep our mind strong and clear."**
>
> **—The Buddha**

Having a creative mind or ADD is a sneaky thing. Things can be going along great, and then BLAMMO! Everything blows up in our face.

Often this is the result of a lack of self-care. Things like diet, exercise, and sleep are essential to keeping us on an even keel and keeping the pistons firing right. Picture your mind as super-complex, highly advanced, and often finicky machinery whirring around ten times faster than other equipment. It doesn't take much to knock the equipment out of balance and cause the thing to hiccup or lock up.

That's how our minds work. So we need to make sure we're fueling ourselves properly, getting enough sleep (especially while in college), and maintaining our bodies and minds so we don't lock up, compromise our creativity (which is truly our "edge" in college), or cause our minds to go into a tailspin—just when we need them the most!

Exercise, diet, and proper sleep can make the difference between an A student who can semi-painlessly memorize, study, and socialize, and the student who's hiding under the sheets, terrified of going to class, and constantly feeling like he's been run over by a truck.

Wouldn't you rather be the A student?

and ADD

a miracle cure for those of us with ADD. ...rcise, built into your daily routine, can transform your college career and your entire life.

Many ADD experts today agree that exercise can be as important and beneficial as medication in soothing the ADD mind! For myself, I believe it's even more important. When someone's struggling with sleep, stress, or daily challenges, one of my first questions is always whether or not they exercise. The answer's typically in the negative, like "I'd love to if only I could find the time." Believe me, I understand this sentiment, but there are ways to overcome it. Remember that exercise makes you *more* productive and creative during the hours you *are* working, and more relaxed during the times you're not. This means any time spent exercising adds to rather than takes away from your scholastic success while at the same time increasing the quality of your life *and* the fun factor at college. By adding exercise to your day, you can start a fun lifelong habit that'll help you for years to come…and really, that's what college is all about.

Below, we'll go over some great ways to find the time to exercise, and reasons why exercise may be that magic ingredient you need to overcome many of your ADD challenges.

Why Should You Exercise?

You may say you don't have time to exercise, but I would argue that you don't have time not to. You can't tell me there aren't dead spots in your day, time when you're staring at your books or computer without being productive. I'm an ADDer as well—I know you zone out and sit almost coma-like at times, unable to get work done. Aerobic exercise, as little as twenty minutes a day, helps stimulate your brain and produces many of the same chemicals as medication. You've heard of a "runner's high," right? When you exercise daily, you gain energy, stamina, and mental clarity. You may have less time to get your work done, but you'll have fewer dead spots, too.

Daily exercise also helps program your body clock. It helps your body learn what to do when—when to wake up, when to work, when to play, and even when to sleep. I used to be an ADD insomniac, and now my daily exercise routine helps me sleep like a baby. Exercise relaxes your mind so you can drift off easily into sleep rather than problem-solve through the night.

Physical Benefits

Vigorous aerobic exercise has been shown to be one of the leading ways to keep us healthy and happy. According to Dr. Edward Hallowell, author of many leading ADD books, "sleep, exercise, and sex" are the three keys to success with ADD. In *Delivered from Distraction*, Hallowell writes that exercise helps with:

- Relaxation
- Focus
- Concentration
- Decreased impulsivity
- Sleep
- Increased energy and stamina
- Increased productivity

Specifically, daily aerobic exercise has some pretty far-reaching benefits. It has been proven to do the following:

- Strengthen the heart
- Lower blood pressure
- Increase energy levels
- Release endorphins, which help you feel better and relax
- Fall asleep more easily—can help reset your body clock with regular (same time) daily exercise
- Increase aerobic capacity, which means less effort for walking, hiking, and climbing stairs
- Increase muscle tone

- Decrease body fat
- Speed up the metabolism
- Keep you younger longer
- Increase bone density

From a physical perspective, there are several key reasons to exercise in college.

1. It gives you greater stamina throughout the day. You'll need this when you're regularly studying late into the night.

2. It helps keep the freshman fifteen—or fifty—at bay!

3. It keeps you pain-free. Sitting in a chair all day isn't as cushy and painless as it sounds. It can easily lead to back and neck pain, among other health issues. Keeping loose, nimble, and strong goes a long way toward being pain-free throughout college and beyond. This is a life habit that will pay dividends when studying now—and when working for years and decades to come!

4. It keeps you healthy. Want to avoid the common cold, the flu, and other nasties flying around in the air? Moderate daily exercise helps strengthen your immune system. This alone is more than reason enough to exercise when your world is a Petri dish.

5. It keeps heart disease, high blood pressure, asthma, and more at bay. These may sound like distant maladies to the college student, but you'd be amazed at the changes your body goes through in your twenties. Staying healthy now helps keep you healthy later on.

6. Sleep, sleep, and sleep. If you struggle to sleep at night (and who with ADD doesn't, at one point or another?) regular, repetitive daily exercise can be a godsend. If you take a short walk, hike, run, or perform some other aerobic exercise for twenty minutes in the morning and evening, you rewire your body to the natural rhythms of the earth (sunrise and sunset). In short, your body will remember when to wake and when to sleep.

7. It gives you greater strength and injury prevention.

Exercise regularly. It's better than an apple a day for keeping that doctor away! And you'll feel great each and every day you do it.

Ahhhhhh. That's the sound of relief, relaxation, and accomplishment you'll make after you've finished that morning workout and are on to the rest of your day!

Psychological Benefits

So there are psychological benefits to exercise in addition to looking great come spring break?

Yes! Exercise can help you focus and stay relaxed throughout the entire day. I know many people who go for a run or a swim first thing in the morning. That's often a challenging routine to get into, but once you're there, it's worth it. After your workout you feel incredible for the rest of your day. Not only that, but you can study and focus better, particularly in those classes that previously put you to sleep. Know how the ADD mind often seems only half awake? Say good-bye to those days after you've done your morning exercise!

Exercise can also give you an increased sense of self-confidence and self-esteem. Exercise builds muscle and helps you get in better shape, and typically the better shape you're in, the more you like your looks and the more positive your body image will be. As you're exercising, you're also probably improving your performance at a sport or activity. As your game or activity improves, you get another boost of confidence and self-esteem.

Better yet, this self-esteem and confidence doesn't turn off when you're finished exercising. You carry around your new and improved body wherever you go, taking your self-confidence and newfound self-esteem with you. This can be just the body armor you need to get you through your day.

Does Exercise Have Medicinal Benefits?

Daily exercise can be as important, if not more important, than ADD meds. Having tried both, I can attest to exercise's incredible benefits, whether I'm on my meds or not. Adderall makes me calmer, more focused, and more relaxed throughout the day. I can get by without my Adderall; I think I'd go insane without my exercise. I'd have too much nervous energy to burn, and I'd never be able to focus in class. Exercise releases chemicals to the brain, the same type of chemicals you get from your medication or even from illicit drugs. There's a reason there's something called a runner's high. It's no joke; it's *real*. Daily exercise changes the chemistry of your brain leaving you more relaxed, happy, energized, focused, confident, and calm throughout your day. As good as meds? In many ways, YOU BET!

How Do You Find the Time?

"I'd love to exercise, but I just can't find the time!"

I completely understand your sentiment. We're all in the same boat on this one. There just isn't enough time in the day, and something has to give. But it shouldn't be your exercise. As you'll see below, exercise gives you more time than it takes. So it's worth including, almost no matter what. (Some people try to skip it when studying for exams, but that's a double-edged sword. For the short-term, they end up with more time, but they're also more anxious and edgy and less productive. So do they *really* get more out of the studying…or are they even more brain-fried come test time?)

So with all the benefits, just where *do* I find the time?

1. First off, you could put it into your morning routine. When the alarm goes off, just roll out of bed, stumble out the door, and run, hike, snowshoe, or drag yourself along for twenty minutes. By the time you come back you'll be wide awake, relaxed, and refreshed.

   Honestly, do you think the twenty minutes after you hit the snooze alarm will let you get any quality sleep?

2. Can't wake yourself up? How about throwing yourself in a pool? Better yet, join running club, swimming club, or fitness class that meets at the same time each morning. Nothing beats meeting a group, having friends to work out with, meeting members of the opposite sex, or peer pressure to get us up and at 'em early in the morning.

3. If that won't work for you, see if you can make time in between classes or possibly take a slightly shorter lunch. Still no luck? How about after your last class? That's typically when intramurals and after-school club sports are held anyway. Where there's a will, there's a way.

4. Many students (myself included) have had to exercise late in the day, after dinner. At first this sounds irritating or disruptive, but actually, it gives quite a boost to evening studies. Working up a sweat at six, seven, or eight at night can keep you studying well past midnight before you fade.

Build It into a Routine

The real trick to getting into the habit of exercising regular-ly is making it part of your routine. You can't exercise spo-radically or just whenever you get around to it—if you don't put it into a routine, it doesn't become a habit and just won't get done. There are several ways to build it in. If it's an individual activi-ty, block off a specific time (set alarm after alarm after alarm) for it each and every day. Usually earlier in the day is better; there are fewer distrac-tions, you're not quite as panicked about what needs to get done, and it can help you wake up and prepare your brain to focus on other activi-ties throughout the rest of the day.

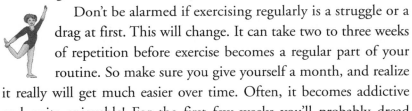

Don't be alarmed if exercising regularly is a struggle or a drag at first. This will change. It can take two to three weeks of repetition before exercise becomes a regular part of your routine. So make sure you give yourself a month, and realize it really will get much easier over time. Often, it becomes addictive and quite enjoyable! For the first few weeks you'll probably dread working out or try to find excuses not to, but if you can muscle through this time you're more likely to keep it up. It becomes a regu-lar part of your daily routine, and you'll miss it if you stop. You'll become addicted to feeling better.

It can also be helpful to:

1. Find a partner. It's often hard to drag yourself out to exercise alone. But if you can find a partner to exercise with you, it becomes much easier. Ask around cam-pus, check out the postings at the gym or rec center, or even check online at websites such as www.craigslist.com. You might even find someone on Facebook, MySpace, or similar sites. Regularly meeting with a partner will keep you motivated when you feel like skipping a day or two.

2. **Join a club.** There are sports clubs for everything from running to rock climbing, cycling to soccer, yoga, skiing, maybe even base jumping. If you join a club you can find people to work out with and try new and different activities. As a result, you'll be more likely to get out and stay active. It's also a great way to meet new people and make friends.

3. **Join a team.** If you like to participate in team sports, join a club team. There will be regular workout times and a coach to help keep you on track. You'll make new friends, and you'll get to burn off a ton of energy. A competitive environment could be just what you need to take your mind off your worries. Just be sure you don't overextend yourself. You don't want to be stressed out because you're spending just as much time with your team as you are with your studies.

Info: A Word of Caution

Don't exercise too close to bedtime—it can keep you awake long into the night. If I exercise after nine o'clock, I might not fall asleep until dawn. Exercise raises my body temperature too much and gets me too energized, which are not things you want to do to yourself late at night. So make sure that you exercise early enough that it won't interfere with your sleep.

What Different Types of Exercise Are There?

Aerobic Activities
Aerobic exercises, those that raise your heart rate, tend to be the best for all of the health benefits described above. That's

not to say non-aerobic activities aren't great too, but they won't give you all of the same benefits. Wondering if your activity's aerobic? Check your heart rate or listen to your breathing. If you're huffing and puffing, or your heart's racing like a rabbit, then it sure is!

There are an endless number of aerobic activities. Try running up and down the stairs of your dorm or a downtown building, or up the down escalators at your local subway station (yes, this *really* works). Or try dancing at a party. Even running from security guards (not recommended counts). Almost anything that continues for at least twenty minutes and gets your heart rate up can become an aerobic workout.

- Swimming
- Soccer
- Basketball
- Hockey
- Tennis
- Racquetball
- Ultimate frisbee

- Lacrosse
- Vigorous walking
- Hiking
- Biking
- Snow-shoeing
- Water polo
- Aerobics

- Spinning
- Tae bo
- Dancing to a fast beat
- Boxing
- Kickboxing
- Swing dancing
- And yes, even sex

Non-aerobic Activities

While aerobic exercises may offer the most health benefits, such as a lower heart rate, lower blood pressure, greater stamina, and reduced weight and body fat, there are some magnificent benefits to non-aerobic exercises, too.

Often your non-aerobic exercises are those involving form, technique, and concentration. While they may not raise your heart rate and burn the fat, they still help build strength, increase concentration, and reduce fatigue and anxiety. They can also help you get in touch with your inner strength, a benefit we address in greater detail in the meditation section. They are absolutely worth doing, either along with or alternating with, your aerobic workouts. For instance, running three mornings a week and doing yoga on the other days is an amazing gift you can give to yourself and an incredible way to start each day!

Yoga, Pilates, Martial Arts, and Meditation

 These types of exercises tend to focus more on strength and body control than aerobic exercises. Perhaps you've seen people doing tai chi early in the morning. This is a perfect example. It helps focus the mind and body, slowing down the endless chatter in your brain. Meditation, while not technically an exercise, also has a strong mind-body connection that deadens the chatter, leaving you relaxed, refreshed, more creative, and less stressed.

All of these activities involve a high degree of inward focus. This introspective concentration tends to relax people with ADD and leave them feeling refreshed throughout the day. While they don't produce the same chemicals or endorphins as aerobic activities, these activities produce long-lasting mental results.

More information on yoga and pilates (along with instructional videos, which I use to help keep me focused while I'm working out) can be found at www.gaiam.com, and self-meditation techniques can be found in dozens of great audio books (including my favorites, *Meditation for Manifesting* and *Getting in the Gap*, both by Dr. Wayne W. Dyer) at www.audible.com. For even more meditation info, check out an amazing number of books and CD's at www.hayhouse.com. There's even a meditation CD specifically for ADDers at www.mindfulnessforadd.com.

High-Focus Activities

High-focus activities are those that require a major meeting of mind and body, and include rock climbing, archery, bowling, pool, golf, target practice, and even car racing. While some of these don't fall under the category of traditional exercise, they have many similar benefits. The focus and exertion necessary can help you block out distractions, relax, and feel calmer throughout the day. (And for all of you climbers out there, this can be the toughest exercise you'll ever do—it strengthens every muscle you never knew you had, and if you get good at it, it can be quite aerobic as well!)

Recreational skiing and snowboarding also fall under this category, as do more risky and extreme activities such as hang gliding, parachuting, or bungee jumping. And for some people, performing on stage, being on a debate team, solving incredibly difficult math or science problems, or thinking ten steps ahead in chess produces these effects. Whatever the activity, if you're forced to focus and concentrate with all of your might, you'll gain clarity, calm, and stress relief that lasts throughout the day.

What about Wii or other video games? you might ask.

Yes, gaming can have the same effect as other high-focus activities. But again, make sure whatever you're doing does *not* become an addiction that takes you completely away from your work. Your extreme concentration and ability to block out extraneous stimuli and distractions is great unless you're using it to block out the things you *really* need to do! (That is, unless you're studying to become a video game programmer and/or are doing tests of a game you've designed for your thesis. In that case, play away!)

Exercises to Avoid

While exercise is a key ingredient for decreasing stress, what you do and when you do it are critical to your success. As mentioned earlier, exercising late at night can keep you awake, which definitely won't help reduce stress. And certain exercises may also make you more, rather than less, stressed. For many people, boxing or sparring can be a tremendously rewarding experience. But for a few ADD guys I know (myself included), such activities make us downright hostile. Maybe it's the repetitive visualization of clocking one's opponent that brings out the ADD rage. One guy even told me, "I'm scared of myself when I'm boxing, so I need to take my meds before I box. If not, I'm liable to hurt someone. Unfortunately, when I take my meds, I'm not hostile anymore, and so I don't box quite as well." Then again, I heard he'd bought a gun while boxing, and sold it after getting out of the sport. So just watch out for signs of violence as you exercise. If there's a potential for trouble, leave that hot potato alone!

But I've heard martial arts are calming for the mind, you might assert.

Yes! I've heard the same thing. Martial arts tend to bring out this Zen focus and control you don't see in a pure slugger-sport (nothing against boxing here, it's just a different beast).

I've known ADDers who have taken up karate, another form of fighting but one very different than boxing. It's given them the body control to be very relaxed and the skills to give them a newfound sense of self-confidence. Unlike boxing, which tends to focus on hitting, martial arts emphasize mental control, focus, and mastery. It also teaches you never to use the art or skills for anything but self-defense. People who take martial arts develop great self-control. They tend to be quite connected to their inner selves, almost rewiring their minds for incredible patience, balance, concentration, and focus. They use these skills in far more than just the exercise they're involved in. Additionally, the training involved makes these trained "fighters" more artist than soldier, and far less likely to fight.

In almost any athletic endeavor, a very high level of competition can stress you out. With ADD and athletics, like ADD and anything else, moderation is often the best approach. If you love competition, don't be scared away by the potential for stress—just realize that if you push yourself too hard, you may lose the stress relief benefit you sought in the first place.

ADD Advantage: NCAA and ADD

I've seen many incredible ADD athletes stop their athletic endeavors when they begin college. They (or their parents) are concerned they can't juggle the top-level sport and college academics.

Well here's a mind bender. Competing in the NCAA in a school with good academics can actually *improve* your scholastic performance!

Why? Because competitive sports impose structure on your life. In a sense, the NCAA is more like boot camp than college. Not only are there specified times for eating and sleeping, there are specific times and places you *must* be studying (you even need to sign in and out). Choose the right program and your athletic career will flourish, your self-esteem will go through the roof, and your grades and ability to overcome challenges will reach an all-time high. Talk to a coach, the athletic program director, trainers, current athletes, and even the RSD for a given school to see if their program falls into this category. Most do, though some are off-the-hook party-athletes…but this is far less likely to be the case than you'd imagine. Don't give up athletics for college. They're part of you and have made you who you are. Just choose the right program. Then go for it, *go for it*, GO FOR IT!!!

Info: Pick Something You Love

Make sure you choose a sport you enjoy doing. Don't set yourself up for failure by selecting something that exaggerates your weaknesses. As ADDers we often martyr ourselves by sticking with things too long before we realize they're not working for us. If you're swimming laps for exercise but find it mind-numbingly painful, join a swimming group or club, check out water polo, or get the of the pool. If running another mile sounds more excruciating than dousing a scraped knee with vinegar, throw away your running shoes and try a new sport immediately.

Remember, in anything you do, don't bang your head against the wall or try to be a square peg in a round hole. You have nothing to prove to anyone, and martyring yourself isn't the way to a happy life. Instead, focus on your strengths. If you love aerobic exercise but hate the drudgery of running along the sidewalk, try cycling, snowshoeing, power hiking, or maybe even barefoot trail running. If you love team sports but can't shoot a hoop to save your life, try soccer, hockey, or water polo. Look to your strengths and make sure what you do emphasizes your talent. You'll be happier and more likely to keep up with what you're doing, and you'll increase your self-esteem.

Give Yourself a Gift

Happiness and well-being are the name of the game, not good grades (sorry moms and dads). If you're unhappy or unhealthy, nothing else matters, and you're certainly not off to the right start in adulthood. This is the time to start healthy habits to last a lifetime, *not* the time to torture yourself, glue yourself to a chair, and fight to enter an existence of misery in a life, career, or lifestyle that's not right for you. As ADDers we tend to have more energy, enthusiasm, and athletic skills when we're doing what we love. We're the Michael Jordans and Lance Armstrongs of the world, so we shouldn't sell ourselves short.

Exercise can be—and often is—as important as medication. Don't think for a minute you can't find the time or shouldn't do it…particularly if it brings you great joy. If it makes you happy, *do it*.

Remember, exercise helps you relax, concentrate, improve your energy, sleep better, and gain a greater sense of self-esteem. And it's easy to do, too, when you build it into your routine. Just twenty minutes a day—that's the same amount of time it takes to write a couple of emails. Whether it's walking in the morning, hockey at night, yoga begin or to end your day, meditation anytime, or scaling a climbing wall anytime, give yourself the gift of exercise and watch your body and mind improve. Now, what are you sitting here reading this for? Go out there and start exercising, *today*!

ADD Challenges: When You're Struggling at What You Love

I've seen many athletes give up the love of their life—their sport—when things start to go wrong. So what do you do if things aren't going your way? First off, determine the source of the problem. Is it a bad coach or a poor program? If so, consider going JV instead of varsity, playing for a city or town league, or transferring schools. If you've always played hockey or football, don't sell yourself short and say it's not important that you're not enjoying the game. Remember, this is part of what made you who you are and something that gives you confidence...self-esteem is the number one factor in your success, so get to where you're happy.

Happy with the coach, but still struggling? Could it be related to diet or meds? Oftentimes, training is scheduled for late afternoons when our blood sugar is at its lowest or we've depleted our meds for the day. I've seen many student-athletes confused, befuddled, and unable to focus after their meds wear off. If this sounds like you, talk with your doc! There may be a simple solution to this problem. And either way, get some high-quality protein and slow-burning fuel into you with a lot of water *before* practice. Going in energy-depleted or dehydrated from class is a surefire way to crash and burn.

Whatever you do, before you give up, brainstorm, talk with others, and listen to your gut. There's a solution to this problem, and chances are, giving up the game you love is not it. So hang in there and be honest with yourself. If it's important to you, keep it that way!

Train on your own? Want your best workouts ever? Invest in cool training devices such as a heart rate monitor or (if you're a cyclist) a wattage meter. These devices allow you to see how hard you're training and keep you from slacking. Many of them are downloadable so you can track your workouts at home (very cool for the ADDer who hates doing boring things). In this way, you can monitor your progress and get a quick picture of your results. Do you run, cycle, or skate, and want to see something really cool? Get a GPS unit (such as a Timex or Garmin watch) and see a map on the computer of where you've been, exactly how far you've gone, your pace, and even your heart rate. Tools and toys like this help keep our ADD minds from frying and dying of boredom during exercise.

 Want to track your progress digitally? There's free or cheap software available online to track your daily, weekly, and monthly progress on your computer or PDA. You can even build workouts in advance to let you know what you should do and when. It's like having a portable coach, helping to keep you from under-training or—as is often the case with ADDers gone mad—from overtraining.

Can't find a way to get to workouts on time? Of course you know the answer by now. Set alarms to help you get there. Set yourself up for success. Have an alarm go off the night before to ensure you've packed your gym bag and placed it by the door. Better yet, keep it in your car and on the

"Leave all the afternoon for exercise and recreation, which are as necessary as reading. I will rather say more necessary because health is worth more than learning."—**Thomas Jefferson**

Diet and ADD

Did you know your diet can radically affect how you feel and perform in and out of the classroom? And I'm not talking about having a "healthy" diet, though that certainly helps. I'm talking about what you ate twenty minutes ago!

"One cannot think well, love well, sleep well, if one has not dined well."—**Virginia Woolf**

People with ADD tend to be more susceptible to blood sugar lows than other individuals are. Our brains are already struggling to keep up with the day's events, and trying to keep them running without fuel is nearly impossible.

When you eat a high-carb meal or snack before class, you're setting yourself up for a fall. When I'd crash, I'd be in trouble. Everything would turn to gibberish at best.

A big part of the solution to this problem is the Atkins diet or almost any diet that reduces your intake of quick burning fuel (carbohydrates or foods with a high glycemic index) and replaces them with slower burning fuels such as protein and fat.

A great way to do move to a more ADD-friendly diet is to try incorporating more protein into your meals and snack. For breakfast, skip the Twinkies or the quick glass of juice. Instead, try low-fat milk, eggs, or a protein shake. For vegetarians (more on this in a bit), try soy milk, egg substitute or soy patties, a soy or vegetable protein shake (notice the soy theme here…it's a lifesaver!), or a high-protein cereal. Add some nuts to your meal if you'd like. And you don't have to skip the fruit and grains entirely—just eat less of them (in comparison to everything else).

Breakfasts like this won't leave you with plenty of energy to get to your first class—and then feeling like you want to pass out thirty minutes later. Instead, you'll feel energized all morning.

Snacks are another area for improvement. Often we have a sugary drink or snack right before class, setting ourselves up for the midclass crash. Instead, consider protein bars (my favorite's the Odwalla Protein Bar, since it doesn't have a ton of sugar or other additives that might make me wacky), beef jerky, nuts, or yogurt (without added sugar or else they'll crash you just as badly).

For meals, make sure you have enough protein with your carbohydrates. Skip the sugars and stick with more complex carbohydrates such as whole grains, vegetables, and rice, which take longer to burn.

Be careful with a quick glass of juice, a can of Coke, or any other sugar without protein to balance the burn. These are great if you just need a quick burst of energy for twenty minutes or so, but if you don't replenish quickly, you'll be jumping out of that plane without a chute. And in the middle of a class, that's not a good idea.

ADD Challenges: Obesity and ADD

While we typically think of ADDers as skinny, wired, and bouncing all over the place, there are many, many ADDers who are overweight. It's an easy problem to end up with. We don't have a very good self-regulating mechanism, it's hard for us to judge what's enough and what isn't, we tend to eat for self-medication, and we can eat impulsively.

Many students who are taking stimulants find the medications have an appetite-suppressing effect. But this doesn't mean those on stimulants are skinny. Once their meds wear off late at night, they can get a big craving for food, followed by gorging before going to sleep.

Obesity can be quite unhealthy for anyone, and even more so for an ADDer. We may already have self-esteem issues. Keeping motivated and energized can be tough, especially if we're carrying extra weight. It can also lead to lifelong health conditions such as hypertension or heart disease. Having a healthy lifestyle and healthy habits now will help prevent such conditions later.

The key here is to watch your medication, learn about your eating habits, visit a nutritionist if necessary, and if you're unsure, keep a log of what you eat. If you log your eating habits for two to three days and then add up the calories, it should be very clear whether you're eating healthily or not. If you're still not sure, take the log to a nutritionist or your health center on campus; they'll be able to let you know.

Diet

Irritable Bowel Syndrome

A few years back, I started to have major stomach problems...bloating of sorts. I couldn't get it under control or figure out what was going on. The best diagnosis (more voodoo than anything) I received was Irritable Bowel Syndrome (IBS). I think this is the name doctors give to any stomach disorder they can't pin down. But what I've found is that many of us are diagnosed with IBS. Why? I don't have a clue. My parents would say I had stomach problems well before my college years (and before I started any meds). But from my perspective, it came on in adulthood with a vengeance, and it took forever to shake.

What worked? A pretty radical diet change. I cut out all chemical preservatives and ingredients whose names I couldn't decipher, went almost exclusively vegetarian (except for sushi), eliminated

all dairy (yeah, calcium pills!), and began eating as many "whole" or organic foods as possible—i.e., foods that were grown locally and still living as recently as possible (this applies more to food growing out of the ground than it does to animals). Exactly how or what did it, I'm not quite sure, but with this diet, my IBS (which hung around for years) is finally *gone*.

Diet Instead of Medicine

First off, IBS or no IBS, I'm no longer consuming any chemicals I can't pronounce or would need to make in a lab.

I try to stay organic, chemical free, preservative free, additive free, hormone free, pesticide free, artificial sweetener free, and even poison free. Difficult? Sure. Near impossible on a food plan? Quite possibly. Worthy of consideration? *Oh, absolutely!* I feel better, I'm fitter than ever, and I've less body fat than ever. I don't have food cravings. My blood sugar's not kicking me in the butt, and I'm sure I concentrate, act, and think better than ever before, without nearly as many impulsivity issues. Oh, and did I mention that this ADD insomniac finally sleeps like a baby?

I take a few supplements (see Chapter 3) that I believe work *for me*. I say "for me" because I don't know (a) if it's simply a placebo affect or (b) if it's like medication, where different kinds in different amounts work for different ADDers. But I use an expensive berry concentrate (Ageless Xtra from Oasis) and a ground up salad powder (mine's Metagreens, but there are dozens out there) in my diet.

One area for personal improvement is fatty acids. There have been studies showing that increasing fatty acids (such as omega-3 and fish oils) in your diet may be helpful for those with ADD. According to a study conducted by Alexandra Richardson and Basant Puri, faculty members at Oxford University and Imperial College, and published in the February issue of *Progress in Neuro-Psychopharmacology & Biological Psychiatry*, adding fatty acids to your diet may also help improve ADHD and dyslexia symptoms.

I now build eating into my routine. Setting an alarm on my PDA at school helps me remember what to eat when. With my new diet, what I eat doesn't change radically from day to day, so I don't have to try adjusting my schedule for particularly big or small meals. But on that note, my new diet seems to help me listen to my body and eat just the right amount—without feeling either hungry or stuffed. Knowing when you'll eat helps you stay on track and allows you to play with your diet, figuring out what works best for you and when. As with anything else, eating should be built into your routine for success.

Eating Well in College

I must admit, a lot of what I've suggested is difficult in school, particularly on a meal plan. To follow such a diet often costs extra and requires additional forethought and careful selection. It often means setting an alarm the night before class to remind you to throw some food in a plastic container or paper bag to grab when you're running out in the morning. It means skipping the junk food and choosing carefully in the meal lines. And it means resisting the temptation of the vending machine.

On that note, if you must grab a vending machine snack, consider something with nuts or beef jerky—something high in protein and fat (yes, some fat is good!) but *not* high in sugars. I must admit, in addition to trail mix, my emergency vending machine food is peanut M&M's. There's a little sugar, but the protein and fat counter it, and there's no getting around my cravings for chocolate.

It used to be said that you'd gain the "freshman fifteen" in college. Today I think it's more like the freshman twenty-five or fifty. With all of the supersizing of snacks and meals available, and with the amount of sweeteners and fat stuffed into everything, it's completely insane. However, a lot of this weight gain is also attributable to alcohol; that's where the true caloric intake comes in. Cut back on the beer or cocktails, and you're cutting back on a *major* source of extra calories!

Info: Chocolate, the Miracle Food

What a crime! After reading Dr. Spock (not from *Star Trek*) my parents believed that chocolate was bad for those of us with ADD. I haven't heard that one mentioned for a while, and I believe quite the contrary. Chocolate has caffeine in it, along with other chemicals that stimulate the brain and calm the mind. I find it helpful for writing, studying, or anytime. Give me any excuse, or no excuse at all, and I'll eat chocolate. Oh, and they say it's good for you now! They say it's an excellent source of antioxidants. Whoo-hoo! To make it work with my diet, I eat organic chocolate or chocolate without dairy (sorry, no milk chocolate for me), but this is one ADDer who cannot live without his chocolate fix!

Info: Grazing—It's Not Just for Cows

My MBA classes were each four hours long. It was insanity. I'd eat a *huge* meal before class, and still crash an hour or two into it. Then I got an idea: What about eating *during* class? Wow. What a difference. Grazing on foods high in protein and fat (such as trail mix) helped me maintain my focus and concentration even while others' waned. After that realization, I'd go in to professors at the start of the semester and let them know I had blood sugar issues and would need to eat during class. Except for science labs, not a single one minded, and it's been a lifesaver. Consider grazing to keep you going!

Eating Well

Eating well is not just for the hoity-toity. It's for college students with ADD who want to be at their best when they need to. Avoiding blood sugar crashes is a major way to improve our concentration in class and keep us from getting cross-eyed or upset. Eating for success means cutting back on sugars while increasing your protein and fat intake. And it means planning ahead. I know it sounds a bit tough, but you'll feel better and look better, and it's one way to improve grades without studying harder. Now that's never a bad thing, is it?

Tech Tip: Struggling with Remembering to Eat

There's an expression in endurance sports: "eat before you're hungry, drink before you're thirsty." If you struggle to get food in on time or are really sensitive to changes in blood sugar, you need to manage your food and water intake just as you would your meds. Ever been in class and had your brain lock down, your gut start to twist, and someone in the back of your mind yelling at the top of his lungs, "I've gotta get outta here, NOW!!!"? That's your adrenal system telling you you're starving. Congratulations, you've just activated your prehistoric lizard brain and now *the hunt* is the only thing on your mind.

You want to prevent this at all costs!

You can use the same strategies you use to take your pills on time. But for some students, this isn't enough. If you're really sensitive to drops in blood sugar, use alarms to ensure that you eat regularly or even "graze" throughout the day. Set a countdown timer on a watch or other device that'll go off every hour or two, or perhaps even more frequently.

Sleeping Soundly

> "Without enough sleep, we all become tall two-year-olds."— **JoJo Jensen, *Dirt Farmer Wisdom*, 2002**

Struggling to fall asleep and stay asleep is a common problem for those of us with whirling, creative minds. Studies suggest that at least 40 percent of teens and adults and 50 percent of children with ADD have difficulty sleeping. Sleep is very important for the ADD brain. A lack of sleep makes focusing and concentrating more difficult, increases impulsivity, and generally magnifies the negative symptoms of ADD. There are some professionals who suggest that the ADD brain needs more sleep than the average mind to recover from the day's activity and be fully functional the next day. However, our troubles falling asleep make it even harder to get this extra rest we need.

College poses some unique and frustrating challenges to getting the sleep your ADD mind needs to be at the top of its game. First off, you're being bombarded with information in and out of class, and you may not get any down time to start processing it all until your head hits the pil-

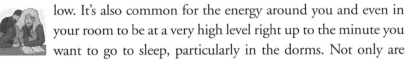

low. It's also common for the energy around you and even in your room to be at a very high level right up to the minute you want to go to sleep, particularly in the dorms. Not only are you attempting to pack everything you need to do into the day, but so are the hundreds of people surrounding you. Couple this with the stress of upcoming assignments, tests, reading, your personal life, and everything else, and falling asleep can seem impossible. And even if you can manage to fall asleep, with all of the work, social activities, friends, and everything else going on, when do you find the time?

The Sleeping and Studying Connection

Sleep is essential to our ADD minds. I'm not merely suggesting that you might be a little groggy in the morning without enough sleep;

I'm saying that you might not even remember your name! Lack of sleep makes focusing two or three times tougher than usual—we're lucky if we make it to class at all, and it's a miracle if we remember our books and assignments when we're there. Problem solving, memorizing, and conceptualizing is an impossibility if we're over-tired. Being even slightly sleep deprived can wipe out our productivity for the entire day.

Unfortunately, sleep deprivation is a constant fact of life at college. There are, however, many simple things that you can do to help regulate your sleeping. And if these don't work, a trip to the doctor may be in order. Doctors can prescribe sleep aids, or they may wish to modify any medicines you are currently taking or the dosing schedule to see if that helps. Daily meditation before bedtime can also help.

Tricks for Falling Asleep

- Don't exercise or do anything else very stimulating late at night. This includes listening to loud music, watching an exciting movie, playing broom-ball in the hall, or visiting your local hangout. Your brain needs a chance to unwind at the end of the day, and exercise and stimulation do the reverse. I try not to exercise after 7:00 p.m. Or, if I know I'll be going to bed late, I just make sure I don't exercise after nine o'clock

- Do get plenty of aerobic exercise early each day. If I get thirty to sixty minutes of aerobic activity a day, it helps my body and mind to wind down and relax late at night.

ADD Advantage: Benefits of Walking

Here's one thing I've seen help many ADD students and adults with sleeping: take a twenty-minute walk each morning when you get up, then another right around sunset. Try to walk somewhere off the beaten path—along the beach, around a lake, in a park. These walks seem to help us set our body clocks to the twenty-four-hour clock of the planet. It conditions our bodies to know intuitively when to go to sleep and when to get up and therefore helps sleep come more naturally. The body will unwind on its own when it knows it's time to sleep, and it will wake you up more gently, too.

- Stick to a set bedtime routine. This is the most surefire way for me to fall asleep easily, as well as the hardest thing to make myself do. There's so much at night to keep us from getting enough sleep. However, going to bed at the same time every night helps the body set its clock for sleep. Consistency is the key.

- Do relaxing activities before bed. This could mean turning a few pages in a boring book, taking a hot bath (a salt bath is awesome if you're an athlete in heavy training, but check with your doctor or trainer first), or watching something mind-numbing on TV. Even surfing the web is fine as long as you don't get sucked into something interesting. Avoid heavy reading, good TV, or Internet-surfing that will make you think (or give you nightmares).

- Don't take your meds close to bedtime. Of course, follow your doc's recommendations. But for me, this means not taking my Adderall after 5:00 p.m. This is a very individual thing and depends on your prescription, but it's definitely worth asking your doctor if your sleep habits have changed since you started the meds. Taking meds before bedtime may help you calm down, relax, and fall asleep. Talk to your doctor and figure out what works for you.

- Avoid caffeine late in the day. Although this should go without saying, soda and other caffeinated products can interfere with sleep.

- Sleep the same way each night. Let's face it—we're creatures of habit, and sleeping the same way every night can help form good sleeping habits. Try to sleep in the same or similar clothing each night. I hide under a pile of blankets that blocks out noise and helps me sleep. Consistency in all things involving bedtime will help your brain shut down for the day.

- Use nature to help you sleep. Try a glass of warm milk or chamomile tea with a little honey if you're having trouble drifting off. Maybe the smell of lavender, scented candles, or incense will help. Of course, don't lay down with burning candles—falling asleep may soon be the least of your concerns!

- Turn down the heat. Your body temperature naturally falls when you sleep. If you start to cool off your body by turning the temperature down in the room a bit, cracking open the window, or opening your apartment door for a few minutes, you trigger your body to unwind, let go, and fall asleep.

- Decrease your daily stress. Around finals and midterms, sleeping may become more of a problem. Reorganizing your life can have an amazing effect on your ability to sleep during these trying times—when I decluttered my environment, built a schedule and routine, and focused on positive self-talk, I stopped overworking my brain at night no matter what was going on, and my sleep naturally improved.

- Don't count sheep, but count back through your day. This is an ancient Tibetan monk technique. After getting into bed, the monks close their eyes and play back the day's events from the most recent to the earliest. They don't judge the events or think about what actions they need to take; instead they simply play the tape in reverse. This clears their minds and helps them to sleep without worrying about the day's events. I've been surprised at how effective this technique is!

Info: Meditation and Sleep

Meditation helps clear your mind, stop the chatter, process the day's information, and gets you in the right state of mind to fall asleep as soon as you lay down. Taking twenty minutes at night to meditate can help you sleep through the night and improve the quality of the rest. It can even help you have pleasant dreams.

Read the chapter on meditation for more details, recommendations, and techniques, but here's a great nighttime ritual. Stuart Wilde, author of a great audio book, *The Art of Meditation*, suggests running through the day's events in your head backwards, from most recent to earliest, before you go to bed. Don't place judgment on things, but just see them happening in reverse. It clears out the mind and keeps you from dwelling on the day. For me it works great, and it's definitely worth a try!

Using Technology to Help

- **Nighttime alarm clock.** A nighttime alarm clock that alerts you when you're getting close to bedtime can help you establish and stick to a schedule. A good calendar program on your computer can work great, too, as it can give you multiple alarms to get you ready. There are even progressive alarm clocks and sound machines with lights built in that will gradually dim and/or get quieter as it gets closer to bedtime, sort of forcing you to go to sleep. Find something that works and try to stick to a regular bedtime—you'll both fall asleep and get moving in the morning much more easily. Time Timer software (timetimer.com) is a personal favorite of mine. I use it to schedule and remind me when to go to sleep, write papers, switch gears between assignments, or jump in at the last minute (snipe) on eBay. It's incredibly visual and has different alarm sounds to help you recognize the alarm and know what to do immediately.
- **Vibrating watches.** You can program these watches to give you the cue to go to bed without having to explain to anyone else what's going on. And if you're a more kinesthetic than auditory person, the

vibrating alarm may help you shift gears more quickly and easily than a loud noise would.

- **Talking watches or alarm clocks.** I love these! They alert you with a verbal alarm, and you can set it however you would like without having to look at the time. It talks to you to help you set the alarm and make sure it's on. (Yes, you most certainly *can* set this watch with your eyes closed!) This is particularly handy when you're getting to bed late and don't want to psych yourself out for the morning. There's a large selection of talking watches and alarm clocks at independentliving.com.

- **Really high-tech.** Want a dozen alarms to get to sleep or do other things at night? If you're a real techie, check out the Timex Ironman Data Link watch. There are up to two hundred alarms with five-minute backup alarms, and the personal organizer function includes a schedule mode and holds hundreds of phone numbers, appointments, events, and notes. This watch will definitely tell you what to do when and can give you dozens of reminders to go to bed.

- **Aromatherapy.** Does the smell of chamomile help you to sleep? Check out the Progression Wake Up Clock from hammacher.com. It provides aromatherapy, dimming lights, and decreasing nature sounds at the end of the day to help you unwind and get to bed. You can set it in reverse to gently wake you up in the morning, as well.

- **The Zen way.** Another clock that can be used to help you fall asleep or wake you up is the Zen Clock (now-zen.com). This alarm clock uses a Tibetan chime that gongs with increasing frequency over twenty minutes to help you shift gears and move on. It's great for getting you off the computer and into bed, or gradually bringing you out of slumber or meditation in a gentle way.

- **Tracking sleep.** The SleepTracker watch tracks your sleep cycles (you can see in the morning how often you were in deep sleep) and wakes you up at the lightest point of your sleep cycle. You give it a window of time—say, somewhere between six and six-thirty—and it waits until you're almost awake to go off. This helps you function better throughout the day, thereby making it easier to sleep the following evening.

- **Ambient noise.** Sound machines, fountains, a fan, or anything that makes a white noise can soothe your mind, helping you unwind and fall asleep. You can also use these devices to block out background noises that could keep you awake.

- **Artificial light.** Another device that can help you soothe your mind and naturally drift off to sleep is a full-spectrum light bulb. These lights create artificial sunlight, which your body will naturally respond to. Artificial sunlight is the creative mind's best friend, particularly when you're studying or writing on dark winter nights. These lights helps you remain creative and energetic long into the night, and once you shut them off, you'll naturally think it's time for bed.

- **Audio CDs.** Experiment with different types of music and sounds to see if there's something that really helps you sleep—nature sounds, water sounds, soothing music, or a guided meditation are all good places to start.

- **Brain wave technology.** Software such as the Generator (bwgen.com) gives you numerous binaural sounds—different, simultaneous sounds out of your left and right speaker that cause a wavy noise when heard together. Choose different sounds for your specific needs. Some sounds help with creativity and focus, while others aid meditation and sleep. I've found if I crawl to my computer when I can't sleep and listen to sounds that help synchronize my brain waves with the pattern of sleep, my eyelids grow heavy, I become incredibly drowsy, and after hitting the hay again, it's quickly into la-la-land I go!

- **Guided dreaming CDs.** I've been playing with CDs that include brain wave sounds that get your brain vibrating at the right frequency for sleep and not-so-subliminal suggestions. They help me fall asleep and may eventually give me some really cool dreams. I've been experimenting with *Brainwave Mind Voyages* and *Brainwave Journey* by Dr. Jeffrey Thompson (brainwave-entrainment.com) and the *Lucid Dreamer's ToolKit* by Stephen LaBerge (luciddreams.ukf.net/).

Get Some Sleep

Having ADD and the highly creative mind that comes with it is a very individual thing. Not all of these tips will work for everyone, but they're worth trying when you're so worried or focused on the events of the day that you can't sleep when you get to bed. Just find something that helps derail the thoughts that keep you thinking through the night. And if you've tried all of this you're still having difficulties getting to sleep, it may be time to visit the health center or a doctor.

> "Above all, do not lose your desire to walk. Every day I walk myself into a state of well-being and walk away from every illness. I have walked myself into my best thoughts, and I know of no thought so burdensome that one cannot walk away from it."
> —**Soren Kierkegaard**

10

Juggling Your Finances

"**Too many** people spend money **they haven't** earned, to buy things **they don't want**, to **impress people** they don't like."

—**Will Smith**

In college our minds are so full that even without ADD it's very difficult to keep our finances in order. But it's essential that we do just that if we want to both stay in school and keep eating. Budgeting tends to be particularly difficult during freshman year. A lack of practice, combined with juggling financial aid, making new purchases, and setting up bank accounts and credit cards often adds up to trouble. We tend to think we have more money than we do because we get it in a lump sum at the beginning. We also often spend money that isn't ours! We receive loan and financial aid checks that must go to the bursar's office, and if we don't realize this we can get into big trouble.

Ways to Watch Your Money

• Visit your financial aid office to understand what you're responsible for—how much you owe monthly, quarterly, etc.
• Keep as little money on hand as possible. If you have it, you'll just be tempted to spend it!
• Keep two bank accounts: one for money available to spend this week, and the other to be drawn from once a week to replenish the first account. If the first account runs out, you're out of money until the next week.

- Throw out the checkbook. This one is optional, but I stopped using checks entirely. Even today I pay by debit card. It lets me track purchases and keeps me from spending what I don't have. While you can still burn through money just as fast as you can with cash, it's much harder to overdraw your account.

- Go back to the allowance. Ask your folks (or whomever) to only send you a certain amount of money each week or month. It may sound silly and immature, but chances are even your parents limit their finances this way—they probably get a weekly or biweekly paycheck. Since you're less likely to spend what you don't have, this can help keep you in check.

How Do You Create and Stick to a Budget?

Making a weekly or monthly budget and sticking to it will keep you from running out of money and ensure that you have extra funds if an emergency arises. Below is a blank budget form you can use to see how much money is coming in and how much is going out. Start one of these at the beginning of each semester, keep it somewhere you'll check it often (or use software on your computer or PDA), and it'll help keep you out of financial hot water.

Semester School Budget						
Income— Money Coming In	Monthly Budget	Monthly Spent (Actual)	Monthly Budget	Monthly Spent (Actual)	Monthly Budget	Monthly Spent (Actual)
Parents						
Work (Job)						
Financial Aid						
Grants						
Scholarships						
Loans (Other)						
Miscellaneous						
Income Subtotal						

Expenses— Money Going Out	Monthly Budget	Monthly Spent (Actual)	Monthly Budget	Monthly Spent (Actual)	Monthly Budget	Monthly Spent (Actual)
Tuition						
School Fees						
Room and Board (Rent)						
Food Plan						
Groceries						
Cell Phone						
Internet						
Health Insurance						
Car Expenses						
Bus Fare/ Transportation						
Parking						
Club Fees						
Movies/ Entertainment						
Eating Out/ Vending						
Clothing/ Uniforms						
Sports Gear						
Nutritional Supplements						
Medication						
Medical Expenses (Doctor's Visits)						
BAIL—Just Kidding (I hope!!!)						
Expenses— Subtotal						
What's Left? Income Minus Expenses						

Making and keeping a budget is tough. However, there is great software available nowadays for both your PDA and your computer that not only helps you budget but makes it simple, easy, and perhaps even fun.

Which software works for you? That's a personal preference. Check out the different packages on Download.com. QuickBooks is an awesome choice, though not the easiest to use. Lately I've been playing around with My Budget Keeper. It seems quick and easy, though I haven't yet tested it for the long run.

ADD and Credit Cards

My folks strongly impressed upon me that I should have a credit card when I went to college. They insisted it would help me build credit, invaluable for my future in the world after school. My intuition told me otherwise. I resisted the temptation to get a credit card for several years before caving in to their advice and succumbing to the temptation. I'm an adult, I thought; I can handle this! But with ADD, just juggling my checkbook was hard enough. Keeping up with my credit card, then my minimum payments, and soon my late fees, I quickly became another statistic, just another student buried under credit card debt.

Play with the fire of credit cards and you could burn not only your credit, but your financial future. Also, since companies can legally look at your credit before they hire you, you could affect your future career options. Imagine having the best grades and greatest degree, but losing out on job opportunities because of the debt you accrued in college. It's insane—but it's true.

So when you're on campus and people are throwing credit cards at you (which, though it sounds strange, really does happen, and all the time), no matter what the freebie, no matter how good the offer, resist it. I beg and implore you.

It's far too easy to get behind on your payments without even knowing it, even with the "great" offers the company will use to entice you—no interest, balance transfer, points and rewards, etc. No matter how good the plastic sounds, turn it down. The only time you should ever even consider it is if you're about to get booted out of school because there's no other way to come up with the money. And even then you should try to secure an education-friendly loan through a bank first. But barring that life-or-death situation, do not dance with this devil. Yes, you need to build a certain amount of credit to function financially in the real world—and you can do it after college.

But If You Must...

I know that the idea of getting and using a credit card can be quite seductive. For an ADDer (and most anyone, really), not having to pay anything back right away is often an offer too tempting to resist. But the problem is that the end of the month rolls around quickly, and it's so hard to track and budget with a credit card that you can quickly bury yourself beyond belief. It's not uncommon to hear of students with ten to twenty thousand dollars of credit card debt—and that's not even counting the student loans they may have to pay.

Credit card companies make millions on fines and interest. They're depending on you to help them out by messing up. In order to make a profit, they need you to make a late payment—potentially jacking up your interest rate from 0 percent to as high as 21.9 percent overnight. Or they're counting on you to wrack up so many expenses that you can't afford to pay them.

If you have a card and your payment's going to be late, call and let them know. It's possible they can offer a one-time extension on your grace period, which beats the twenty-five, thirty-five, or even fifty-dollar late fee. Not only that, but did you know you're reported to the credit bureau if you're even thirty days late? There's no sense hurting your credit if it's at all possible to avoid it.

Credit Cards and Tuition

Try to avoid using your credit card to pay your tuition bill unless you're absolutely sure you have the money to pay it off right away. For instance, if you get frequent flyer points and have the money, pay with the credit card, then make an instant payment online to your credit card company. Now you'll have the points and no worries about being late, falling behind, or watching your finances implode.

What if you're stuck and have to pay your tuition with a credit card that you can't immediately pay back? Before you do anything, check into the school's financing programs to postpone payments. There might be some fees associated with this, but they'll be a lot less than the interest a credit card company will charge you.

Getting Help

I blew up my bank account over Christmas break my freshman year and ended up owing more than five hundred dollars. Later on I fell prey to the seduction of credit cards and the allure of building credit. The thousands of dollars of debt I accumulated made the five hundred dollars look like child's play. And I thought I was responsible.

If you're like me and have just buried yourself, don't panic—there's a lot of help available.

- First off, you can talk to your folks—it may be ugly and they'll probably be disappointed in you, but they're your parents, and if they can help, I'm sure they will.

- See a financial aid counselor on campus. Go to an experienced counselor, a pro with years of experience. Chances are they've seen it all and can point you in the right direction.

- Look for a consumer credit counseling agency. They can help you build a sensible budget and come up with a repayment schedule. They'll even contact the credit card companies and get them to stop harassing you, reduce your payments and interest rate, and reduce or eliminate as many penalties and late fees as possible.

- If you're in a large town and your spending's out of control, seek help from an ADD counselor, coach, or support group, or from Debtor's Anonymous, a support group specifically for those in debt.

Don't worry about these groups or individuals judging you. They're there to help you get back on track. And don't judge yourself too harshly—credit cards are given out like candy today, and once you have one, it's criminally easy to spend and get yourself in trouble. Don't beat yourself up. Take a deep breath, find the help you need, and concentrate on fixing the problem.

The trick? You've got to be up front with whomever you've found to help you and then *stick to the agreement*. The good news, though, is that you tell them what you can afford, or they'll help you determine it, so you're never making promises you can't keep! I wish I'd seen these guys early on. They helped me greatly later in the process, but that's their job: they're there to help.

The Bottom Line on Credit Cards

In many ways, credit card companies make loan sharks look like the good guys. If you owe three thousand dollars on a credit card and you pay back a hundred dollars a month, it will take you three years and cost you more than four thousand dollars! If you pay just the minimum balance, you could be looking at ten years and five or six thousand dollars. It's just not the kind of burden you want to saddle yourself with. I've known students who've had to take crappy jobs after college just to pay back their credit card debt before they could even begin to think about the future. I strongly recommend avoiding the problem altogether.

> "If you think nobody cares if you're alive, try missing a couple of car payments."
>
> **—Earl Wilson**

11

Organizing Your Life

"As you **simplify your life**, the laws of the universe will be simpler; **solitude** will not be solitude, **poverty** will not be poverty, **nor weakness weakness.**"

—**Henry David Thoreau**

Whether you like it or not, organization is essential for college success. The demands on time and space in college go well beyond the challenges you faced in high school, and your mom and teachers aren't there to provide the organizational structure you're accustomed to. Small piles in your room can quickly lead to lost homework, keys, hours, and then days. Without frequent assignments to keep you neat and organized, you can rapidly fall so far behind there's little or no hope of turning things around. And the disaster in your room can get you lynched by a roommate faster than you can say "good-bye."

Though we dread organization, rail against routine, and fight for our freedom and spontaneity, if we want to remain sane and succeed in school, we need to structure our environment and our time.

Organizing Your Environment

Did you ever play connect-the-dots as a child? Slowly but surely a picture emerged from the formless potpourri of numbers, and in the end you had a finished drawing you could have hardly imagined before you started.

Organizing your life works much the same way. In the beginning it's difficult to picture the end result. But with a plan comes simplicity and success, order and efficiency. Breaking organization down into manageable pieces will help take the pain out of the process, reign in the chaos, and make you a happier and more efficient student.

> ## Info: Packing for School
>
>
> Here's the cardinal rule of packing for college: leave behind at least half of what you plan on taking. You won't need it, and it'll only end up cluttering your breadbox of a living space. Ask yourself how much you'd stuff in your suitcase if you were going on a week's vacation. That's how much you want to take with you to college, and all you want to have in your room. Any more than this, and like a virus, clutter will quickly spread out of control. Leave anything you're not going to use this week at your parents' house.

How Should You Organize Your Room?

So you're already at school, your room is a disaster, you have no time to organize, and you get stuck in the details whenever you try and end up accomplishing nothing. What do you do?

Not to worry—we'll get you through this quickly. Let's grab some supplies and get to work.

Organizational Supplies

- 4–8 new storage or office boxes with lids, or transparent Rubbermaid-type boxes
- 1 package colored permanent markers
- 1 package colored index cards
- 1 package colored sticky notes
- 1 package colored dry erase markers
- 5–6 binders of different colors (1 per class)

- 5–6 colored notebooks punched for 3-ring binders (colors should match the binders)
- 20–24 colored folders (4 per class; colors should match the binders and notebooks)
- Stackable trays for inbound/outbound mail and inbound/outbound homework
- 1 giant dry erase board and eraser

  - 1 bottle of correction fluid
  - 1 box of paper clips
  - 1 desktop stapler
  - 1 mini stapler
- 1 portable hole punch
- 1 filing cabinet (unless your desk has a drawer to hang files)
- 1 package of 1″ x 2″ (or larger) labels

Info: Critical Mass

 The more clutter you have, physical or mental, the more likely you are to attract even more. If you don't quickly rein it in, it'll soon reach critical mass, the point at which you're so buried you completely lose control. Avoiding critical mass is essential to your survival!

Why Are You Cleaning?

College is a lot more complex and demanding than high school, so you need to adopt better and more consistent methods of organization. Putting lots of effort into creating a structure will help make every day life that much easier. Below are a few key reasons to keep things in order.

- **Happy roommates.** If your room looks like a science experiment gone awry, your roommates will not be pleased with you for long. Even if they're smiling now, eventually they will be annoyed at your disorganization and uncleanliness. Sooner or later they'll have had enough, which will likely result in confrontation or a terrible cold war. Roommate difficulties can be a major cause of academic disaster—they can ruin a class, throw an entire semester offtrack, and even affect your cumulative GPA. Like it or not, it's in your best interest to have an environment that helps keep your roommates happy.

- **Decreased stress.** In the typical college dorm room, there's stuff piled up all over the place: dirty laundry, beer bottles, backpacks, papers, books, and scary things best not identified. Important stuff's buried, and you're least likely to find it exactly when you need it the most. You may forget to take completed homework to class or lose your keys when you're already running late. It's also just hard to relax and unwind at night when you can't even find your bed. Clutter greatly elevates stress and can lead to a total meltdown.

- **Clear thinking.** Clutter acts like a virus, infecting and multiplying. It infects our brains, saps our mental energy, robs us of our creativity, blurs our focus, and jumbles our thoughts. In order to think clearly and work at your best, you need to get clutter under control and keep it at a minimum.

Info: Test Your Mind!

Ever do homework on a cluttered desk? Try this experiment to see the difference between working in a clean and a dirty environment: Grab a homework assignment and head for your desk. Do half of it with your desk as is, then take a break, temporarily remove all of the clutter from your desk, and do the second half of your homework. See the difference

Our minds respond to our environments. Just as a computer bogs down when it has too much going on in the background, we have a hard time staying focused or descrambling our thoughts if we're overloaded by clutter and stimulus around us. Our minds mirror our environments, and a jumbled environment often means a jumbled mind.

Cleaning and Organizing

The First Step

After you have all the supplies you need, walk around your room and throw out all the trash. Next grab all of your clothes and put them in a pile. Then grab anything and everything else that isn't paper and throw it into a box. Leave out only what you'll need in the next week; when in doubt, it goes into the box. Put your clothes in a separate box.

Put these boxes in your closet or storage area. If you don't have storage, stow them under your bed—just try to put them as far away from you as possible, and definitely out of sight. This reduces the temptation to constantly dig through them. I guarantee you forget all about those boxes in a week.

Desk Time

Now that you've cleared the majority of your room, it's time to head to that dreaded mountain of stuff piled on and around your desk. Start putting all nonessential papers, notebooks, etc. into a box. Once again, when in doubt, it goes into the box. After you've attacked the outside of the desk, do the same to your drawers—the drawers aren't supposed to be permanent storage: they're there to keep things you use frequently within arm's reach. After you've cleaned up your desk inside and out, take the box of clutter and whisk it away to storage.

Finishing Up

Now that you've removed everything you can from your room (or at least your sight), assign places for whatever's left. Using your colored flashcards, magic markers, folders, and trays, label and make a home

Organizing Your Life

for everything you own. Have a set place for your keys, books, toothbrush, wallet—everything. If you're really ambitious, get shelving from your local hardware store to put more stuff up and out of the way. Then label and hang index cards from the shelves with a specific location for each item that goes on them.

Don't worry if you don't keep things perfectly in order at first. It takes two to three weeks for an average student to make something a habit, and for the average ADDer it can take even longer. Work to make it automatic by putting everything in its home the minute you see that it's out of place. Over time you'll catch yourself as you're putting it where it doesn't belong.

Info: Cool Space Savings

Want the coolest room on your hall? Need more space to get things out of the way? There are two surefire ways that help accomplish both:

- Get a loft. A loft is like a one-person bunk bed with no bottom bunk. Good ones run from sixty dollars to a couple hundred, are supersturdy, and create plenty of extra open space for shelves and anything else.
- Build shelves. Often students are quite surprised at how easy this is.

Filing

Now that you've gotten rid of the major clutter, it's time to find a home for your important paperwork. Does your desk have a drawer for hanging files? If so, great; if not, head to your local thrift or department store and buy a filing cabinet, the larger the better.

Stay away from cramped plastic filing boxes and the accordion file systems. The more compressed or squashed your files are, the less likely you are to see what you're looking for—or to continue filing things.

Filing One, Two, Three

Designate or block off three different filing sections, one for school work, another for bills, and a third for miscellaneous.

Assign a color to each subject, bill, etc., and use colored tabs and files to designate them. For instance, you could have a red tab for your algebra work and use a corresponding red binder and notebook for algebra. Need to find something algebra-related? Just look for red.

Fill your files. Go through your stack of papers to be filed and put them away. Find something without a home? Simply make and label a new file.

It's that easy! And once you're accustomed to filing everything, you can adopt systems of alphabetizing, staggering labels, or creating extra-large tabs—whatever makes sense to you.

How Do You Organize Your Schoolwork?

I know college work seems overwhelming, but don't panic! Your home environment should be in better shape now, and that's half the battle. Now we'll look at how to carry your books and paperwork around while keeping things sorted and easy to find. That's the second half of the battle.

The Backpack

Want to remember everything you need for class? The right backpack can help you do the job. Get a backpack that has as many pockets and sections as possible. Brighter backpacks stand out more and are easier to find (i.e., harder to lose), so consider one that's colorful.

- Once you have your backpack, designate each pocket for a specific item or task. At a minimum, have a separate pocket for textbooks, notebooks, and binders, and specific places for your cell phone, keys, lunch, pens and pencils, and PDA or handheld computer.
- Whenever you're done using an item, be sure it finds its way back to its designated pocket in your backpack.

- Each night before you go to bed, make sure you've gone over your schedule and are packed for the next day. Then place your backpack by the front door—right where you'd trip over it on your way out.

Whatever you do, be consistent—that way you can always find what you need.

Binders, Notebooks, and Folders

The secret to having what you need when you need it is to always keep the right thing in the right place. Like a great backpack, binders help you keep things in their places and allow for easy access. The key is to systematize your binders to allow for maximum organization with minimum thought.

- Use a separate binder for each class. Like everything else, these should be color-coded with a different color for each of your different classes.
- Fill each binder with correspondingly colored folders: red folders should only go with the red binder, and so on.
- Designate separate folders in each binder for incoming assignments, outgoing assignments, graded work, and photocopied reading materials.
- Use large labels on both the inside and outside of each folder for quick identification, and always keep folders in the same order in each binder.
- Carry a small three-ring hole punch with you in your backpack, and make sure each document gets to the right place immediately after you get it. If you're using the papers at home, make sure everything's repacked each night before you go to bed. Resist the urge to say you'll put something in a binder later—later often becomes lost.
- Insert a correspondingly colored notebook into each binder. Use whatever type of notepad paper works best for you. Many ADD students like graph paper for the natural order and organization it provides.
- Designate and label a specific shelf space in your dorm room for each binder. Color code the shelves for easy access.
- After everything is set up, practice keeping the exact same thing in the exact same place. Struggling to remember where things go? Make

bigger labels or even signs. You should get to the point where when you put an item down, you automatically put it in the right place.

• Don't get down on yourself if you struggle at first. Just keep practicing and over time it'll become second nature.

Info: The Mail

You must keep up on your mail—after all, it's how your bills and important notifications get to you. Consider hanging mail slots on the wall, or vertical slots on your desk. Avoid horizontal trays if possible; they tend to pile up. Have assigned slots for incoming and outgoing mail.

When you handle the mail, try to touch each piece only once. Take immediate action on each item—file it or throw it away. Don't even waste time opening junk mail; it should go directly from the mailbox to the recycling bin.

Loss Prevention

We ADDers tend to think about what we'll be doing next, not what we're doing at the present time. When you come through the door you're thinking of what you're going to do with your evening, not what's in your hands—which can lead to forgetting where you may have put your keys or homework assignment.

If you can, try placing a small shelf in direct view and reach of the front door. Have an assigned place on the shelf for your essentials, such as your keys, wallet or purse, cell phone, and PDA. This way, when you put things down right away, they're already where they belong! Practice placing your belongings in their homes each and every time you come in, or whenever you see them out of place.

Organizing Your Life

If that still doesn't work, don't fret. Try using index cards or sticky notes as reminders. For example, do you keep finding yourself at the microwave, TV, or computer right after you enter? Try posting index cards where you tend to end up, with giant, colorful statements such as "Hey You! Did You Put Your Keys by the Door?!?!?"

Have a sense of humor about it. Strategically place notes to yourself, like, "Don't Even Think About Putting Those Down Here!!!" in the various places you tend to leave things. Get creative. A dangling ball with a message attached that hits you in the head when you enter your room is a great reminder. Sure, your roommate will hate you, but it's guaranteed to get your attention!

Tech Tip: Key Finder

Do you keep losing your keys, wallet, purse, or other important items, no matter how hard you try to keep track of them? Instead of beating yourself up, go high-tech: There are dozens of products out there today that can help you find your keys and other essentials. There's one product you can attach to your keys, and when you clap, your keychain will chirp back to you. Press a button on another and your wallet's located instantly. A quick search on the web for "key finder" yields dozens of these products, and they're cheap—many are ten dollars or less.

The Most Important Thing

ADD makes organization an extreme challenge, but you must master it to thrive in college. Just keep trying, and keep your sense of humor—you'll get it eventually. And when you still lose your keys, you'll be able to laugh about it.

Have you built your routine and yet still struggle to get to class on time?

It's time to let technology go to work for you. There are many time tracking devices, alarm devices, PDAs, PDA phones, and even PDA watches that can help you do the trick. Simply enter the time you need to start preparing to leave into one of the above devices (make sure it's one that you're always carrying with you, such as your cell phone, PDA, or an alarm that's attached to your keychain or bonded to your body). Set a second alarm that's the drop-dead time you need to leave for class. When the first alarm goes off, drop everything and start getting ready. When the second goes off, *head out the door*. Don't even grab that second shoe, just get moving! (Keep a spare pair in the car!)

Don't like carrying an alarm with you? If you're on the computer all of the time, you can use appointment tracking software such as MS Outlook, the ADD Planner, Life Balance software, or dozens of other scheduling softwares you can find online at websites like download.com. The question is: will you look at these when it's time to go? If not, here's one last option: a screaming loud alarm like the Screaming Meanie (well over one hundred decibels) or the e-pill minder. This little devil is designed to remind you to take your meds, and is ridiculously easy to set, and scary loud. It'll get you out of the door on-time, every time, because soon enough your roomie,

Organizing Your Life

housemates, or neighbors down the street will make *sure* you turn that thing off! Hey, it won't give you an electric shock to get you moving, but it's pretty darn close!

"The harder the conflict, the more glorious the triumph."

—Thomas Paine

12

Academic Success

> **"Circumstances do** not make the man, **they reveal him."**
>
> **—James Allen**

If you're reading this, you already know college academics are tough. The good news is that any challenges you face can be overcome. And what seems tough today might be no sweat tomorrow...once you've figured things out.

In this section we'll take a look at the challenges, see why things are so difficult, and then arm you with the tools you need to jump over any hurdles that may (temporarily) stand in your way. You'll overcome these challenges and succeed; I know you can do it. Just take it one step at a time.

So have fun with this. I'm sure the positive results will shock you. Don't be surprised to find yourself staring at an A and thinking, "Who the heck am I? Did I do this?" Yes, you did, and yes, you can!

What to Do in Class

Are you struggling in the classroom? Is it boggling your mind?

Whether you're just starting college or have already been around a year or two, if you're struggling, chances are you haven't mastered the transition from the high school to the college classroom. It's not your fault. High school courses rarely prepare you for the hurdles you'll face in college courses.

Why Are College Courses Tougher?

I did well in high school, even in AP courses, so why are college courses straining my brain?

Specifically, college classes are harder than high school for several key reasons. First off, class periods are longer, and more information is thrown at you. Secondly, the information isn't spoon-fed to you—you have to sift through it and figure out what's important and what's not. Third, professors, unlike teachers, may offer you little hands-on attention; college classes are very much sink-or-swim situations.

There also is little—if any—external accountability in college. Many professors never take attendance, and you can skip class and come and go as you please. You may only have one or two tests, papers, reports, or any other assignment due in a semester.

Sound like heaven? Think again. External accountability keeps us ADDers focused and on our toes. It keeps us from falling behind. Without it, unless we have a strong accountability system, routine, and great coping mechanisms in place, we can become hopelessly lost in the blink of an eye. Catching up in high school is tough enough; in college, fall behind just a little bit and catching up isn't *ever* happening. Unfortunately, keeping up isn't optional. To survive, you've got to keep up with the reading and the workload in class, plus prepare for monster exams and giant term papers and projects.

The good news is there's a formula for classroom success. It's not rocket science, but it will take some work. Let's look together at the different ways we can make your classroom endeavors into your greatest successes.

Going Back to Basics

Many ADD students believe classroom success will result from trying harder or focusing more intently. And that's what we've been told by the "experts" or our well-intentioned folks. So we bang our heads against the wall when "trying harder" only achieves the opposite results. We pick on ourselves for our failings, blaming it on weakness or lack of moral character. But that's like telling a beginning runner he just needs to push harder, focus more, and push through the pain and he'll win a marathon. It just doesn't make sense. Instead, like the runner who works to perfect his stride, we must go back to basics and rebuild your classroom techniques.

How to Make It through Class

Class drives me insane…I feel like I've landed on an alien planet…they're speaking a language I don't understand and I'm lost from minute one. Here's what to do.

Be Prepared—It's Not Just for Boy Scouts

Whether a class is daunting or comfortable all depends on how prepared you are for it. If you're prepared, you'll be able to focus, absorb the information, and perhaps even have an enjoyable time. If you're ill-prepared, you'll understand nothing, you'll become terribly frustrated, and you may even leave mid-class, desperate to quit. In all honesty, I've walked out of more than one class to try and figure out which end is up *before* going back in.

How to Stay Ahead

Read and Review the Night before Class

Try to prepare everything the night before, while you're packing things up, so you don't forget anything. Skim the reading again, go over a paper you're turning in, or review practice problems. If it's been a little while since you did the work, it may already be foreign to you. Getting things together the night before helps prevent you from forgetting something in the morning. Equally as important, reading, reviewing, or skimming your notes the night before class helps keep the subject fresh in your mind. This way you're not backpedaling during the first few minutes of class trying to figure out what planet you've landed on.

Download Notes or Presentations in Advance

Professors today often post their presentations online in a PowerPoint-type slide show. If you use a laptop or tablet PC in class, download the slides onto it and write your class notes directly on them. The professor has already made the outline for you; it's almost as simple as filling in the blanks. If you don't use a computer in class, double- or triple-space the presentation and print it out. Punch holes into it, enter it into your three-ring binder, and take notes directly onto your pre-made outline!

Read and Do Practice Problems in Advance

If there's assigned reading, make sure you do it before class. Not only will this prevent the lecture from sounding like gibberish, but it will help you retain more information and participate in the classroom discussion. Along the same lines, if there's homework to do, especially if there are recommended practice 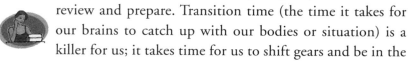 problems, do them. For us ADDers, optional problems are never optional. In fact, if you really want to set yourself up for success, do them with a tutor or schedule a regular time with your professor to go over practice problems. This ensures that you get them done and get them done correctly, which dramatically increases your chances for success.

Doing this also helps you build a routine. Whether or not you see your professor, make sure to have a regularly scheduled day and time for doing each course's homework or reading. For instance, if accounting's on Monday, make Sunday night accounting time.

Regularly Show Up Early for Class

Do your best to get to class early. Set the class time in your PDA or calendar twenty minutes to an hour early to give yourself time to review and prepare. Transition time (the time it takes for our brains to catch up with our bodies or situation) is a killer for us; it takes time for us to shift gears and be in the moment. So get to class early, set up, even briefly go over any PowerPoint slides or the previous day's notes. Be ready to begin when the class starts, instead of thinking about the walk over or other things you have to do that day.

Tech Tip: Early Birds Don't Get Wormed!

I've known some ADDers, myself included, who used competition to get to class early. They'd want to be the *first* one to class to prove to themselves they were committed to the class. If someone else was there five minutes early, they'd start showing up ten minutes early...if someone was ten minutes early, they'd be fifteen...and so on. Surprisingly, there seems to be a direct correlation between getting to class early and higher grades! Being early doesn't just mean that you're prepared in advance and your mind's in the moment, but also that you don't miss that all-important comment the professor mentions in passing just as the class begins. Be the early bird—and don't get wormed!)

Hide in the Front of the Classroom

Lots of students have a tendency to try to escape notice by sitting in the back of the classroom. While I understand this desire, I also know that we are constantly on the lookout for stimuli—if you're sitting at the back of the room and the slightest distraction catches your eye, you'll lose your train of thought and end up having no idea what the professor is saying. Instead, hide from stimuli up front. If you're sitting up front, all you see is the professor. Not only does this eliminate distractions, but now you're drawn to the movements of your professor, which is perfect for paying attention.

What if your attention still wanders?

Explain your situation to the professor and ask for a visual cue if she notices you drifting off. Perhaps the professor tugging her ear could mean, "Michael, please draw your attention back to the class."

Are you in an enormous class or seminar? Consider switching to a smaller version (taking the class in the spring instead of the fall, for example, at an odd time, or with a different professor). No way to switch this late in the game? Do your best to get up front. If you have to, take notes word-for-word to keep your mind from drifting...

Work on Your Notes

Good note-taking skills are critical to success in the classroom. Experiment to find the technique that works best for you. A laptop is ideal for the fast typist; it facilitates multitasking and is great for later review. A keyword search in your notes can help you find information in a jiffy and is amazing for the rare open book test!

Make friends with fellow classmates. Offer to share your notes, and don't be afraid to ask to see theirs if you missed something. If nothing seems to work and the RDS office feels it's a reasonable and necessary accommodation, they'll provide you with a note-taker free of charge. If need be, you can even hire a private note-taker.

Record Your Classes

Think about tape recording your classes; a digital recorder is fantastic for this. Make a file for each class on your computer and simply download your recordings. If you need clarification on something that was said or if you missed something, your recorder is your second chance to find the information. Play it back when you review your notes and you'll be amazed at how much more you remember and retain.

MY STORY

How a Recorder Saved the Day

I spent my final semester as an undergrad studying abroad in France. These were the last classes I needed in order to graduate. While the majority of the faculty members for my program were great, one professor was extremely eccentric. He had a requirement that we use fountain pens, and he insisted we use proper "Oxford English" at all times. However, the biggest problem became apparent after the first of only two tests: test questions did not come from our reading but directly from class lecture. Unfortunately, he had written his lectures for class years ago and just read them to us in a fast monotone. Even if an ADDer like myself could pay attention long enough to follow such a lecture, I couldn't have typed fast enough to keep up.

I got a two out of twenty on my first test. As there were only two tests, there was no mathematical reason to continue showing up, but the professor assured me that if I scored near perfect on the second exam, I wouldn't flunk the class.

I started studying in the insane, hyperfocused, ADDer way. First, I recorded each of my classes. Then I reviewed and typed up the notes after class. Then I made flashcards on everything I thought could be a possible test question. I blocked out everyone and everything in my life to concentrate on the material. I spent countless hours reviewing and re-reviewing flashcards. I did not want another semester in school!

It worked. I aced the exam and passed the class. The moral of the story: record it. Because you never know when you'll absolutely, positively need to know exactly what was said in class.

Picture This

If it's okay with your professor, use your camera, camera phone, or PDA to snap a photo of the board when you can't draw a diagram or list quickly enough. We're often great at notes, yet stymied by diagrams. With the technology available today (and if your professor is okay with it), you could even consider video recording your class with your PDA or video camera. Many professors and schools are scared to have videotaped classes in the public domain—they fear something may be taken out of context—but if you're highly visual, you could have your RDS office advocate for you.

Modern technology has come so far that you can now easily video record your entire class on the fly and on the cheap. A cell phone with a memory card or a digital camera with video (I've seen some as cheap as fifty dollars) will do the trick. Again, ask for permission in advance. However, if you're stuck in a seminar or lecture hall and are lost in the crowd, check the rules, but then don't feel too bad about letting the camera roll. It may not produce the highest-quality results, but when you space out, it won't. Replay the video when reviewing notes or studying for a test, and prepare to be amazed at the results (particularly if you're visually inclined). Wow!

Wear Good Glasses

If you have scratched or dirty glasses, they impede your ability to focus and concentrate more than you think. You may even find yourself a bit dizzy, cranky, or queasy. Keeping your prescription up to date and your glasses well-maintained is important.

Keep Your Blood Sugar Up

If you're in a long class and the professor allows food in the classroom, bring snacks with you: protein bars, nuts, something like beef jerky, or even a protein shake. Any of these will help keep your energy up and keep you focused on the class instead of on your stomach.

The next step: read up on the glycemic index. This number shows you how much quick-burning sugar is in that rocket-fuel you call food. It compares slow-vs.-fast burning foods and shows you which foods will spike your blood sugar and which ones won't. Also, avoid nonorganic sugars and any foods superhigh in starches, like white bread or other white flour products. These spike blood sugar levels and get you craving more! Eliminate the basic sugars and white flour products from your diet, and you'll find yourself less spiky, less moody, better able to concentrate, and hap-hap-happy!

Info: Index Cards and Duct Tape

We are notorious for asking far too many questions in class. When you have an idea, grab your arm before it raises and fight the urge (if you lose the fight, grab the duct tape, and use it liberally).

Write the idea down on an index card before you say or do anything. Then ask yourself two questions:

1. What value does asking this question add to the entire class?
2. Have I already made a couple of comments or asked a couple of questions today?

Don't ask questions just for yourself, to share your great knowledge, to impress others, or for your class participation grade; this does *not* work with sharp college professors. Instead, think about what it adds to the discussion for your classmates. And if you've spoken more than twice, perhaps it's best to hold any further comments until after class, no matter how good you think they are.

Review, Review, Review

Reading and reviewing your notes (or playing back audio, video, or other recording devices) right after class or later the same day will easily double your retention of the material. If possible, budget time immediately after class to go over your notes. You can reorganize them if you need to, draw or redraw a mind map, color code important points, make bullet points, or add any other modifications that will aid in your understanding and retention. Chances are, you'll remember points you missed in class. This process will remind you to look up something you didn't understand, and your notes will become clearer and more effective. Want to really maximize your review? Form a study group and go over the class lecture each day or quiz yourselves based on the day's class or reading. Time consuming? Yes. But if the group's friendly and productive, it'll be more than worthwhile!

Class Participation

If you can show your professor you've gone above and beyond the call of duty, and that you have something meaningful to offer, it'll go far in helping your grade. Better yet, work to make your comments helpful to the professor *and* to the class—this makes the professor's job easier. Not only will you help a potential participation grade, but you'll also give yourself some breathing room in case you have unexpected problems further down the road.

How to Excel at Class Participation
- Think quality, not quantity. More is less when it comes to class participation.
- Appraise the value of your comment or question. If you're still unsure what good your idea does after writing it down and thinking about it, wait until you have a better one.
- Bring questions in advance. If you've done your reading and thought of something of interest, write it down as you go through your notes. If you use a PDA or Outlook, set a reminder to pop up at the beginning of class. Asking a question at the start of class shows that you have done the work, are very interested in the topic, and can demonstrate your knowledge.
- Do additional research. If you've done additional research for class, bring it up in a question. Just make sure it's relevant and adds value to the class.

- Do research during class. If you're a multitasker, look up the discussion topic online during class or bring a second book on the topic with you. This may give you a leg up in further discussions and will greatly add to your academic experience. Trying to discover information that would lead to a value-adding question or comment before the end of class can be a fun game. Just be careful. No matter how tempting it may be, if you find information contradicting the professor, *never, ever* mention this in class. If it's driving you insane and you see it as absolutely necessary, discuss it in private with him afterwards.

- Get your professor talking. If you get the professor talking about your question for quite a while, you've done your job. You've asked something that is of value to the class or of interest to the professor. In either case this goes a long way toward helping your grade.

What Do You Do When You're Struggling?

Sooner or later, we all run into trouble in a class or two. Either we're constantly behind, we can't follow the material, or we miss one or two critical lectures and suddenly we're on an out-of-control downward spiral. This happens to the best students, and for ADDers, it happens twice as fast and twice as often. When the going gets tough, the going takes action, yesterday! Do not hesitate, or assume things will get better. When your gut starts twisting, take immediate evasive action…before you're flattened by the bus.

Get Help Immediately

What action should you take? The first thing I'd do is immediately get a tutor and talk to the RDS office and/or my professor. Use all the help you can find to get back on track and keep Humpty Dumpty from falling off the wall. Use the questions and resources below to discover the source of the problem and get it corrected before it gets any worse.

Many students call me when they're in trouble...they're weeks behind, they've missed yet another class (they didn't want to show up without that late assignment or because of the test they'd have to take), and they don't know where to turn for help. First off, if this is you, check out the section on talking with your professor, because that should be step one in rectifying the situation. Next, find a tutor, and pronto. Where? First, ask your professor if he knows of one. The professor may even have an assistant who does tutoring on the side, or on rare occasion the professor himself may be willing to help out. Where else can you look? Check with the department secretary and on the department's physical bulletin board or website; also check with your RDS office, which may even have tutors available free of charge.

How do you get the ball rolling now? Slowly back away from this book, and look up your professor's number on the computer or directory. Call first, try email second, but take action *now*, and not a moment later. This will put things in motion to right the ship before it sinks, or before potential shame or embarrassment sets in further, causing even more disastrous delays.

Wake Up Your Brain

If the class begins really early in the morning, even if you get there on time you may not be fully awake. The ADD mind often takes some time to stir. And many ADD meds, particularly the long-acting ones, take a while to kick in. Since ADD symptoms are often magnified by exhaustion, unless you're a real morning person you should avoid early classes at all costs. If you're stuck in a morning class, however, there are things you can do to help.

- Keep your meds next to your bed and take them before you even hit the snooze alarm in the morning, to start waking your brain up even while you're still sleeping.

- Meditate after you wake. Ten or twenty minutes of deep breathing and meditation can wake up your mind more than another hour or two of sleep. Just roll out of the bed onto the floor, put on a guided meditation CD, and follow along.

- Build an exercise routine into your morning. Yes, this does mean you're stuck getting up even earlier, but morning exercise has many benefits. For instance, if you take a morning walk each day, you'll feel calmer and more connected to the world, and you'll be more awake and focused for class. Plus, regular morning exercise will help you fall asleep faster each night, which may improve the quantity and quality of your sleep.

Fuel the Mind for Success

 Think you ate a good breakfast? Ask yourself this: was there any significant protein (such as chicken, fish, meat, dairy, cheese, soy, or nuts) in your meal? If not, you're starving your brain and setting yourself up for a quick crash. Pop-Tarts, instant waffles, bagels, donuts, Danishes and even fruit are all set-ups for disaster. Without protein you'll burn through almost all of your energy before you even make it to class. Protein and fat are the slower-burning brain fuels that will keep you going and keep your blood sugar up.

Forget To Do the Reading?

- **Don't panic.** There are some simple ways to bluff your way through.
- **Begin emergency skimming.** If you have your book with you or can borrow a classmate's book, it's time to get busy. Thumb through the reading you were supposed to have done. Go first to the end of the chapter and look for a summary, or read the last paragraph. If there's time, skim through the chapter. Try reading anything in bold, or read the first sentence of each paragraph.
- **Grab your laptop and get on the Web.** If you have your computer with you, you're way ahead of the game. Hop online and look it up—depending on the book, you may find term papers, class discussions, or even a CliffsNotes-type summary posted online.
- **Get out your syllabus.** If you know the general topic you're reading about, grab your syllabus (if you have it). Look ahead and try to figure out where the discussion is headed.
- **The best defense is a good offense.** If you can tell from the discussion or the syllabus where things are headed, try to add value by asking a key question about the topic soon to be at hand. This gives the impression that you're thinking ahead of the game, and also moves the discussion forward to a point that has not been covered in the reading. But beware: this is a powerful technique only if used on very infrequent occasions. If a professor catches on that you're doing this, you could be found out.
- **Appear busy.** Okay, this is a very high schoolish thing to do, but if you're desperate and the ship is sinking, it may be worth a try.

Info: The Dog Ate My Homework

If you don't have an assignment or forgot to do it, don't skip class or make excuses. Instead, the best solution is to talk with the professor. Begging forgiveness may buy you some time if you've already established a relationship and rapport. Just don't lie about it. Offer the professor a reasonable compromise or solution: "Professor, I forgot my homework at home, but I can get it and put it in your mailbox later tonight." If you give her something to work with, often times she'll be reasonable. And if this is the first time it's happened, she may be fairly accommodating.

Believe It, and You'll See It

If you're struggling in class, visualize it going well. Picture yourself doing better. Show up with a smile and the belief that things will improve, even if you're shaking in your boots. Then take some steps to help you improve. Changing one small thing could make things easier, and the more success you have, the easier it'll be to achieve more. Dog-ear or mark this chapter and don't be afraid to refer back to it often. This is one area you'll be able to improve for years to come—and one with great rewards.

Tech Tip: Messenger to the Rescue!

Need to talk with a classmate about work without disturbing the entire class? This is one place where instant messaging can be quite handy. You can discuss the lecture, your practice problems, a group project, rebuttals, or anything else class-related without disturbing the professor.

However, be careful what you chat about—there are eyes all around. Get off the subject or chat with someone who's not in the class and you're not only disturbing those around you, but seriously asking for trouble.

Take Your Meds before Class

Your medicine acts as eyeglasses for the brain, helping to clarify your surroundings and enabling you to see the material more clearly. Make sure you're taking your meds before your classes. You'll focus better, be able to concentrate on the lecture, and be less fidgety and impulsive. You're also much less likely to over-participate in class discussion or blurt something out if you're on your meds, and you'll retain what was discussed in class.

Find a Way to Get Involved

If you're bored out of your mind, fidgeting, and unable to pay attention, look for ways to immerse yourself in the class. Can you work on your class participation grade? Can you read ahead in the book to see what's coming next or to catch the professor tripping up on something (whatever works to keep your mind engaged)? Could you make drawings that reflect what the professor is talking about? If you can find a way to get excited about the topic or engaged in the material, it'll become a lot easier to focus on it.

Inspiration: Remember This?

One time I took a class called Enterprise Resource Planning, which was basically about efficiency and production. This was not on my top ten list of exciting topics. So I went to the professor to try to boost my interest level. We talked for a bit, and he mentioned an author whose ideas clicked with me. In this boring class, I actually asked for extra reading. And it turned out to be really cool. I became excited about the material, and the professor even asked me about my reading in class. Now I was engaged and felt like a part of the class rather than a part of my desk or the wall.

Multitasking and the Laptop

Are you the type of person who needs a radio or TV on to study and pay attention? Does doing one thing at a time bore you, while doing multiple things at once sounds fun? If so, you are probably one of the many ADDers who is a great multitasker. If you're lucky enough to have a laptop with you, the need to multitask can be a huge advantage! Remember, though, not to disturb those around you.

Good Uses of a Laptop in Class
• Going over class notes
• Looking ahead in the lecture
• Brainstorming discussion questions
• Doing your homework for the class you're in
• Surfing the Internet for information that would aid the class discussion

- Online discussions (keep it brief) with other students on relevant topics
- Doing research online for a paper or project for the class you're in

Bad Uses of a Laptop in Class:
- Surfing the Internet in areas unrelated to class
- Emailing or instant messaging friends
- Playing games
- Appearing completely disinterested in the class and professor
- Working on homework that was due at the beginning of class or giving the appearance you're working on something that was already due
- Working on other subjects. Be careful—I did this a lot and later found out it upset other people in the class. My recommendation: make sure there's no one behind you or around you that might be disturbed. Err on the side of caution and assume that, if there's someone behind you, they're bothered by you constantly doing something else.

Going Forward

Success in the classroom can be yours. Follow the advice above, and experiment. If something's working, keep doing it. If not, try something else. I'd recommend rereading this section from time to time to help you continuously improve. Your creative mind gives you a greater willingness to problem-solve, tinker, and discover what works for you. Too simple to be true? Sure sounds like it. But have fun with it and amaze yourself with the results!

> "The classroom, with all its limitations, remains a location of possibility."—**bell hooks**

Studying

> "The more you understand, the less you have to remember."
> —**Craig A. McCraw**

With your creative ADD mind, getting good grades is not a matter of studying harder—you have to study differently. There aren't enough hours in the day to muscle through your studies on brute force alone, and college tests are much more comprehensive, lengthier, more challenging, and trickier than the ones you took in high school. You need a strategy for success.

What Are the Basics?

There are some great strategies for studying with ADD, but first you need to cover the basics—what you need to do before studying to make sure your efforts will be effective. We study best when we're well rested and properly fueled, and when our minds are at ease. To set ourselves up for success, we need to:
- Have a fairly regular sleep time.
  - Get daily aerobic exercise.
  - Eat foods and snacks that are high in protein and low in quick-burning carbs and sugars.
- Keep your study environment free from clutter.
- If you're on meds (or using supplements) take them as prescribed, not just during class time.
- Be kind to yourself. Schedule shorter, more frequent study sessions, and reward yourself for your efforts.

Once you've got the basics in place, you're ready to start studying!

What Is Your Studying Strategy?

There are eight key elements for successful studying:
- Study routine
- Study environment
- Making time
- Reviewing

- Doing the reading
- Quizzing yourself
- Study buddies
- Getting help

Let's look at each element in detail to learn how to get the most out of your studies with the minimum amount of time, effort, and pain.

Info: Start a Study Routine

To make your studying time more effective, you need a standard routine in place that gets you into the groove and learning as soon as you sit down.

- Study right after class. Try to review your notes immediately after your difficult classes; this has been shown to dramatically increase retention of class material. Schedule studying time when your mind is functioning at its best.

- Study your most difficult subjects first. If you save the hardest for last, you're likely to be so fatigued or behind schedule that you never get to it or only do it halfheartedly. Put activities that require the greatest brainpower first, while you're fresh, and save the mindless work for last.

- Try to schedule only one difficult class per day. This allows you to put the majority of your efforts into studying or home-work for one major class each night, rather than to have to cram lots of reading and studying for several hard classes into one evening.

- Build snack time, meals, and breaks into your studying time, to allow yourself to recharge and refuel to keep your energy up while you're study-ing. A consistent schedule will let you fine-tune your eating so you know how to be ready to work at your best.

Determine Your Ideal Study Environment

To find the place that works best for you, ask yourself where you concentrate the best. This can be anywhere—your dorm room, the library, a computer lab, a coffee shop, outdoors—just as long as it's a place where you can shut out distractions and really focus. Also, make sure

that the place is available during your peak hours of performance. If you know you retain information best around
11:00 p.m., and the library closes at ten, you'll have to find
somewhere else to study.

Build this spot into your study routine. This makes it automatic
and ensures you get the job done. For instance, if you know you'll
blow off studying if you head back to the dorm after class, take your
study materials to class with you. This way, you can totally avoid the
dorm and its distractions and head directly to your studying spot.

Organize Your Study Time

Don't needlessly force yourself to study for four hours straight
or tie yourself to a chair until your studying is done—you
may get through the material this way, but I doubt your retention will be all that good. Stretch, walk around the block, send an email
or two, grab a snack, or pick up a magazine every thirty minutes or so
during your studying. Keep the breaks short, but make sure you give
your brain a rest every now and again so it can refresh itself. You could
also reward yourself (with a little block of chocolate, or a half hour of
video games) for each block of time that you study.

Review

Reviewing your notes on the day you write them can double your
retention. Here are some easy ways to review:

- **Daily review time.** Schedule a regular time to review your
  notes each day, either immediately after class, during a
  break, in a study hall, or after school. Building it into your
  routine means you'll remember to do it and makes it seem natural,
  not extra work.
- **Rewrite.** Consider transferring your notes onto fresh paper. This not
  only makes them clearer and easier to read, but it helps you determine
  what information's most critical and what you might have missed.
- **Make them visual.** Create a visual map or flow chart of your notes,
  or color-code them for quick and easy recall. If you're a highly visual
  person, this can be invaluable.

- **Highlight, highlight, highlight.** No time to rewrite or draw? Highlight key information as you reread your notes to burn the material into your brain and help you when it's time to study for a test.
- **Read them out loud.** If you're an auditory learner, read your notes out loud to sink the ideas into your mind, or read them into a recorder for later review.

Tech Tip: Electronic Reminders

The minute you have a great thought or an emergency thought, *take electronic action*.

Write yourself an email and send it to yourself right away, or set an alarm on your calendar software. Don't have your laptop? Set an alarm on your PDA, watch, or even your cell phone. The minute you remember something, get it down. If you don't remember *when* something is due, but you know you forgot about it and it's due soon, set an alarm for later in the day to check.

Do the Reading

Some classes will definitely have more assigned reading than others, but rest assured, you'll be doing at least some reading for every class you take. And no matter what you might think, it's crucial to read everything the professor recommends. Here are some ways to ensure you do it:

- Schedule daily reading time. The easiest way to get reading done is to have a set time and place for it each day. Experiment to figure out where and when you read best, and then make it a part of your routine.
- Put your most difficult reading first. If you put the hard stuff off until later you risk never getting it done or being too tired to really concentrate on it when you finally get around to it. So set a time for each subject, hardest to easiest, and stick to that order.

- Break it into bite-sized pieces, and take breaks. Don't fry your brain by tackling too much at once—give yourself frequent breaks and reward yourself for your accomplishments.
- Color-code your reading. Just as you do with your notes, highlight the key portions of your reading for quick and easy review.
- Take notes. Take notes while you're reading so you don't have to reread the material later—you'll have the important points already distilled in front of you.
- Read out loud. If hearing it will help you remember, find a secluded place and read out loud.
- Note what you don't understand. Make a list of any information from the reading that you don't understand so you can ask about it in class or talk it over with your professor.

ADD Challenges: Staying Stimulated

Sometimes our brains are moving so fast and processing so much that one stimulus at a time just isn't enough. If we focus only on the professor, or the boss, or any one object, our brain ends up with too much idle time and we start to drift. Adding stimuli—for instance, a blaring radio—to the situation can help bring us back into the moment and keep us on track.

Stimuli come in many forms. For one person it may be pacing; for another, fidgeting. I've heard squeezing Silly Putty or a stress ball helps some people to concentrate and stay on task. For other people it may mean having a TV or radio on in the background.

For still others, the preferred tool is multitasking. While those with ADD are said to have an inability to focus, this is far from the case—it's actually an inconsistency of focus. We often have the ability to hyperfocus on interesting tasks and may do quite well with multiple things to focus on simultaneously. This may mean following a class lecture while doing homework and reading or doing research at the same time.

Understanding your need for stimulus helps you build the right study environment. When searching for the right place to take a test or study and do homework, it's important to understand how the amount of surrounding stimuli affects your productivity. Don't look at what works for others or worry about how you might appear to observers. Just find out what works, fine-tune the process, and use it to your advantage.

Quizzing Yourself

Quizzing yourself is a great way to remember difficult material—you'll never forget what you get wrong in self-examination and end up looking up and concentrating on. Here are some self-quizzing tools to consider:

- Flashcards. Make flashcards for key concepts and terms as you read chapters or review your notes.

- Sample essay questions. If you have an essay test coming up, make up practice essay questions and write out the answers. Time yourself so that it's as much like the actual test as possible.

- Computer software. There's software available that you can use to make flashcards or self-quizzes or take sample ones. Check out download.com to see some of what's available.

- Visual quizzes. Make a drawing of each key concept from memory, then compare it to your notes. This is a good way to see if you have a grasp on the main ideas.

- Practice problems. Do as many sample problems as you can before a test. Write big, use graph paper, and write each step down so you can catch your mistakes and keep the problem from becoming a jumble of numbers. As with anything, the more you practice, the better you'll get.

Tech Tip: Download Slides for Organized and Searchable Notes

 Today more and more professors are posting outlines or notes online before a class begins. They expect you to download the slides and print them out to follow the lecture in class. But you can do much more with these tools.

Instead of simply printing out the slides or outline, copy and paste them into a Word document. Then click the "outline" feature on your word processor and you'll have everything organized by Roman numerals, numbers, and so on.

Now add enough room between each of the topic headings to add your own notes, and you've got the perfect outline for in-class fill-in-the-blanks.

With your laptop handy and your customized file open, kick back and relax. Simply fill in the details of the lecture on the outline you already have prepared!

And it's searchable!

Not sure which day you studied mitochondria? Simply type the term into the "search" field on your computer and ask it to find any documents with "mitochondria" in them. Soon you'll have the exact class discussion you were looking for.

Study Buddies

Sometimes the easiest way to get something done is to have someone else there. That person doesn't need to help you specifically, but sometimes his or her presence can be enough to help get you back on track, focused, and moving in the right direction.

Other times it helps to have someone there to bounce your ideas off of. I know many students who feel stuck until they start talking to someone else about what they're doing. Having someone to talk to about what you're doing often helps release your ideas from the hidden corners of your brain. It's almost as if the other person is giving suggestions, but they're coming out of your mouth.

Here are some ways that working with others can help you study:

- **Physical presence.** Just the physical presence of someone can sometimes help you get focused and productive. In *Driven to Distraction*, Dr. Hallowell mentions a business owner who hires someone to sit in his office with him so that he can get work done.

- **Better studying environment.** This can be particularly helpful if you know you don't study or work well at home. Plan on meeting someone at the library or a computer lab; setting a meeting time forces you out of the house and gets you into the environment you need to be productive.

- **Group studying.** It can be helpful to meet a group for studying—if there are multiple people focusing on one thing, it's hard to get distracted. You can also try these group techniques:

  - **Divide and conquer.** If you have a big test coming up that covers multiple subjects, have each person take a section to study and prepare notes on for the group.
  - **Quiz each other.**
  - **Tackle problems.** You can work together to solve math and science problems, and then to compare answers and methods.

- **Meeting the professor.** This can be very helpful in organizing your thoughts. It forces you to prepare in advance, and describing things to your professor makes clear what you know and don't know.

- **Helping others.** Teaching the material to others in your class can help solidify the information in your head—before you can teach other people, you have to thoroughly understand the material yourself.

- **Writing center.** You can use writing centers to help with outlining, organizing, or completing a paper. And setting an appointment has the added bonus of forcing you to work on your paper so that you have something to show them when you go in.
- **Working with a tutor.** A tutor can help you organize your thoughts and focus on your assignment. Tutors are good not only as instructors that help you understand the material but also as sounding boards for your own ideas.
- **Proofreader.** Having someone else read your paper is always a good idea—they can catch mistakes you might not see on your own. You may have been too close to the subject matter to realize something key was missing, or you may think your structure is good and discover that it confuses the reader. A reader can also challenge your ideas, which helps you better formulate your arguments.
- **Resources for disabled students office.** There is often a staff member who can help you study, get you started on a paper, or find a place where you can work productively.

Getting Help

Don't ever feel bad about asking for help, and it's always better to do it sooner rather than later, maybe even before you need it. In fact, people are often more likely to help when you don't appear too desperate and when you've clearly been working your way through the material. Just show the professor or whomever you're asking for assistance that you're already working on the problem, and ask them for specific help on exactly what you're stuck on.

If this isn't enough, get a tutor and get one early, as soon as you sense you might need a little extra help in a class. And if you know what you need to do but can't motivate yourself to get it done, make a tutor, a coach, or your RDS office hold you accountable for your work. You've worked too hard and come too far to flail unnecessarily. If you need help, don't be afraid to ask for it.

Studying

ADD Challenge: Find What Works For You

Don't be afraid to try things on and see what fits. This is especially true with studying. It can be a huge challenge for your creative mind. You have to try different ways of approaching the material until you find exactly what works for you. If you're struggling, try changing your environment, turning some music on, inviting a friend over, or taking your work to your professor and asking her for clarification.

Once you figure out how to work with your mind, you'll find new confidence, achieve beyond your wildest dreams, and find that many areas you previously struggled with will become your areas of greatest success and passion.

So if you're struggling, tinker, try things out, believe in yourself, throw out the limits, and above all else, don't be afraid to ask for help. Why bang your head against the wall when you can simply ask for the help you need? Don't try to reinvent the wheel; learn from others to shorten the curve!

Tech Tip: Tutorial Software

For almost any course you can think of, there's likely to be interactive software available to help you learn the material. There's an amazing amount of this software online. First stop, go to download.com. Type in the subject you're studying and see what comes up. A quick check on

"Spanish," for example, shows over 450 different programs! There were tutorials, dictionaries, conjugation games, speaking games, flashcards, interactive quizzes, and so much more!

If you type in "chemistry," fifty-four results come back. You can download the table of elements right into your PDA. There's Chemlab to simulate a chemistry lab and interact with animated lab equipment. There's a bunch of software and games to learn elements, symbols, and equations, and even solutions calculators to help you solve problems and check your work.

"Study lends a kind of enchantment to all our surroundings."
—**Honoré De Balzac**

Test Taking

"Third Law of Applied Terror: 80 percent of the final exam will be based on the one lecture you missed and the one book you didn't read."

College quizzes and tests are much harder than those in high school, particularly with a creative ADD mind that can so easily get away from you (as mine did during my accounting quiz). However, you can overcome these challenges and turn these daunting quizzes and tests into successes. You can actually use your ADD mind to excel on these tests once you understand some basic strategies and know how to effectively employ the accommodations available to help you over the hurdles.

ADD Challenge: Stop Cramming

 It's often a huge surprise to find that the same studying techniques that gave you A's in high school could cause so much grief, heartache, and poor grades in college. You can't cram your studying into a two- or three-day period when you have five, six, or even seven classes, all with comprehensive exams covering hundreds of pages of material. All-nighters and cramming can be miracle techniques for one class or test at a time—but they don't work when you have multiple classes and assignments and an overload of information and complexity.

This is a major reason that successful high school students bomb when they hit college. You have to learn how to break your studying down into manageable chunks, how to prepare for tests, and how to get the material into your long-term memory in advance so you won't need much studying at all the night before. Succeeding on college tests and exams requires study habits and planning above and beyond cramming. Good results often have little to do with your studies the night before an exam or your test-taking performance—and everything to do with long-term preparation.

Seven Strategies for Test-taking Success

Test taking in college requires preparation, planning, and strategizing. As with anything else in life, to achieve mastery over taking college exams you must learn, understand, and practice, practice, practice. Here are some simple ways to vastly improve your study habits.

1. Start studying today.

This is the simplest, easiest way to help yourself and improve your results. As the saying goes, don't just study longer and harder, but study smarter. As soon as you know an exam's coming, begin studying for it and build time for it into your routine. Starting today (or, preferably, yesterday) has the advantage of getting the material programmed into your long-term memory, where it's more likely to stick. Cramming only gets it into your short-term memory, which can fail you during a stressful exam.

Starting right away also allows you to see pitfalls ahead. Are you having trouble understanding something? Might you need a tutor? Starting now leaves you time to take action on any issue before it becomes a problem.

2. Understand the material and know what will be on the test.

Perhaps it's Murphy's law, the law of the creative mind, or a jinx of ADD, but whatever it is, the harder we study, the more likely we are to miss the one key element, term, section, or chapter that's the key to the entire exam. It's guaranteed—you'll either study everything except what you needed to study, or you'll realize that you missed something crucial and it will upset you, throwing off your performance.

This is a problem that's easy to prevent: Ask your professor what's on the test. But don't just ask—prove to the professor that you've put some thought and effort into it by bringing some work to show her. That will make her much more willing to help you.

3. Create the right environment.

If you need complete silence, see if there's a private room or an out-of-the-way cubicle you can use in the library. And it's not out of the question to make your study area the basement of your dorm, the bottom or top of an empty stairwell, or someplace even more unorthodox. Make a habit of studying in any place you can find that works well for you.

If you need stimuli, try to find a place that's full of interesting sights and sounds but doesn't have so many friends around that they'll pull you off task. This could be a busy library area, a study lounge, a coffee shop, or a computer lab.

4. Choose the right studying tools.

Do you have a lot of terms to memorize? Make flashcards and quiz yourself right up until the exam. Do you have a lot of facts and concepts to memorize? Write a review sheet. Not only is a review sheet a great reference, but just the act of writing it down ingrains the information.

Cater to your own needs and style and be creative. Are you a visual learner? Make colored flashcards and use different colored pens as you rewrite or outline material and key points. If you're more auditory, read and study out loud or quiz yourself on tape for later review. Try recording the class review session and listening at home.

Use mind mapping and other memory devices, such as mnemonics. You've probably used mnemonics before in grade school. An example is the popular rhyme that can help you remember how to spell "success": *Double the C, double the S, and you will have success.* Be sure to check out the section on mind mapping.

Info: Memory Tool

Here's a fun tool to try. If you're a visual person and have a bunch of terms, formulas, or numbers to memorize, try picturing the house you grew up in. Put a term or two in each room of your house. The mind remembers well in pairs, so you could put two formulas for acids on the couch downstairs, two formulas for bases on your bed upstairs, and so on. It sounds crazy, but our minds think geographically by location and physicality, so making concepts into physical objects and placing them around the house might just do the trick.

5. Enlist assistance from your professors or peers.

You can meet with your professor, study with a friend, instant message a friend, or call in a professional (such as a tutor or ADD coach) who can help you learn the material, stay on track, and get the job done.

Conversely, another fun way to work with others is to tutor other students on the material, even (or especially) if you don't know it well yourself. This is particularly helpful for people who know the material but test poorly. Tutoring others forces you to find the information, do the research, quiz yourself, and reason your way through until you understand it thoroughly. It burns the information into your brain and makes you comfortable with concepts, ideas, and problem sets whether they come at you forwards, sideways, or even backwards on the test.

6. Simplify and skim.

When it comes time to review for a comprehensive exam in college, you don't have time to read everything over again. Instead you need to be smart and learn effective skimming. If you know what key concepts and ideas to look for, you'll better know what to read thoroughly, what to skim, and what to skip altogether.

Here are some skimming tips:

- Focus on key concepts and ideas.
- Read paragraph headings, key words, or italicized material in each chapter.
- Read chapter summaries.
- Quiz yourself on chapter summaries. How much do you remember right off the bat? Does everything make sense? If not, consider going back through the chapter in more detail.

ADD Advantage: Creative Studying

Above and beyond all else, be creative each step of the way. Make a painting or collage about your English test, or write a story about a fictional quest where the character gets all the information she needs along the way. Don't just memorize chemistry; crack out the molecule set and build things as you go along. The more touchy, feely, and artistic you get, the more incredible your recall will be.

Remember to reward yourself for your accomplishments and have fun with studying. Despite what everyone's told you, one test, grade, semester, year, or even degree will not make or break your life—but attitude will. Go easy on yourself, have fun with this, give it your all, and let life work out the details.

Info: Visualiztion Exercise

Starting a week or so before your exam, take ten minutes of study time each day to visualize the test. Try this exercise:

Find a quiet, comfortable place to sit or lay down. Begin with a few minutes of slow, deep breathing. Breathe in, counting slowly to four. Breathe out, doing the same thing. Think about a positive experience you've had in the past, and link that experience to the word "yes."

After a few minutes see yourself sitting down for the best test of your life. Now see yourself clapping your hands together and saying loudly, "Yes!" Now, actually say "yes" three times out loud. Feel the positive emotions of the experience you've linked to this sound. Now go back into your breathing. As you take slow, deep, relaxing breaths, see yourself having the most amazing experience you've ever had in an exam. You're prepared, you know it, and the answers reflect all your hard work.

Actually picture in your mind how happy you are at your progress on the test. Feel your confidence, be amazed at your test-taking prowess, hear the pencil as it dances across the pages with effortless perfection. Imagine, believe, and see yourself doing well, and that feeling of confidence will follow you into the actual test.

If you start feeling stress during your visualization, follow it to see what you end up imagining. Stress can be your gut's way of telling you where to focus future study efforts—maybe you'll see a section that you forgot to review. Then replace the negative thoughts with positive ones, such as the "yes" from earlier. Focus on the end result: you getting a good grade.

Taking the Exam

So now you've studied, visualized, tested yourself, and prepared in more and better ways than ever before. For a well-prepared athlete, the race is the reward for all of the hard training…and a great exam experience and excellent grade will be your reward here. Follow the advice below to make test day go smoothly and ensure a positive result. I know a lot of this is plain common sense, but that often eludes us during exams.

What Do You Bring?

Spare Writing Instruments

If you'll be writing, bring several pens and pencils—you never know when one will run out of ink or break on you. If you don't want to have to sharpen your pencil and risk disrupting your concentration, bring pencils with replaceable lead. Also, it may sound silly, but if you have a favorite pen or pencil for doing your homework, or if you prefer a particular color of ink, bring it to the test. It'll help you think.

Extra Scrap Paper

Make sure you bring tons of scrap paper. You don't want to worry about doing calculations in a tiny space; this leads to careless errors like missing steps or transferring numbers or answers improperly. You want to see giant letters and numbers in front of you for accuracy and so you can think—and a cluttered page equals a cluttered mind.

Food and Drink

See if you can bring a protein bar and a bottle of water with you. Be sure to ask first, and if it isn't allowed, discuss it with the RDS office. As a last resort, I've been known to keep a protein bar in my pocket, excuse myself for a bathroom break, scarf it down in the hall, drink some water from a fountain, and then head back in.

A Study Guide or Notebook

It's not uncommon to want to check one last thing before the test. Rather than get flustered because you thought of it and couldn't check, take it with you; even if you never need it, it'll make you feel better.

A Digital Watch or Timer

While this can be intimidating if you focus on it too much, it can also be a valuable tool. If there are twenty-five questions and you have an hour to take the test, knowing you have about four minutes per question can help. Noticing you've been stuck on one question for twelve minutes is a clear indication that it's time to move on.

Your Electronics

If you need to make calculations or type your exam, make sure to bring your calculator, laptop, or whatever electronic devices you're allowed to use during the exam. If you'll be using a laptop, make sure you charge the battery the night before!

Final Preparations

Keep Everything by the Door

Pack everything you need (pens, pencil, laptop, calculator, books, etc.) the night before the test and leave your bag by the door. That way, you can just quickly double-check it before you leave in the morning. Make sure you keep your keys, wallet, phone, and other personal belongings ready to go as well. The last thing you need is the stress of searching for your keys before heading out to an exam.

Get a Good Night's Sleep

Getting the sleep you need may be more important than that extra hour of cramming. It will keep your brain from being in a fog and allow you to problem-solve more accurately.

Do One Last Visualization

Give thanks for an awesome exam as you step out of bed, or do a ten-minute visualization exercise and use all your senses to picture the exam going well.

Fuel Up

Eat a high-protein meal but don't eat too much. Eating protein will help prevent a sugar crash, but if you stuff yourself you may feel sleepy during the exam.

Budget Quiet Time

Set aside quiet time before any test—build it into your schedule and guard it with your life. It's best to have a chance to shift gears, unwind, and clear your mind before taking your test. Try to schedule quiet time before you leave for the exam, then arrive five or ten minutes early to get your mind back in the zone.

During the Exam

Get Set Up

Give yourself time to look over your notes one last time, get your pencils or pens out, get your scrap paper situated, and take a few minutes to relax and breathe deeply.

Write Your Name

When the exam is distributed, put your name on it first thing. This is frequently overlooked and can sometimes create big problems.

Listen to the Professor

If the professor starts talking, stop what you're doing and listen—these instructions could be critical to your success.

Make a Rough Time Breakdown

Look over the questions and figure out the amount of time you should be spending on each one.

Read and Reread Questions

Read each question twice to avoid misinterpreting it or giving the opposite of what the professor is looking for. Figure out what he or she wants, and if you're still in doubt, ask.

Don't Rush

No matter what, a panicked pace isn't necessary. Move slowly and methodically. Try to remain relaxed and limber. It may help to keep repeating a positive phrase in your head, such as your "yes" from earlier or "thank you for my awesome results."

Move On

If you're completely stuck, star or leave some sort of mark on the question and move on to the next. If you've budgeted five minutes per question and you're on fifteen, just move on. If you come back, great; if not, at least you've gotten through many others because you moved on.

Stay Loose

If you get stuck or stymied, remember your breathing and visualization techniques. Get up. Stretch. Take a bathroom break. You aren't losing time with these activities; you're helping re-energize your brain and getting back in the game.

Do the Easy Stuff First

If you feel like you can answer some questions but not others, go with the easy stuff first. Positive momentum builds positive results. Do one section well, then go back and tackle the harder stuff.

Review Your Work

Go back over your problems, preferably twice if you have the time. On tests involving calculations, go through your steps one by one (and number them) if at all possible. Make sure you haven't missed something easy.

Document Your Process

If you have most but not all of what's being asked for, jot a note at the end of your answer. This way, the professor knows where you were going and you might get substantial partial credit.

Go Back to Your Starred or Marked Questions

It's best to get into the habit of putting down any answer first, even one you're not sure about, and then coming back to it when you've finished the test. This is essential in case you run out of time— at least you have a shot at getting the answer right.

Taking Different Types of Tests

There are many different types of exams out there, each with its own most effective approach. Here we'll look at three of the most common types, along with valuable ways to focus your efforts to get the best results on each.

Essay Exams

To succeed on essay exams, it's best to practice in advance: write out answers to potential questions or practice questions and work out their organization before the real thing.

If you're in a science class, you may have exams with long problems requiring detailed answers and calculations. These exams are quite similar to essay exams and the same kinds of strategies can be used.

1. Skim the exam, plan ahead, and then jump in. Look at all of the questions or problems first. Are some simpler than others and therefore likely to take less time? Decide in advance whether you want to hit the complicated or easy questions first.

2. Read and reread the questions. Read them quietly out loud if you have to. It's often not until the second or third read that you truly grasp the meaning of a question or that the best answer pops into your head. The worst thing you can do is misinterpret or read the question wrong, write out the greatest answer in the world to the wrong question, and receive zero credit.

3. Structure your answers. Science professors are more lax about properly worded or structured answers. On essay exams in more literary disciplines, such as English or history, however, your structure, organization, and writing style can be almost as important as your answer. Unless the professor instructs you to answer in a paragraph, it is typically best to use an intro, body, and conclusion. Check with your professor in advance to see what kind of format he or she prefers.

4. Do your best to use proper grammar and spelling. If you're just stuck on one or two words, choose similar words you know how to spell. And if your spelling is particularly horrendous, see if writing the essay on your laptop (and using spell-check) is an option.

5. Try not to repeat yourself in your answer, which is really just another way to fill space. Also make sure you're not using the same sentence structure line after line, such as repeating "the author says" in several consecutive sentences. This will drive your professor batty.

6. Keep it brief. Clear and concise answers are valued far more than rambling answers, no matter how eloquent they are. It's much better to have one tight paragraph than three crammed with filler. Think of how much professors have to read—the more direct and to the point you are in your answers, the less time your professor has to spend looking at your exam and deciding what to mark down. Keep 'em happy for a better grade!

7. Read and review your answers as many times as possible. Perhaps you've missed something or made an obvious mistake, or maybe rereading the essay will jog your memory and remind you of something crucial you need to include. If you have the time to go back through the entire test, do so; if not, go back through the questions that were hardest for you (mark them with a star or letter as you're going through).

8. If they're math problems, check your calculations again and again and again. Perhaps you moved a decimal point one place or wrote 87 where you should have written 78. Errors like this happen, and you shouldn't beat yourself up for it—just try to review your calculations and catch mistakes when you can.

Do you have a linear-thinking professor who wants straightforward, concise answers? Or would he appreciate a little humor, creativity, or ingenuity in your responses?

Though sometimes risky, there seems to be good karma associated with making things more interesting and entertaining for professors, who are stuck reading and grading exam after countless exam. Sure, occasionally you might bomb if you totally misread an instructor, but overall this can be a very effective technique. Not only that, but professors who enjoy your answers are far more likely to give you rave reviews, great letters of recommendation, and may even offer you a teaching assistant position in the department (or recommend you for an internship) further down the road.

ADD Advantage: Extra Time for Math

Always ask for extra time on math exams, even if you're relatively sure you won't need it. After you've finished your first pass through the test, relax, take some deep breaths, and perhaps even do a short meditation. When you're through, take the test again. Do it entirely on scratch paper and check over each step and your final answers carefully. Even the best of us have been known to

Test Taking

transpose numbers, copy answers incorrectly, miss a positive or negative sign (or reverse them), or make other small mistakes that can quickly take an A exam down to a C. Use your time and take the test again.

However, it is important to note that you shouldn't change your answer unless you're absolutely sure it's wrong. When in doubt go with your gut, and that's generally your first answer.

Multiple-Choice Tests

Of all possible test formats, the multiple-choice exam is the sneakiest. Questions seem straightforward enough, but many college professors indulge in a bit of sport. To see if you truly understand the material rather than having just memorized it, they ask questions backwards and sideways with tricks and pitfalls aplenty.

While I don't believe we ADDers are careless (as some people claim), we do have a penchant for moving quickly. On multiple-choice tests we must read, reread, and then read the question again to determine what answer really is the best. It's a process of elimination, and with practice you'll get quite good at it.

- **Read each question carefully a couple of times before reading the answers.** Questions can often be misleading—make sure you're paying careful attention to whether they're asking for the best response, the one that is least likely, or the option with the most correct answers included in it.

- **Read all of the possible answers twice before putting pencil to paper.** Read each answer out loud (but quietly) if you have to, but make sure you thoroughly understand them all. Make sure you've found the one that most closely matches what the question is asking.

- **Be sure to ask your professor for clarification if you do not fully understand a question.** However, if you feel the need to ask about each and every question, not only will the professor stop helping you, but by disturbing the class each time you get up, you're liable to make some enemies amongst your classmates.

- **Mark troublesome questions, put down your best guess, and then move on.** You don't want to spend too much time on any one question; if you find you're struggling with one, put down your best guess, mark the question, and come back to it later.

- **Review the test.** Go over the entire test if you have time. Read the questions again to make sure you've put down the exact answer the professor is looking for. This is also a good opportunity to verify you haven't missed any questions or recorded answers somewhere they don't belong.

- **Trust your gut.** When in doubt, go with your intuition. Overthinking something can do more harm than good, so go with your hunch, which is generally the first answer that comes to you. Maybe your subconscious mind is telling you something that your conscious mind just doesn't remember, but either way, you'd hate to have gotten the answer right the first time, then changed it because you talked yourself out of it.

Online Exams

Many professors post timed exams online. Often they can be taken at the student's convenience (which usually means right at the last minute). Most are open book and can be taken from your dorm room. Their timed nature, however, can trip you up: if you haven't created the proper environment for concentration your mind may be scrambled before you even begin.

Nevertheless, if you choose the time and place where you take online exams wisely, you may really enjoy them. They're more interactive, which keeps ADD minds stimulated; typing often helps us keep things straight; and we don't have to rush to a classroom and deal with everyone and everything around us. Here are some tips for conquering online exams.

- **Arrange for extra time.** Make sure you request extra time for online tests in advance—you may run into some technical complexities during the setup that could affect the time you have for the actual exam.

- **Pinpoint the best time to take the test.** In essence many of the same rules apply to online tests that apply to standard exams—try to take it when you know your mind will be sharpest.

- **Find the best place.** Make sure you're taking the test in the right environment. This could be your own room, a computer lab, the library, or perhaps even a coffee shop. Just make sure you won't be disturbed. If you need a very quiet environment to concentrate, see what provisions your RDS office can provide.

- **Keep the environment clean.** You should have a clear, clutter-free environment for taking the test. If you're using your computer at home, clear the desk of anything that isn't essential—the less clutter on your desk, the less clutter that will be in your brain during the test. (If you have to, take everything on the desk, sweep it into a laundry basket, and stuff it into your closet. This method has consequences later, but it will definitely help during the test.)

- **Have all the essential resources at hand.** Make sure your books, notebooks, and any other study materials that could come in handy are out and fully accessible on or near your desk.

- **Consider using a second or third computer.** If you keep your notes on your computer, you may want to use two or even three computers for your test (this generally means heading for a computer lab). For one online test I took, I had one Word file of class notes and a second that contained all of our reading documents. I went to the computer lab on a quiet Sunday afternoon (which was miserable for my weekend but ideal for my needs). I set up on three computers in a quiet corner of the lab: the middle one had the test on it, and on each side I pulled up my Word files. I could search, scan, find, and write all at the same time—it allowed me to answer questions quickly and thoroughly, and also fed my ADD need to multitask.

- **Prevent interruptions.** Let others know you'll be taking a test. Disconnect the phone, shut off your cell—do whatever you can to prevent interruptions from robbing you of critical time. If you're testing in a computer lab, sit away from everyone else and plan to be there when few people will be around. Consider making a fold-over sign saying "test in progress." Just keep people away from you so you don't have to spend test-taking time shooing them away.

- **Consider having a friend present.** If it makes you feel more comfortable and helps keep your mind from wandering off, you could ask a friend to sit in the room with you while you take the test.

- **Prepare to take a timed test.** First, of course, make sure you're granted extra time; but then break things down. Do you need to answer twenty-four questions in two hours? That means you have four or five minutes per question. You don't need to watch a timer to make sure you're on track, but having one with you can help you determine when you need to give up and move on to the next question. And if the on-screen timer is bothering you or making you panic, shut it off—it's not a bad idea to check it between sections, however.

- **Move if you need to.** Even during a short test taken in your own room, getting up and stretching can help you refocus and energize. This gets your blood flowing and helps ease the pressure on your mind.

Info: Step Outside

If you can, take a short break from your test, step outside, take off your shoes and socks, and scrunch your feet on the lawn a few times. It's amazing how this can reset your mind, calm you down, and ground you. It can help alleviate panic or anxiety and give you greater concentration and ability to focus for the rest of the exam. Some professors, time limits, or lawn squirrels won't allow this, but it never hurts to ask.

ADD Advantage: Making a "Cheat Sheet"

For some classes, you're allowed to bring a "cheat sheet" or crib notes into the exam. This is typically one piece of paper that you can fill front and back with notes, formulas, or whatever you want to help you through the test.

I've found that the most effective tool for making cheat sheets is Microsoft Excel. It allows me to shrink fonts and put tons of material and information on one page. Whenever I make sheets like this, other students want to copy mine. I happily let them, both because they'll return the favor and because I know I'll get the most out of it—the process of making the sheet is an awesome study tool. It forces you to look up the information and understand it clearly. And since we often remember things spatially, or by location, you're basically making a map of the most pertinent information.

If you take the time to make a great cheat sheet, you may find you don't even need it much. The effort of deciding what should go on it, tracking down that material, and then organizing it into a sensible order burns the material into your brain. Resist the urge to copy someone else's sheet; that cheats you of its entire value.

Going Forward

Acing exams is an art. It's something that takes skill and practice, but it can be learned. Keep working at it, have a sense of humor about it, and realize that no matter what, it's not the end of the world if you don't perform well. We often lose perspective, particularly around grades and exams. Don't forget to have fun and keep things in balance. A healthy, happy student is far more likely to do well on a test.

Remember that there are no limits in life; you truly can become whatever it is you desire. With your mind, you can overcome any challenge and turn any "weakness" into your greatest strength.

> "I have only one question for Mr. Melon . . . in twenty-three parts."—*Back to School*

Writing Papers

> "Writing is an exploration. You start from nothing and learn as you go."—**E. L. Doctorow**

Until you get the basics down, writing a paper can be a very frustrating and daunting task. Picking a topic, planning your time, creating a structure…there are so many decisions to make and directions to turn that it's easy to feel stuck—or to procrastinate until you're out of time.

But there are some steps you can take to make paper writing much less painful and more productive. No, it doesn't involve hiring someone to write the papers for you or purchasing papers online (do *not* do this!). There are tools and techniques you can use to help you get going and get your best words down on paper in a way that's to your professor's liking.

Info: Know What's Expected

 Writing a good paper is not as simple as having a great topic and perfect grammar and being well-organized and to the point. This won't get you a good grade if it's not what your professor wants. This is a common mistake that students make—they assume they know what the professor is looking for and write the wrong paper. Don't fall into this trap! If you're only 99 percent sure you know what the professor is looking for, this is a good opportunity to get to know him better.

Pick a Fun Topic

The first step in writing a good paper is to have a good topic. In high school, topics were typically assigned to you, but this is generally not the case in college. Professors want you to think, explore, and come up with your own ideas.

Make a list of interesting topics. Pick a topic that fascinates you and, obviously, that relates to the subject. If you're writing about nineteenth-century America, what was the most interesting part of that time for you? Was it the Underground Railroad? The world's first submarines? Civil War uniforms? The origins of baseball? Writing about something that interests you will make it easier for you to stay on top of the research, and your professor will be able to see your passion for the subject in your writing.

Use what you know. Narrow down the list by looking for a topic you already have experience with or know a lot about. Perhaps you wrote a paper about the Underground Railroad years ago, or maybe you still have informational booklets from visiting a Civil War museum. This is a good way to make writing the paper a little easier on you.

Find out what's available. Now start looking online and through the collection at your library to see what's available. If you're interested in how buttons on army uniforms changed between the American Revolution and the Civil War, it's possible there isn't much out there. If you don't find information readily available, you may want to think about switching subjects.

Info: Be Able to Support Your Topic

It's very easy to say you want to write an amazing and unique paper on a subject that no one else has ever written about. But if you can't find resources to back up your paper, you may be in trouble. This could lead to a bad paper or a last-minute change in topic. Remember: This is likely not the only assignment you have due. When it gets to crunch time, you won't have the forty hours to spend on it you once thought you had. So don't make it hard on yourself—pick a topic on which you can find articles, books, and websites that support your ideas.

Find Your Thesis Statement

Look through your initial research and make a list of some of the interesting ideas that fall under your topic. Read the list. Do you see a common theme? Perhaps you're writing about farriers (horseshoers) in the 1800s, and everything you're reading mentions how they were essential for the country's westward expansion. Are there other details on the list that support this idea, such as the fact that horseshoes allowed horses to travel farther and carry heavier loads? If so, you may have found your main point.

Randomly talking about horseshoes without a point is not only boring but also fatal to a good grade—you need to focus on one main point and back it up with your research and ideas. For instance, this hypothetical paper could be called "How Horseshoes Made America." It's a big idea that you're able to support with facts.

Such an idea is called your thesis statement. It will go in your first paragraph, typically toward the end, and will be a strong statement that says exactly what you're writing about. Here it could be something like the following: "In this paper we'll discuss the history of horseshoe-ing and how it supported the westward expansion of America."

Check with the Professor

Now that you have a solid topic and thesis and have done a little bit of research, run it by your professor. Make absolutely sure she approves of the idea and feels that you're heading in the right direction with it, and find out if there's anything else she thinks you should include. Verifying that you're on the right path could save you a lot of time and frustration (not to mention a bad grade) down the road.

Make a Timeline

 Now that you know for sure what you're writing about, it's time to make a schedule to ensure you're not researching and writing it the night before it's due. Break the paper down into the smallest pieces you can and list them; you can cross the first one off already: picking the topic.

1. **Research.** Break it down into manageable steps. Perhaps you could research farriers first, then westward expansion, and then supporting evidence for your idea that horseshoes made westward expansion possible. Decide how many hours you'll need for each step.
2. **First draft.** How long do you think it will take to write the first draft? First determine how long you'd like to spend on the actual writing. Then budget extra time—once you get started you'll discover you need to go back and do more research.

Info: Practice Makes Perfect

Don't be intimidated by the timeline process—it's all a matter of practice, and you may not be very good at it when you start. That's okay! It's a matter of trial and error, sticking with it, and fine-tuning the process. Before you know it, you'll be breaking down your papers quickly and efficiently.

The rewrite. Estimate how long you'll need to rewrite and edit. Personally, I find it much more difficult to write the paper the first time, but it always takes me much longer to edit it. Be realistic—this is the stage where you'll really be fine-tuning on your work, and you may have to add additional information. You should plan to spend a good amount of time on this.

The final stages. Decide how long it will take you to compile a bibliography, footnotes, a cover, or any of the other finishing touches your professor may require.

Now that you have your timeline, enter each task onto the corresponding date on your calendar. Just as with anything else, ask yourself when you work best: Perhaps you can do research late at night when your brain is half-asleep, but you need to write midday, when you're most alert. Or maybe you need to write in a quiet environment, and the library or computer lab doesn't settle down until late at night. Plan the environment and time of day and schedule it all on your calendar.

ADD Advantage: See the Librarian

If this section has your mind melting and your eyes watering, and you're contemplating manufacturing toothpicks as a profession, don't fret! Go see your local librarian! Your school librarian will help you with all of the above! You'll be amazed by his patience, generosity, and ability to help a student who wants to help herself. If you're struggling, I guarantee your librarian will keep you from drowning and help you in more ways than you can imagine!

People often don't realize how much a librarian can help until late in the game (if ever). But librarians have worked with hundreds of students on writing papers, so they know how you should budget your time and even what pitfalls to watch out for. They're great for far more than just research and can help you almost every step of the way. The only thing they won't do is spoon-feed you the answers, but if you're willing to put in the work, the majority of them would love to help!

After everything's scheduled, you should try to meet with your professor again. Show her your plan, and ask if it looks realistic, if there are any steps missing, or if there's anything to look out for that has tripped up other students in the past. If you've done your work in advance and have something concrete to show them, don't be afraid to ask professors as many questions as you feel are necessary—they're a valuable resource with tons of experience and are generally happy to steer you in the right direction.

This would also be a good time to visit with your RDS office, a tutor, a librarian, or an ADD coach to make sure this is a realistic plan and timeline (or for help if you're still struggling to come up with either).

Create an Outline

Find and Organize the Main Points

Go back to your thesis and initial research and decide what each of the main supporting points of the paper should be. For example, if you're writing about horseshoeing in the 1800s, what are the key facts you need to mention? Write them down, then check that you haven't missed anything important and that they all relate to your thesis. Do you think one or two might be interesting to you but not necessary to the paper?

Whittle down your list to three to five main points. Put them into chronological order or an order that makes sense for your point. For example, your main points might be:

- The history of horseshoeing, which assumed prominence in the early 1800s with the first patent
- History of the westward expansion
- How the expansion would not have been possible without the rise of the modern horseshoe

This is a logical order: the points lead into one another, and it's easy for the reader to follow. If you're having difficulty at this organizational stage this is another great time to ask for help. You have the hard part down—what the main ideas are—but you may need help defining how they come together. Talk to your professor, a writing center, RSD office, tutor, librarian, coach, or preferred 1–800 hotline if you need to.

Fill in Your Outline

Now that you have all the main points in order along with your thesis, you have your basic outline.

- Intro paragraph (includes thesis)
- Point One
- Point Two
- Point Three
- Conclusion paragraph (wraps up all main points)

Next use your preliminary research to add the supporting pieces of information for each point. Your outline should look like this:

Intro paragraph (includes thesis)

- Point One
    Supporting Point A
    Supporting Point B
    Supporting Point C
- Point Two
    Supporting Point A
    Supporting Point B
    Supporting Point C
- Point Three
    Supporting Point A

Supporting Point B

Supporting Point C

Conclusion paragraph (wraps up all main points)

Do the Research

Now that you know exactly what you need to find to support your topic, it's time to get into the heavy research.
Research for college papers used to be quite difficult: You'd have to go
to the library and dig through books, scouring each one. If your
library didn't have the information you needed, you'd typically have
to order materials from other libraries (interlibrary loans), which
could take weeks, or you'd just have to go to another library. Then
there'd be a time crunch to get the paper written before the deadline.

Today, of course, we have the Internet. This has made
research a lot easier, but it does have a few pitfalls: it's much easier to find oodles and oodles of information about a very wide
range of topics, but now you must sift through this mountain of information to find what's valuable, what's legitimate, and what's useless or
untrue. You should make sure to include plenty of time for this sifting.

Tech Tip: Researching on the Internet

The first thing you want to do is run your topic
through a basic search engine. If you don't get any
usable results, try similar but different words. For
example, if searching "horseshoes" only gets you
websites that want to sell them to you, try searching for "history of horseshoes."

Metasearch Engines
Search engines like Google and Yahoo are great
sources of information, but metasearch engines are
a bit more efficient. Each search engine has its own
high-tech techniques for finding websites. They

---

each look for different things, and no two search engines will put up exactly the same results. Metasearch sites sift through many search engines (such as Google) at the same time. My favorite is dogpile.com, but there are many good ones out there. Each search engine has its own bias, so this is a great way to pull info from many different places at the same time.

Library Databases

There are dozens of databases available for you to search on your school library's website or computers. These sites range from the very broad (such as a search of all journals, magazines, newspapers, etc.) to the very specific (trade journals within a particular field, industry, or discipline). In the beginning it can be hard to determine which databases best meet your needs, and you can burn a lot of hours sifting through irrelevant periodicals. This is another great reason to attend a seminar or session on research or using your school library during orientation or at the beginning of the school year (if one is offered) and another great reason to make friends with your librarian and ask for their guidance!

I always choose the option to show only articles or books that are available online. If I don't, I often get results that I may have to order from another library, and I don't want to know about what's out there that I can't read immediately. For periodicals or newspapers, try ProQuest—they've digitized many journals and newspapers, so you can pull up all the articles pertaining to your topic dating back to the 1800s.

There are so many great databases that it's worth your time to make a quick trip to the library and ask your librarian which databases would likely give you the best results.

Portals, Magazines, and Online Groups

If you're writing about the history of the railroads, there may be a website dedicated to collecting all the information online about railroad history. There may be an online railroad magazine that regularly writes about history, or there may be a railroad history trade group. Portals, magazines, and groups will all have their own search engines that allow you to look through their materials.

Info: Use the Library Website

Your school library's website is one of your most valuable tools. Not only will it have online resources and databases, but it can cross-reference what's physically available in the library. It may have great how-to tips for research, possibly even tips specific to the class you're taking. Even better, it may include lists of resources that students who have taken the class before may have used. Be sure to utilize this underappreciated resource.

Organize Your Findings

You're going to find a massive amount of information—don't try to include it all! Look for three to five main sources (or however many your professor has requested that you have) and stick with these. If you try for too many, chances are you'll drown in references, lose track of what came from where, and make it impossible to cite anything correctly.

Once you've determined your main sources, read through them and highlight key points. I like to do all my research electronically. I cut important points and facts out of the original and paste them into a Word document to be sorted through later. Make sure you label (consider color-coding) where everything came from!

Start to put the main points you're finding into your outline. This way, you'll be able to visualize where each piece of the puzzle fits. Eliminate pieces that don't fit—they're probably unnecessary. After this is done, you're ready to start writing.

Info: Use Acceptable Sources

 Your professor will likely discuss acceptable and unacceptable sources for your paper. This may be very specific (certain scientific journals or authors) or more general (no more than three Internet sources). Pay close attention to these guidelines, and if you're unsure, ask. If you reference only online material and your professor wanted otherwise, you could receive a bad grade despite having written a worthy paper.

Remember: Good professors aren't looking for the best paper in the world; they're looking to give you the skills you need to write good research papers. And if you continue to graduate school or beyond, these research skills are essential both for class and for anything you may later publish. Also keep in mind that online sources aren't always as reliable as those in print. Until we can ensure the accuracy of everything referenced online (and who knows if that will ever happen), professors want to make sure you get reliable references.

Writing the Paper

Once the research is done, start writing. Break the paper down into sections and write them one at a time.

The Intro Paragraph

 Your intro paragraph is very important: think of it as the first five minutes of a movie, or the first few pages of a novel. The intro paragraph draws the reader in or scares him away. If you keep your professor's attention and interest from the beginning, he'll be much more likely to relax and enjoy the content. If he's bored, he'll reach for the red pen.

Start with an intro sentence that hooks the reader. In our example about horseshoes, you might try "In the 1800s thousands of horses struggled with their bare hooves as they traveled across the wild, wild West." Make it interesting, draw in the reader, and leave him wanting more. Sentences that are visual and create a picture in the reader's mind are often very effective.

Your next few sentences can provide a bit of background information or briefly touch on the main points your paper will mention. For example, you might have the following "Shoeing horses in the West went from a small trickle to a flood as westward expansion hit high gear. Once gold was discovered and the Gold Rush began, horseshoes and shoers were in high demand. As farriers headed west, America's manifest destiny to conquer the continent shifted into overdrive. America's growth was now in the hands of the humble horseshoer."

Finally, rein in your intro paragraph with your thesis: "In this paper, we'll look at the specifics of how horse farriers were essential to the westward expansion of America."

The Meat of the Paper

The structure of the typical college paper is very simple. Think of it as a sandwich. The bread is the intro and the conclusion, and the meat is the middle. The "meat" of the paper is where you provide the main points to support your thesis or argument and where you provide details to support each main point.

In this simplified format (which can also be used in essay exams) you'll generally write paragraphs in the same basic form:

1. An introductory sentence which lets the reader know what the paragraph will cover and how it relates to the previous paragraph: "In addition to raw material needs, industry demands transportation to get goods to market."
2. After your intro sentence you'll discuss your main points—in the example above, you would address the transportation demands of industry.
3. Then you'll wrap it up with a conclusion sentence: "Industry needs transportation to get goods to major cities, distribution centers, and retail outlets for…."

The Conclusion

Your conclusion is another key element of the paper. To compare reading a paper to watching a good movie, it's the first five minutes and the last five that hold your attention and stick in your memory. A good intro gets you rolling and into the story, and a great conclusion wraps things up and leaves you with a strong feeling or takeaway message. That's exactly what your conclusion should do here. Look at it this way: the conclusion is the last thing your professor reads before she grades your paper! So you want to make it good and leave a great lasting impression.

In a sense, your conclusion is very similar to your intro. You want to:
• Summarize your key points.
• Have a wrap-up statement that's similar to a thesis statement. For instance, "Now you know how farriers were essential to the westward expansion of America."
• Either leave this as your final sentence, or (highly recommended) use your creative mind to its max! Wrap up with an amazing takeaway, something that's funny, that's fun, or that leaves the reader thinking.
• For instance, modify the above sentence to "Now that you know the importance of farriers to America, you'll never again think of horseshoes in quite the same way."
• Or better yet, add to it: "Perhaps we'd never be the great country we are today without the humble horseshoe!"

I'm sure you can do even better than my two examples! So have fun with it, leave your readers thinking, make them happy, or play with words. Whatever you do, use your creative mind to catch their attention and make them think "This student did a great job!"

Editing and Rewriting

Ever seen Michaelangelo's David? According to Michelangelo, David was already in the marble—all the artist had to do was scrape away the excess. That is what rewriting and proofreading does. In college the difference between a C and an A can be rewriting and editing. Carve away the excess and fine-tune your sentences, eliminating extraneous words and even whole sentences. Create a paper that's sharp, to the point, and filled with solid, well-documented and strongly referenced information. Don't just look for typos or misspellings at this stage; look for ways to make your paper better.

Info: Footnoting

It's very important to properly acknowledge information in your papers that did not come from you. If you got something from your research, footnote it. If it's an exact quote, footnote it. When in doubt, give credit to someone else—it can keep you from being accused of plagiarism.

Make sure you're consistent with your footnotes. Don't use one style one time and another the next. If not, you can find standardized formats on the Web or in a reference book or textbook. Just make sure it's consistent.

It took me years before I learned to cite sources as I went along; I always assumed I'd take care of it afterward. Unfortunately, "afterward" was always hours or minutes before the paper was due. I would panic, and I could never figure out what came from where. Avoid this by making a detailed reference or even the actual footnote as you're writing. Don't save it for later; you may run out of time or simply forget where each item originated.

Tech Tip: Use Your Creativity to Make Killer Presentations

As ADDers or owners of highly unique minds, we tend to have an amazing gift for creativity and visual presentation. Use this to your advantage the next time you have an individual or group presentation. If you have to give a talk and need to use slides, let your outside-of-the-box creativity and imagination take over. Don't just make a PowerPoint presentation. Instead, make an audio and visual experience—sort of like your own music video or movie for class—and blow everyone away! Find music, movie clips, animation, or sound effects, or even shoot your own movies to make a powerful statement. If you have the time, interest, and resources, you could even make a website for a class presentation and walk the class and professor through your presentation while you're online.

Not only will your efforts help set you apart from the crowd but often the extra effort in making something fun and creative is *easier* than doing something plain, boring, and simple. Your mind really is your greatest asset; use this opportunity to let it shine!

Info: General Rules for College Papers

Use quotes from the articles in your text to support your arguments and make them stronger—it proves that your ideas are based in fact.

Employ correct paragraph structure, which includes:

- An introductory sentence which lets the reader know what the paragraph will cover and how it relates to the previous paragraph
- Discussion of the main supporting points of the paragraph
- A conclusion sentence that reiterates the ideas of the paragraph and leads into the next

Tech Tip: Technology Tips for Writing Papers

- Speech-to-text software. Are you highly creative when you verbally describe what you'll write but struggle to put pen to paper? Speech-to-text software such as Dragon NaturallySpeaking lets you talk into a microphone or digital recorder, then types up what you've written. This can help get your creativity flowing, get your ideas on the paper, and get you over that initial hurdle. Plus, you don't have to worry about typing the paper!
- Text-to-speech software. Many creative and ADD minds struggle with reading or are officially dyslexic. If reading stymies you, get software that will read your text or books out loud to you. Many programs will read websites, PDF

files, or anything you scan into the computer out loud. You could also find textbooks and other research materials on CD or audio format. Inquire with your librarian to see what's available and works for you. The right solution is out there for your challenge—you just have to find it.

- Mind mapping. If you can see ideas, the big picture, or the concepts involved but can't make order out of the details, software such as Inspiration or MindManager by Mindjet can help. They let you diagram your paper or use pictures to lay out ideas without words; they can even take your diagram and convert it into an outline. (That's how I got this book rolling!) If you're highly visual or organizationally challenged, this is a great way to go—it's like laying out all your ideas on the desk, and then seeing what you'd like to put where without worrying about what you're missing or not looking at.

If You're Still Doing Poorly

If you've followed these rules, written numerous papers for your professor, and still can't seem to get it right, you may not be giving the professor what he wants. Remember that it's not what you know that gets you the A; it's showing the professor that you know what he wants you to know!

Get the professor to tell you exactly what he wants—it's not always easy, but there are a few things you can do. The first option is to bring him your completed paper well ahead of time and ask him if it's what he's looking for. Professors don't want to read your whole paper in advance—it takes up their time, and can give you an advantage over the other students—but they are often willing to discuss your ideas and whether or not you're heading in the right direction. They could also offer guidance on what you could do to make it better.

If this doesn't work, look to your classmates or other students who have taken this class and professor before. Do they still have any of their papers that received high grades? Look at how they wrote them: Are there major differences between theirs and yours? Is there a basic format, formula, or structure you could follow?

You should also look at the comments on your previous papers. Are you making the same mistakes over and over? Are there clear guidelines as to what you did wrong and what needs improving? If you can't tell, try asking your professor for clarification.

The Advantage of a Good Example

Throughout my MBA, I got good grades on my papers—then I took marketing. On the first paper I got an A, but on the next one I got a C, then another C, then a C-...what was going on? After each paper I went to the professor and asked for suggestions. One time I got "not enough specifics," so on the next paper I added more detail. On the next one I got "too much detail." No matter what he said, I couldn't figure out what he wanted.

Then another student offered to show me her papers. She'd gotten a B+ , then an A, another A, and another A. She was obviously doing something right, and something I wasn't doing. Looking over her papers I found two things. First, she gave very specific titles to each section of her paper that highlighted exactly what the professor was looking for. Second, though the professor required three pages max, he had said that appendices were optional. I thought this meant to write a three-page paper, but he was looking for charts, graphs, quotations, and other supporting information in appendices.

On my next paper I incorporated headlines into the text and compiled charts and graphs in an appendix. I got an A...then another A, and on the biggest paper of the semester, another A. The key to this success, and all paper-writing success, was figuring out precisely what the professor wanted and giving it to him. The help of a class-mate (and my ability to accept the help) saved the day.

Follow the Formula for Success

College papers can be daunting, complex problems, but if you break them down, follow a basic formula, and keep your writing fun and to the point, you'll do fine and may even enjoy the creative process. Just remember to start early, ask for help when you need it, and, most important, figure out exactly what your professor's looking for.

Do all this, and you can end up with a great paper.

Tech Tip: Word Predictability Software

- Penfriend XP can predict the next word and read it out loud as you type it.
- Instant text mobile allows you to take faster notes by abbreviating almost everything you type.
- Speech-to-text and mind-mapping software like MindManager and Inspiration add a whole slew of tools specifically for students, such as Word Guide, a built-in dictionary and thesaurus.
- Solo is a very proactive way to organize writing, reading, thoughts and notes, and studying and even works with electronic books in the NIMAS standard to help eliminate scanning.
- Wordq word predictability software will not only give you a drop down menu but will read back

individual sentences to ensure you aren't making any mistakes (such as missing words or pronunciation—because you can hear mistakes instead of seeing them).

"The desire to write grows with writing."—**Desiderius Erasmus**

Working with Professors

"Better than a thousand days of diligent study is one day with a great teacher."—**Japanese proverb**

Have you ever written a paper you thought was great, excitedly turned it in, and then received an unexpectedly low grade? How about studying hour after hour for an exam, only to start taking the test and discover that what you concentrated on wasn't what the professor was looking for? Ever been completely perplexed by a class discussion and left in total and utter frustration?

Times such as these demand that you turn to your professor for extra help. At certain times during your college career, the clarification, understanding, and direction you need can only come directly from the horse's mouth. Generally you should look to your professor for help if you're having trouble understanding the class lectures or discussions, assigned reading, or homework, and for test preparation.

Here are some ways to approach professors and get exactly the help you need.

How Do You Build a Relationship?

I was once in the middle of a midterm when something went wrong, terribly wrong. Before the exam I felt thoroughly prepared and had even helped other students study for it. But when I started the test all of my preparation went out the window. I had a complete and total meltdown, running back and forth from my desk to the professor, asking questions, offering blank stares, and trying to figure out how to get back on track—all to no avail. I got an F.

I went to see the professor a couple of days later to apologize for my performance and discuss what occurred. He knew I had been working very hard, doing extra reading, and actively participating in class. After he and I talked for a while he decided to consider the test an anomaly and threw out the results.

I've known many students who've received extra time when needed to complete assignments or who've gotten one-on-one attention when they were struggling. They all had one thing in common: a strong relationship with their professor. Now I'm not in any way suggesting that you skip preparing for your next exam and then see if you can talk your way out of it. However, spending time cultivating an open and trusting relationship with your professors *can* help you get these kinds of benefits.

Going the Extra Mile

It's the extra mile that's most important in building a relationship with your professor. When I had my midterm meltdown, I had already proven to my professor that I was a hard worker and dedicated to doing well. Early on I found a topic within the class subject that was of particular interest to me and discussed it with the professor in great detail. He suggested some extra readings for me to do and loaned me some books. Even though I only had time to read one of the books, I was able to refer to this reading in class. This showed the professor I was committed to the class, wanted to learn even more about the material, and wanted to help others by sharing my newfound knowledge. If you go out of your way to show a professor that you are interested and committed to learning the subject, he will be more likely to help you later on.

Think of it as putting money in the bank. Each time you go the extra mile you're making a deposit; then, if the time comes when something goes wrong or you're desperate for extra help, you have the savings to withdraw.

Meaningful Participation

When you're in class you should concentrate on asking insightful questions that you think may benefit everyone present. Review the questions after class and try to learn more about the material to share with everyone next time. I know this seems like kissing up to the professor (and it may be), but this type of attention to the subject makes the class more valuable, helps you understand the material, and builds a partnership between you and the professor.

ADD Challenge: Discussing Your Disability

 If you didn't need to ask for accommodations before class started, you may not have mentioned to your professor that you have ADD. The day may arise when you need to discuss this with your professor, however, and doing it after you've established a good working relationship will make it easier.

First impressions with professors are very important. I do my best to look and act professional in the first few classes, I pay particular attention to the material, I look ahead, and I ask a few key questions. All of this helps send the message to my professors that I'm a smart, hardworking student who is thinking carefully about the material, trying to do my best, and going that extra mile. After you've painted this picture of yourself in their heads, they'll already want to help you—and telling them about your ADD now will put them in your corner even more.

Info: Meeting with the Professor

If you're nervous when meeting the professor and don't know how to begin, try showing a genuine interest in something he's passionate about. For instance, if you go into his office and see golf paraphernalia, ask about his golf game. If you see pictures of his family, ask about the pictures. This is the first step toward building a great working relationship with your professor—and indeed, toward building any relationship.

How Can a Professor Can Help You?

Once you've established a relationship with your professor, he can become an invaluable resource; there are many, many things a professor can do to make a class easier. But remember that it's a give-and-take relationship. Do your part to make things easier for the professor (like asking key, guiding questions to keep a class discussion going), and he will be more willing to help where he can.

Clarification

Ever been in a class where the lectures made no sense? This can be a huge problem, as not understanding one class discussion can mean you won't understand the ones that follow, either.

However, you can't just go up to a professor and tell him that you didn't understand or that you got lost; you have to help him help you. Take notes on the lecture and make sure to note where you didn't understand something and what you didn't under- stand about it. That will also help pinpoint exactly where you got off-track, so you can revisit the lecture from that point onward. If you can't explain to the professor what the problem is, all he can really do is go over the main points with you and have you reread the relevant chapters.

Also, taking copious notes during a lecture and recording exactly what you don't understand will impress a professor; it shows both that you're trying your best to learn the material, and that you don't expect him to do all the work for you. This will help reaffirm that you're trying to go the extra mile.

This same advice holds true for help with understanding assigned reading. No matter what the question, if you show the professor your work and ask specific questions about what you don't understand, he will try his best to help.

Info: Hanging around after Class

You may think that students who linger after class are just trying to butter up the professors, but, they've actually latched onto a powerful technique for classroom success. A brief chat with a professor after class gives the professor the opportunity to offer guidance, often suggesting in detail where you should focus your efforts and where it's not necessary. You can also learn valuable additional information about class material, find out which material is the most important, and get tips for upcoming tests.

Test Preparation

As with clarification on lectures and reading, if you go to a professor and say, "I don't know how to study for this test," chances are you'll get nowhere. If you ask, "What's going to be on the test?" she may ask if you were paying attention in class or if you read the syllabus. But if you go in with an outline of what you're planning on studying and ask her to go over it with you, she'll likely be more than willing to help. Again, it not only shows effort and motivation but also gives your professor the structure she needs to provide the answers you need. Furthermore, since you've obviously put in time and work on the test preparation already, your professor probably won't hesitate to make it pretty clear what you should study and what you won't need to.

Info: Always Thank Your Professor!

At the end of the discussion, thank your professor for his help and ask if you could come back to see him if you have any questions after going over the various sections. If you find areas of difficulty and need to approach the professor again, do it in the same manner: discuss what you do understand about the topic, then try to show him what you don't understand or where you've gone off track. If it's a class with problems, such as science or math, do practice problems and bring them in to show the professor exactly where you're getting stuck. The important thing is that your professor knows how hard you've tried and doesn't feel like you're just looking for a handout.

Paper and Project Guidance

Large projects can easily leave you feeling overwhelmed or intimidated. Many professors can help in these situations. The first thing you need to do is read the assignment several times to try to determine exactly what the professor is looking for. If it's a paper and you need to pick a topic, try to think of something that will be fun for you. Outline the process you'll use to write the paper; you might have: research x, then research y, then research z, and then rough out the intro, body, and conclusion. Bring whatever you've put together to your professor. Even if it's only a topic, bring it: the point is to show up with *something*.

Your professor can help guide your approach to the topic. She'll typically tell you if you have a good subject and which subtopics you should be sure to cover or stay away from entirely. Then you can discuss your strategy and how you actually plan to write the paper. Your professor can give you insight into whether it's a good plan or not, what pitfalls to avoid, or even some areas of thought you hadn't considered yet.

Key questions for professors about papers and projects:

- Is this a good topic, or am I offtrack?
- If I'm offtrack, what do you suggest for a topic, or where should I look to find a better one?
- Is this a good way to organize my time to get this done, or is there a better strategy?
- What are the common pitfalls to avoid or the mistakes that students often make in this assignment?
- Have I forgotten anything?

Info: A Quick Warning

Professors often don't like reading a paper in its entirety before it's turned in. It's a pet peeve they all seem to have, probably because they don't want to appear to give you an unfair advantage over the rest of the class by giving you two chances at it. However, they're more than willing to discuss it in the abstract—critiquing your research or your main points, or pointing out areas that might need improvement. So even if you have the whole paper written, it may just be best to bring in your outline and make sure your research and basic ideas are on target.

Other Times to Ask a Professor for Help

- When a project's gone awry
- When your group for a group project is falling apart
- When exams, projects, or papers in multiple classes overlap in a horrific fashion
- When you get sick or have an emergency, or something goes wrong and you need a plan to catch up (see your professor as soon as there's an inkling of a problem)

- When the dog really did eat your homework!
- If you need additional books, resources, reading, or sources you can't seem to find anywhere
- If you're struggling terribly in the lab, with practice problems, or in any area where you need further understanding badly
- If you need a tutor or extra assistance and don't know where to turn

Often professors grade well and fairly, but their assistants want to prove they're being thorough and can become more than a bit overzealous. If you feel you're being evaluated unfairly, politely bring it up to your professor. If you're calm and not accusatory, they'll be more likely to look at the facts.

For a crisis outside of the classroom, find a professor you can confide in if at all possible: he will help you through almost any problem. And if he can't help, he know where you can turn.

Remember that in life, it really is your relationships—not your knowledge—that helps you overcome obstacles and open doors. Professors can help you with so much—both school related and professional—as long as you prove to them that you deserve their attention.

ADD Advantage: ADD Accommodations

Though there's a great section in this book about asking for accommodations from the RDS office, most accommodations come directly from your professor—yet another great reason to build that relationship.

Here are some of the most common accommodations to ask your professor for:
- Extra time on tests
- A quiet place to take tests
- Extra scratch paper to use during tests
- Help in breaking large assignments or projects down into manageable pieces
- Extended deadlines for certain assignments

Building Relationships for Success

Want to succeed in the classroom? Build a relationship with your professor, and then don't be afraid to ask him for help. This isn't about buttering up your professor to weasel a good grade out of him; it's about showing a true interest in your course and in the professor himself and about using all the resources available to you to do the best you can.

If you show your effort and your concern for the class and be specific in your requests for assistance, professors will go out of their way to help you any way they can. Taking an incomplete, getting assignments done over winter or summer break, erasing a midterm or even a final that you bombed, being able to turn in a paper late, or leaving a group project that's turning into a disaster are all possible when a professor trusts you and knows how hard you're trying to succeed.

> "One of the greatest discoveries a man makes, one of his great surprises, is to find he can do what he was afraid he could not do."—**Henry Ford**

Summer Courses

> "Success comes from taking the initiative and following up...persisting...eloquently expressing the depth of your love. What simple action could you take today to produce a new momentum toward success in your life?"—**Tony Robbins**

Ahhhh, summertime...a chance to kick back, earn a few bucks, hang out at the beach, chill, and just relax. Or is it?

Taking courses over the summer, whether your goal is getting ahead before college really begins or catching up between years, can be an amazing way to jump-start college success. Summer school is a low-pressure, high-octane way to prepare for college or fill in any gaps in your coursework. It's also a great time to learn about yourself and discover your passions, both of which are arguably vastly more important than anything you'll learn from one particular class.

Why Take Summer Classes?

- To experiment or dabble: try subjects that aren't in your major or tract or ones that you wouldn't dare try during the regular semester
- To learn about yourself and discover your passions
- To complete prerequisites you couldn't fit into the regular semesters
- To take a very difficult class (or a course with a lab or other time-consuming side work) without other courses distracting you
- To brush up on your math or other skills before jumping into the required courses
- To retake a course you bombed
- To finish an incomplete
- If you're toying with the idea of changing majors
- To take advantage of a cool course taught by a visiting prof that's only offered during the summer
- To save money: summer courses are generally less expensive
- To take a community college class: they tend to be less expensive, easier, and closer to home
- To take a semester abroad or a creative/hands-on program such as acting, film, an internship or study program, etc.

Prerequisite Courses

Summer is a great time to get your prereqs out of the way! Prerequisites, or courses that you need to have taken to be eligible for other, higher-lever courses, are often also offered over the summer. This gives you the opportunity to take the courses you want to take, rather than the courses you have to take, in the fall. It may even be a way to take your prereqs in a less pressured environment—your professor may be more laid-back, and those five-hundred-person freshmen in the typical lecture hall may amount to a much more manageable eighty-five instead! This all adds up to a greater chance of success (and far less pain) for you. You'll be able to concentrate better in smaller classes with more relaxed professors, and a dreary fall course may actually be fun in the summer.

Prereq not offered over the summer? Maybe there's a similar class available that you can use as a substitute. It never hurts to ask!

Talk with the department head or your advisor about getting a waiver to substitute a similar course as a prerequisite. Explain why you need the prereq, how and why the course you're proposing as a substitute would work, and see how it goes. If they still don't bite, offer to do an extra paper or project to fill in the gaps between what's being taught and what you need to know. Don't offer anything you can't handle time- or work-wise, but this suggestion may do the trick.

Info: Independent Study

If you're really self-motivated and up for a challenge, see if you can do an independent study to cover your prereq. You'll need to find a professor in the correct department who's around over the summer and willing to work with you, but it's more of a possibility than you might think. Consider this your opportunity to teach yourself the material and show your professor what you've learned. One word of caution: Along with the freedom comes the responsibility of getting your work done and the material mastered without the routine of class.

Make sure that's something you're willing to do and capable of doing. (The secret may be to get a mentor, coach, or accountability partner to check in with you at least once or twice a week to ensure you have a plan to stay on track.)

ADD Advantage: Difficult Classes

Taking a difficult class over the summer greatly increases your chances for success. Yes, it may still be quite difficult or stressful, but survival (or a higher grade) is far more likely. Why? First off, you probably aren't taking other classes, so you'll have far fewer competing demands. You'll be able to get more help from the professor (or adjunct professor), since there are fewer students in the typical summer course. The other students may also be more relaxed and eager to help you. These factors add up to a much greater probability that you'll survive and even do well.

And here's the best thing: next fall will be less stressful. If you put off a tough course, it may be wearing on your psyche, hovering over your head, constantly taunting you. In the summer you can just get it out of the way, remembering that a little summer stress can make for an incredibly relaxed and even fun fall semester.

One last thought: Whether or not the course is unusually tough, if it requires a very long lab, frequent field-trips, or any other big time commitment, taking it in the summer is the best way to do it. You won't have to worry about other classes, being somewhere else on time, or any other distractions. Instead you can jump in, have fun (relatively speaking), and not sweat the time involvement. Chances are you'll make great friends in your class—sharing a common challenge builds great relationships, as does spending the summer together—and have fun in the common experience, no matter how hard the class is.

Brushing Up on Math or Other Tough Essentials

This is one of the best options for summer school—you'll be able to get tons of one-on-one attention in areas that are particularly difficult for you. You may need to take a math, science, or English prerequisite, or you may want to brush up on those skills before taking the prereq. Perhaps you'd just like to feel out the difficulty level of a particular subject or even try your luck at another school, which doesn't affect your GPA and may save you tuition money. Then the summer is the time to do it. If you've been putting off a tough class and it's time to face the music (remember, depending on the situation, there is a chance you can get a waiver as a student with a disability; check with your RDS office), taking it in the summer can definitely ease the pain of the fall.

Retaking Courses

As with any course—and particularly one in a subject you've already had some trouble with—check who the professor is and whether she's ADD-friendly before signing up. Then seek help (such as a coach or ADD specialist) to determine why you failed the first time around. Whether you take a course in the summer, in the fall, or on the moon, *you* are responsible for setting yourself up for success. But in general, as I've mentioned before, summer courses provide you with more time to concentrate on the one class you're taking, more one-on-one attention, and less pressure. One thing to watch for, though: If it's an accelerated summer class in which you have twice the work in half the time, be careful. Though you won't have competing interests, these classes can be extremely intense. You want to set yourself up for success, not a coronary!

Finishing an Incomplete

Summer is the best time to finish incompletes. In fact, this can be an extremely useful strategy. If you're struggling in the spring, bogged down with reports, projects, and assignments that you know you won't be able to finish, you can see about getting an extension to finish up over the summer. (Talk with your professors about this option far *before* the courses end.) Just be careful: you only want to give yourself an extra week or two, or your incomplete could easily morph into a failing grade if you don't get the work done. But the summer can be your spring semester pressure-relief valve for an overflow of work. Get permission from your professor as far in advance as possible, and let some of your assignments spill into the summer by a week or two. Again, get a coach or accountability partner on your side to ensure you quickly get through the incompletes, rather than let them linger and turn into Fs! Remember that out of class can quickly become out of mind.

Try New, Exciting, and Different Courses

> "Live as if you were to die tomorrow. Learn as if you were to live forever."—**Mahatma Gandhi**

The summer is a great time to check out new and different types of courses. Stick your neck out. Go out on a limb. Discover your passions. Try wild, crazy, or "out there" classes. This could (and should) be a life-changing experience. Don't forget that education is meant to help spark the flame that burns through your life. Summer's a great time to look for inspiration.

There are several great options:
• Audit a course to see if you like it—you you won't be tested, you won't receive a grade, and technically you won't even have to show

up (danger!). However, the trouble for us ADDers is that it can be hard to remain focused and on track if we're not held accountable for the material (and good luck showing up if you're not required to be there...this means you'd better make *sure* it's a course in a subject you'd love).

- Just take the summer course for regular credit. Have fun with it and just give it your best shot; if it's outside of your major and not a required basic class, you can always drop it if it's not going well so that it doesn't count against you.

- Take the course at a local community college: it's likely to be less expensive and more low-key, and you won't need to stay at school over the summer (which is a plus if you're far from home and want to spend the summer there). Best of all, you don't necessarily have to transfer the grades back to your school (check this in advance, however). This gives you the opportunity to try something new, take some risks, and not have to worry about falling flat on your face and having it haunt you. Taking risks builds strength, courage, and creativity, and taking risks without the potential for permanent harm is an added bonus.

- Get an alias, travel outside the country, and pretend to be someone else. This way, if you fail, it won't appear on your record. Then again, if you work this hard to take the courses, chances are you're *not* gonna fail...so reconsider the first three suggestions!

Saving Money

See if the courses you need are available at your local community college over the summer—they're often less expensive than a four-year school. Just check with your school and make sure the credits will fully transfer. This is a great way to try out classes or eke by on a tight budget. Many students have taken a full year or two worth of classes at community colleges over summers or before transferring to a university. It can be a great way to save money, ease into college with less pressure, and ultimately still end up with a degree from am expensive university. You're likely to be surprised at the quality of the courses—as with any institution, no matter how prestigious, it's not the name of the school that matters but the quality of the professors.

Semesters Abroad and Other Special Programs

There are some amazing opportunities to take incredible programs both domestically and abroad over the summer. It's an opportunity to try something radically different. Are you a premed major who's always interested in the movies? Take a film course! Or travel the world while getting college credit. Check out your school's study abroad office for more possibilities.

This isn't just about "play" or frittering away your money or your folks' money. It's about finding your life direction and passion, which is arguably more important than almost anything else!

ADD Advantage: Playing Sports

Want to get into JV or varsity sports in the fall? There may be programs to help you keep up on your skills while attending a summer program. Check with your coaches and teammates to see what options are available. Often a little extra work over the summer can make the difference in making the team or even getting a scholarship. If sports are your game and you want to improve, look at ways to make it happen through a summer program.

Conclusion

Sure, summer's a great time to kick back and relax, but if you really want to have fun, use it as a time to find yourself, discover your passions, get ahead, try out new courses and subjects, and take the pressure off your fall semester. Positive momentum's contagious. A great summer could ignite the fire that carries you throughout the rest of your college career. It's also a great way to save money, make friends, and take courses in a more relaxed, reduced-pressure environment with greater one-on-one attention. Use your summers to enrich your life—not with a minimum wage job but with an experience in or out of college that helps bring happiness and success to your life. With rare exceptions (be careful of those accelerated courses!), I encourage everyone to invest at least one summer in their future. Try it once and see what you think—just make sure you do something fun!

> "Always do what you are afraid to do"—**Ralph Waldo Emerson**

Choosing a Major

> "Your work is to discover your world and then with all your heart give yourself to it."—**Buddha**

Do you want the secret to lifelong happiness and choosing the right major? It's unbelievably simple, despite the hundreds (if not thousands) of chapters and books that have been written on the subject. And for our creative minds, it's quite binary—it really is all or nothing.

Do what you love. Period. End of discussion.

CHAPTER OVER.

Seriously though, forget about fancy tests (though they may help). Forget about studying trends, the marketplace, listening to friends and family, following in the family footsteps, or doing what anyone else wants you to do or even what you think you should do. This decision has nothing to do with thought. Instead, you have to trust your gut, even if, like me, you have (or had) no faith in your own decisions whatsoever.

What have you got to lose?

So here's the single most important advice I can give you for your college education, and the rest of this book is just footnotes and details: do what you love and take the fun classes. If basket weaving's your thing, go for it. How about parks and recreation? Or flying? Or scuba diving? Bird-watching? Painting? Drama? Photography? Ancient civilizations? Spirituality? Tennis? It doesn't matter. As ADDers we're always looking for reasons to shoot things down. As soon as someone tells us that our major is wrong, that it won't make us money, that there aren't any jobs, etc., we take that opinion as our own, forgo our real opinion, and then try to make a square peg fit into a round hole. If instead we do what we love, we'll find success by having fun each and every day. If we don't, we're a miserable lot indeed.

How Do Majors Work?

Declaring a major is as much about the subject matter as it is about the department. For example, if you want to study quantum mechanics or the theory of relativity, you'd likely be studying in the physics department. Want to focus on poetry? Chances are your major would be in the English department.

Majors are a way of helping you focus your studies. For instance, if you want to become a quantum physics major you may be told to take general English, math, history, a language, and one or two other general courses. Then you're given more specifics: take three higher-level math classes, statistics, logic, and eight physics classes, including Physics 301, 315, 327, 403, and so on. Then you have several open credits, courses, or electives where you can choose perhaps one or two courses that have nothing to do with quantum mechanics or the major at all. (Yes, you could still take that basket-weaving class.)

Schools vary in deadlines for declaring a major. Many liberal arts institution allow you (or even encourage you) to wait until you're

Choosing a Major

Michael Sandler • • • 229

beginning your junior year. Other institutions let you take generic core curriculum courses for your first year, then require you to decide after a certain number of courses are taken or units/hours are achieved. I was surprised to find out years ago that many schools, perhaps even the majority (at least of the larger ones), require you to declare a major or career track right away, though they fully expect you'll change majors at least once during your college career.

The more general a major, the less specific the requirements. For instance, you could be a general physics major and still take a few quantum mechanics courses, but then you'd be free to study a wider selection of physics courses instead of honing in. Why would you do this? Well perhaps you like physics, but no one particular concentration has piqued your interest yet. Or perhaps some of the requirements of quantum mechanics scare you. Frequently, the more general the major, the fewer high-level courses (which are typically reserved for specialists in the area or field of interest) you have to take.

What Are the Steps to Choosing a Major?

Here's a timeline to help you out with choosing your major:
• Before college look for schools that offer what you'd enjoy studying.
• Know what you love to do or study. Make sure the colleges you're applying to offer these courses, majors, or areas of interest.
• When you start college declare your major right away if you must—if not, keep your options open. At some schools you have to declare right away. Know what you want to study? Great! Declare with gusto! Don't know, or not sure of the specifics? Then choose a more general major to keep your options open. Seek advice, and take a general studies major until you're ready to get specific.
• Take the general education or core curriculum courses that are required for the majority of majors early on; this helps leave the door open for future majors or a change of heart hiding around the bend.
• Take fun courses—in addition to the general or "generic" courses, you *need* to take fun courses and electives early on. College is the

time to "find yourself," the time to figure out who you are and what you like to do. Have a hunch you'd like something? Try it.

Talk with others—your RSD, professors, departments, friends. You need to determine your school's policy for choosing a major, including what forms to fill out and what signatures will be required. This office can also offer guidance to help you choose your major. However, a word of caution here: realize that asking an administrative employee or a professor for career guidance might not point you where you want to go. A professor may suggest becoming a professor. An administrator might suggest administration (or at least a major or career direction that leads you there). Why? Because either they enjoy what they're recommending or they don't share your creative mind—a creative mind that requires living life a little more on the edge, with passion, or "going for it." On the other hand, what they suggest may be perfect for you—there are many professors and administrators who love their jobs more than anything else in the world. And that's what you want, passion for your direction in life.

Nevertheless, you'll need to visit this office *immediately* and get some direction. Not registered with them? Then you'll need to meet with your academic advisor or counselor or visit the registrar's office to find out what you'll need to submit, by what date, with whose signature, and anything else that may be involved.

Take internships or participate in other creative programs over summers or winter breaks to gain experience and see what you enjoy (or eliminate what you thought was fun but isn't!).

Still unsure? Sooner or later you'll have to make up you mind, so here are some options: take time off, travel, see the world, or work at a local convenience store. You may not be ready to declare, or even have a clue where you want to go or what you want to do, and there's *nothing* wrong with this. It just means you'll either have to get a degree that may or may not be helpful in the future (for instance, if the folks say "finish now or we're not paying") or put on the brakes and take a look at your life.

Can't stop and take the time to look or hate that idea? Then choose a very nonspecific major that'll still allow you to find yourself, determine your interests, and focus more specifically down the road.

When in Doubt, Leave Your Options Open

If you *still* don't know what you want to do, I'd recommend that you find the major that allows you the most room for exploration. In other words, don't trap yourself. This gives you the greatest ability to explore and change majors later on. If you take decide on premed because medicine's where the money is, you may discover there are so many requirements that there's no room in your schedule for other subjects you might find interesting. If, on the other hand, you choose an English major, you may have more room to explore.

ADD Advantage: Get a Coach

It's too easy to choose a major, fill in the blanks, and wind up with a generic degree you'll never use. So how do you avoid this? Seek professional help.

No, you're not crazy. This is just a great time—perhaps the best time—to become proactive, take charge of your destiny, and begin working with a coach or other ADD professional who has experience in helping creative minds and students like you find themselves and find direction. A professional can help you to ferret out what you enjoy and what to try next. Notice I didn't say "career"— now's just about figuring out the fun. Then you need to explore and have a system in place (such as a monthly meeting with your counselor or coach) to help you bounce around ideas and keep moving forward. Having a system in place is one element in saving yourself from the comfort rut, which can lead you to a degree you do not want and classes that meant nothing to you. And at three to five thousand dollars a class, why throw your money away?

It still all comes down to doing what you love.

Info: Major Mistakes

I didn't get into my major.

Remember that everything happens for a reason. Maybe you didn't get in because there's something else out there for you, or perhaps you didn't get all the prerequisites done (or put them off) because somewhere inside, your gut was screaming that it didn't like that major or those courses. Consider this an opportunity to reevaluate, or to look closely for the first time at where you want to go and what you'd like to do. Not getting in could be the best thing in the world.

If you have to declare but didn't get into your major of choice, see your RSD, talk with a professional, and determine whether you'd like to select a fairly generic major that allows you to take the prereqs you need to get into the major later on. If not, find out where else you can go with your interests.

I chose the "wrong" major.

There is no "wrong" major. Any major and any degree is a stepping stone to your future. It may just take you longer to find your way depending on the major you choose, but sooner or later, you'll get there.

So don't freak out, and don't feel this decision is life-or-death. As we all know, you *can* change your major later, and many students do, in fact, time after time after time. So you can choose now, and you always have the option to change later on. Just give it your best educated guess from your heart or from your gut, not from your brain. Go with your hunch.

No matter what you choose, after college you can still go anywhere, do anything, and be anyone you want. Sure, you may have to take some extra classes, perhaps even go back to school for a year or two, but in the long run, I'm sure you'll benefit from the courses and major you thought was "wrong" for you. If nothing else, you'll be on fire, motivated, and more appreciative of where you're going and how you want to get there!

Conclusion

Ideally, choosing a major is something you should begin thinking about the day you begin studying for the SATs. But that's not exactly fair or realistic, particularly with our ADD minds. So the best we can do is to take long walks, meditate, and dream into the future each and every day. Choosing a major isn't the most critical decision in the world, but choosing wisely helps you reach your dreams quite a bit sooner.

Whether you start early or late, choosing a major will help you reach for the stars and achieve your dreams. Follow your passion, and you can't go wrong!

"There is no greatness without a passion to be great, whether it's the aspiration of an athlete or an artist, a scientist, a parent, or a businessperson."
—**Tony Robbins**

13

Life Outside of Class

" **There are** two ways to live: **you can** live as if **nothing is a miracle;** you can **live as if** everything is a miracle."

—**Albert Einstein**

Negotiating the pitfalls of college life outside of the classroom can be far more daunting than negotiating those inside of it! Making friends, keeping friends, staying out of trouble, having a "life," keeping your clothes from crawling away, finding the floor in your room, juggling employment, participating in sports—there's so much to college life.

So take some deep breaths, and let's have fun with this! You're on your own, flying free from the nest, free to do whatever you want to do, and yes, you can reinvent yourself.

Let's look at some of the basics.

Social Life

> "Man is most nearly himself when he achieves the seriousness of a child at play."—**Heraclitus**

Having an ADD mind can seem like both a blessing and a curse. It feels like we're always overachieving or falling impossibly short of a goal, with no comfortable middle ground. And this is particularly true in our social lives. We're generally either the most popular kid or the one struggling to make or keep friends.

I was a social disaster as I was growing up. I thought it was a wiring problem, that I just didn't understand others and that no one could understand me. I also thought everyone was out to get me, and judging from the fights I was in, it would have been hard to prove me wrong.

But the honest truth was that I spoke before I thought. Without realizing I was doing it, I'd insult others, even (or especially) my friends. I didn't understand social cues, couldn't follow conversations, and was a terrible listener because I always wanted to jump in with my own anecdote or story. It was quite tiresome for my friends.

Antics like these can make you feel all alone at best, or hated at worst. And when you get to college, there's no greater sense of loneliness than the one that comes from having your social problems continue hundreds or thousands of miles away from your hometown. It's vital to have a social safety net in order to survive and thrive in college. Without one we can feel lost, confused, or disconnected from the world.

However, we ADDers have one big social advantage: when we figure out how to slow down, listen to others, maintain eye contact, and show that we really, truly care, people begin to notice what big hearts we have. Suddenly, things turned around—and in a big way. By the time I got to grad school, I was one of the most popular students in my class. People loved me, or perhaps they loved the way they felt around me, because I genuinely took the time to care and let them know it. Everyone wants to feel loved, admired, or at least heard, and when we put our minds to it, we can be incredible at this. By caring you go from zero to hero.

ADD Challenge: Don't Compromise Your Values

 Unlike some people I've known, I was lucky enough to have my social nightmare finally turn around in college. Many students, however, turn to drinking, drugs, or doing things that they don't want to do (or that are quite harmful) in order to fit in, make friends, act cool, or just have a life. Doing things you're uncomfortable with for acceptance is always foolish, but it can be a particularly bad idea in college, where almost anything goes.

Instead, you need to be yourself, do what you love, and listen to your intuition. If your intuition would rather go rock climbing early on a Saturday morning than stay up late at a crazy party on Friday, stay in. Do what you love, and others who love the same things will come into your life. Show them that you care, be their friend, and watch the magic happen.

Making Friends

As ADDers we often have trouble reading people. If we're not careful, we may also talk over others and forget people's names. If this sounds like you, consider practicing social interactions with a friend or coach. Practice remembering people's names and something small but thoughtful about them. Learn how to read nonverbal clues and signals and be aware of the ones you're sending—you can ask your friends to help you or read one of the many books on this topic. Be sincere; people can spot a fake a mile away. And above all else, listen to others. We often have an easy time making friends, but then lose them just as quickly when all they talk about is themselves. Take a sincere interest in someone's concerns and you're likely to make a friend for life.

Also put yourself in a position to meet as many people as possible. Get involved in clubs, team sports, fitness classes, extracurricular activities, poetry readings, anything that will get you out and talking to like-minded individuals. Doing this has the added benefit of making you a more interesting person to befriend!

ADD Challenge: Talking to Your Friends about Your ADD

Your new friends are eventually going to notice that you have special accommodations for tests, that you regularly take medication, and that, well, you're a bit on the quirky side. Sharing your challenges with your friends can help them get to know and understand you better. Plan out what you'll say in advance; be sure to share not only the challenges but the humor of ADD and the creativity, intelligence, quick thinking, and intuition. Tell them about the famous people who have had ADD (like Einstein and Edison), or steer them to a website such as thecreativelearninginstitute.com, where they can learn more about ADD.

Keeping Your Social Life under Control

Of course there's always the opposite of having trouble making friends. Way too many of us find social success early in college, be it through friends from orientation or the dorm, or through the Greek system, and because things are going so great socially we don't realize we're having problems in class until we've bombed the semester. This is a great way to end up out of school and on your way home.

The trick here is to have a plan in place to keep up with your classes and homework, not sacrificing too much of your time to making friends, attending events, and building your social life. It's all about balance. And if you're reading this at school and realizing you're already way behind, seek help and take action now. Take some steps to correct the situation—get a tutor, talk to your RDS office—and then go explain the situation to your professor. He'll likely be far more sympathetic than you imagine, because you realized there was a problem and you're working to fix it. Don't fall into the ADD trap of hiding when there's a problem; it'll only get worse.

Balance and Boundaries

It can be hard enough to juggle the bare minimum; being pulled in a thousand directions by new friends, schoolwork, jobs, etc., only adds to the complexity of life with ADD. You need to plan ahead, set healthy boundaries, and work hard not to over commit yourself. For example, make sure your friends know they can't call after a certain hour and have a set time when you turn off your phone and barricade the door. Talk with your roommates about these rules in advance and then stick with them. If you can't crawl to your morning classes without six full hours of sleep, make sure you find a way to get them. If you need three hours to study each night, don't promise your friends you'll hang out with them after dinner. Setting these types of boundaries will ensure that you dedicate enough time to your studies.

I also recommend making a little cardboard wheel with an arrow on it that denotes when you're in, studying, available, or ready to have a great time. Then put it on your door. Friends will respect this, particularly if you have it from the beginning. Be aware of your boundaries and needs at all times, listen to others, but don't ever be afraid to say no.

Think Ahead and Seek Help

Think ahead about the social challenges you'll face in school. Will you be able to handle peer pressure when it comes to drinking, going out instead of studying, rushing, drugs, or just keeping everyone happy? It's a lot to think about—and even more to juggle. If you're like me, you'll handle some of these situations well, and be clueless on quite a few others. If you're unsure, ask friends, older siblings, or upperclassmen who've gone through this before.

Don't be afraid to ask for help or counseling at school. That's what it's there for, and the majority of students will have social challenges that spill over into their academic careers at one time or another.

ADD Challenge: Learn the Unwritten Rules

As ADDers we often have a hard time setting limits and following the rules—doubly so when it comes to the unwritten rules of high school. Who sits at the back of the bus or at which cafeteria tables, or when you can wear what are some of the seemingly silly unwritten rules that can trip you up at school. We should do everything we can to guard our reputations; the simplest of transgressions can get us in the biggest of trouble. Make friends with upperclassmen who can mentor you and teach you the rules. Ask your friends, and don't try to take on the entire world. Ask yourself if breaking a rule is worth the potential consequences.

Recognizing and Steering Clear of Dangers

Recognize dangerous or derailing hobbies and addictions. Think a drink or two on Friday night is fun? What do you do when you start needing six to have the same effect? Are you skipping class because you stayed up too late drinking again? How often do you gamble online? More importantly, how much money have you lost?

ADDers have a hard time recognizing trouble until it's far too late. We can put our academic careers, physical well-being, and even the lives around us in peril if we don't take extra effort and care to think ahead. If you can't stop doing something that's unhealthy, or even if you think you may be headed in that direction, seek help immediately. And choose your friends carefully so you can trust them to steer you away from danger if and when it's necessary.

If you find yourself involved with the wrong crowd or unsure how to get out of bad habits or activities you're involved in, go to your counseling center and be open and honest—they can help. Breaking the cycle may take restructuring your life or finding new friends. In the worst-case scenario you may need time off or a new environment to get away from the bad influences before you can start afresh. But your health and well-being are far more important than anything else. It takes a big person to admit she has a problem on her hands, but many of us have been there before, and with courage and determination you can turn it into a positive life experience.

Peer Pressure and Staying out of Trouble

The impulsivity and lack of inhibition that go along with ADD make it easy to get into trouble. To overcome this, we must be proactive—it's important to think about possible situations in advance and practice how we're going to respond to them. Peer pressure can be rough, but if you've thought of the scenarios before they happen, you're more likely to make the right decision. Oftentimes a small bad decision today can add up to big problems tomorrow. When in doubt trust your gut—it's that little voice in your head that starts yelling and screaming at you when you're about to do something you know is wrong, anything from stealing to cheating on a test to taking a foolish daredevil risk on your bike.

Info: The "Think Twice" Rule

Before you do something that seems like it might be risky, ask yourself if you're comfortable with what you're about to do. Ask why you find it so exciting. Is it because it'll be fun, or is it because it's illicit, illegal, risky, sexy, or something else? You may see that the allure stems from the fact that it's dangerous and to be avoided.

> Then ask yourself the same questions again. If you still can't honestly say that you're doing it just because it's fun, and if it's not perfectly safe, stop. We are thrill seekers, and that can get us into heaps of trouble. If you're unsure about an activity, ask yourself twice if you're doing it for the right reasons to ensure that you've really thought about it.

Remember to Have Fun

With our creative ADD minds, we have the ability to go from wallflowers to social butterflies. If you're struggling to make friends, don't panic; just be courageous and start introducing yourself to people. Join clubs, take fitness classes, try intramurals—and above all else, do what you love. Others will see your passion and be attracted to you for it.

Remember, too, to take it slow and seek balance. Your studies always need to come first. Get your scholastics in order, and then worry about establishing a fun and healthy social life. After all, it will be hard to hang out with all your new friends if you fail out of school!

A parting thought on the social side of things: As with everything else, hitting the pause button on your social life and taking time to reflect is the best way to success. Don't be afraid to take time alone, go hiking by yourself, meditate alone, or simply stroll around the river at sunrise. Be your own best friend—this will give you the courage, initiative, perspective, and clear mind to see where you're going and any pitfalls that may lie ahead. The clarity that comes from time on your own will always help steer you straight and get you where you want to be.

> "You can discover more about a person in an hour of play than in a year of conversation."—**Plato**

Getting Domesticated

> "Cleaning: a job in the moment, a joy in the morning."
> —**Michael Sandler**

ADDers often say that domestic responsibilities aren't important to us. But that's not the case at all (admit it!); it's really that it's very difficult for us to get these things done. They take more time, effort, and organization than we have the energy to give them. They remind us of our failings growing up or consume valuable time we'd rather spend on something fun.

The trouble is it's very hard to be happy, productive, and at peace when your environment's in disarray, your clothing's threatening to walk away, and you haven't had a decent meal in days because you don't cook or can't find a plate from which to eat.

MY STORY

Laundry Lessons Learned

I really thought I knew how do to laundry before I went to college. After all, my mom hadn't cleaned my clothes for years. But once school began, reality set in. There was no laundry room available 24-7, fully stocked, where I could leave piles of clothes to deal with when I wanted to. And doing laundry at school required forethought and planning, such as having sixteen quarters on-hand. This led to some key tactical mistakes.

First, I didn't realize you can't wash what you can't carry. Sure, a laundry basket or at least a bag would have been a great idea. But then again, washing my clothes on a regular basis would have been a great idea, too, and I wasn't exactly doing that. However, if I'd had a basket, I wouldn't have used quite so many articles of clothing as carpeting or donated nearly so many to the halls of my neighbors.

Second, I thought the best time to do laundry was on Sundays. You know what? So did the rest of the world. This guaranteed I doubled or tripled the time it should take.

Third, I selectively chose what I would and wouldn't clean each week. Can you see the folly in this? Don't ever elect to wash just some of your dirty laundry. When you bring your clean, unfolded clothes back into the room, they'll just mingle and hang out with their soiled brethren. By Monday morning I could never tell what was clean and what was dirty. Wash them all and throw the clean clothes on hangers before you even get back to the room. Then all you have to do is hang them and you're done.

Fourth, I didn't regularly check the washing machine's basin before putting in a new load of laundry. One simple little tie-dye left behind did its best to turn all of my clothes pink. And trust me, pink is *not* my best color. Remember to check the machines every time.

Here's another secret: If you've washed your clothes a bunch of times already, you can probably throw everything in together on "cold" and "permanent press." But if they're new, wash them separately—the color will bleed!

Info: Lighten Your Load

Too many clothes to wash? Can you live without some? Donate them to Goodwill, right away. Everything you own has a hidden overhead cost associated with it: the time and money it takes to wash it, hang it up, and put it away over and over again. Don't wear certain clothes in a typical week? Then you probably don't need them! Keep what you use and get rid of what you don't.

Laundry

Laundry Preparation

- **Keep a spare key handy.** Make sure you cannot leave your room without a key, or have a sign on your laundry basket to remind you to grab it. (Better yet, can you make a copy and permanently attach it with bailing wire or superglue to your laundry basket?) There's no more common time to forget your key than when your hands are full and you're thinking of something else.

- **Have a permanent home for dirty laundry.** Keep dirty laundry in a hamper or a bag that's raised off the floor and out of the way. Keeping clothes in the closet can work, but an even better idea is to hang a hamper or laundry bag on the inside of the closet door for easy access and three-point shots.

- **Advanced tip:** Remove all items from pockets before things are thrown in a pile, hamper, or bag.

- **Very advanced tip:** Have several laundry bags, one each for lights, darks, and whites.

- **Exceptionally advanced tip:** When you take clothes off your body, immediately put them into a laundry bag. (Better yet, keep your laundry bag concealed but out, preferably right near where you'll take off your clothes).

- **Set a weekly laundry date.** Decide in advance whether you'd prefer to do laundry with others (which might be fun but often requires waiting) or by yourself. Try to choose a day and time you know you won't want to be studying.

- **Collect quarters in advance.** No, not for the drinking game! Whenever you get quarters, throw them into your coin jar for laundry time. Find out where else you can rolls of quarters in advance (try your dorm's front desk or a local convenience store).

- **Attach a laminated laundry checklist to your basket.** Your laundry checklist should include:
  - Coins/dollar bills for change machines
  - Detergent
  - Fabric Softener

- Bleach
- Stain remover
- Book or homework
- Something in which to place the random contents of the pockets of the clothes you'll be washing
- Food to munch
- **Remember:** Do not leave clothes unattended!

Info: Make It a Routine

A good laundry routine can help you get all your laundry cleaned, folded, and put away in a quarter of the time it would otherwise take. Sure, hanging out with friends while doing laundry can be fun, but save the good times for something other than chores and get your laundry done fast.

Leaving for the Laundry Room

Empty your hamper into a bag or basket. Taking two or three laundry baskets (one each for lights, darks, and whites, which can also be used for transporting between machines and for folding) to the laundromat makes things easier to sort and keep straight.

Walk around your room, looking under the bed, under the sheets (don't forget your sheets and pillowcases), in your closet, in your gym bag, and anywhere else dirty clothes may be lurking. If you have a car, check there as well. Get all the clothes that need to be washed.

Go over your laundry checklist and make sure you have everything you need.

Don't lock yourself out, but don't forget to lock up, either!

Doing Laundry

Find as many empty machines as you need and throw one or two items into each of them to reserve them while you set up.

If you're in a real hurry, make sure you grab a dryer that's just been used or warm it up for a few minutes in advance to save you a little time. (But don't do it for too long; let's take care of the environment and conserve energy!)

Make an assembly line. While one load is going in, another can be coming out. This way you can feed, remove, and then fold everything in one steady process.

Sorting

- As you sort clothes into piles of whites, lights, and colors, go through each pocket and pull out anything inside.
- Do you have any new clothes? If so, and if they have colors, wash them separately so they don't ruin your other clothes. After the first wash, you should be safe throwing them in full loads.
- If you have exceptionally soiled clothes keep them separate from everything else. You don't want to ruin your other clothes.
- Pull aside anything that's been stained and use a stain remover and spray or scrub the spot. Follow the directions, and then let the clothes sit as you sort the rest of the laundry.
- Do all whites together. Use hot water and bleach to help keep them white.
- Do all light colors together. With most detergents they can be washed in cold water, but if you really want to keep them bright, consider warm water.
- Do all dark colors together. Cold water is fine.

Drying

- The safest way to dry is to use low heat, but this takes much longer. Remember that if you do use higher heat, you increase the chance of shrinking or melting your garments. Read your clothing's instruction tags before you go up on the heat.
- If you have special fabrics, like formal wear or cycling clothes, make sure they can handle the heat before you dry them. A lot of stretchy materials melt in the heat.
- You can nuke old clothes on very high heat to finish faster—you're not going to hurt them!

• Use fabric softener sheets for soft clothes. To save money tear them in half—they'll last longer and still do a great job.

Folding

• Folding clothes while they're warm helps prevent wrinkles. If you wait to fold them until later on, even if they're clean, they'll still be wrinkled when you go to wear them.

• Try to keep pants in one pile, shirts in another, and socks and underwear in a third...or however you stuff them into the drawers in your room.

• If you hate folding, throw everything possible on hangers. Bring the clothes immediately to your room and hang them.

• You can even use color-coded hangers; for instance: black for pants, green for short-sleeve tops, blue for jackets, etc. It makes it easy to see what you have that's still clean with a glance into your closet.

Info: Be Enviro-Friendly

You wouldn't believe the stuff that contaminates our water and our planet. Spend the extra quarter or two, and get earth-friendly, organic cleaning supplies. Many of the chemicals are that we're washing our clothes and bodies with extremely potent—not only are they unhealthy for the water and the planet, but they can also compromise your health. Do you really want to put harsh substances against your skin, an organ with a huge surface area through which the body absorbs chemicals? Take care of yourself and the environment. Buy cleaning products you'd feel comfortable buying for a loved one, and use them for yourself.

Heading Home

Look at your checklist before you leave the laundry area. Are you leaving with everything you arrived with? Double-check all possible machines to make sure you didn't leave anything inside and cast one final glance at the area around where you were.

Finishing Up
- Try your best to put the clothes away immediately when you get back to the room. Fight the urge to drop the clothes and run. (This may be because you're starving to death—bring food with you when you do laundry.) Make sure you budget enough time for this to get done, or your clean clothes will soon end up back on the floor and dirty again without you even wearing them.
- Take socks and put them in a specific drawer.
- Put undergarments into their specific drawer.
- Reward yourself for a job well done.

Info: A Few More Tips

Keep all the clothes that you don't use in a given week but that you don't want to give away locked away in a trunk or storage. This way you'll have fewer clothes scattered about.

Store your clothes close to where you dress and change. That way they're more likely to start and finish where they belong. Keep moving something aside that you rarely (if ever) wear? Give it away!

Don't go too crazy at the laundromat. I know that sounds silly, but I've seen people bored out of their minds at laundromats do some pretty stupid things (such as breaking giant glass windows playing indoor laundro-soccer). If the laundromat's off campus, the trouble you could get into could be far more severe than just a window repair.

Plan on bringing a book or homework with you, unless it's close to your dorm room or in the same building. If you go back to your room, make sure to set a timer to remind you to come back down. In some schools or laundromats, clothes are stolen from machines. If that's the case at your place, you may wish to stay by the machines until your laundry is done.

If you've got the funds, consider laundromats that will do your cleaning by the pound. Simply drop off your laundry in the morning, and they'll have it washed, folded, and sorted by the evening. Plan to do this once a week and schedule it into your time and budget.

Not feasible? Live close to home? Many students have survived college by bringing their clothes home on the weekends or short breaks. Sorry, moms!

Cooking

Here's the good news: Until you're off campus, it's unlikely you'll have to cook or even have the opportunity to cook. However, you might still bring a microwave with you, so some of these tips will be applicable. Oh yeah, and if your roomies bring a bunch of food into the place and a few weeks later there's a foul smell in the air, check to see if there's a moldy pizza or old Chinese food under the couch.

Tips for the Chef

- Keep it simple—consider a food plan if possible to cut down on the workload (especially if you're a big eater).
- If you live off campus or have a hot plate, stove, or toaster oven, use timers to make sure you shut your appliances off. Get in the habit of always checking anything hot (such as the stove) before you leave! You wouldn't be the first ADDer to torch a room or even an entire dorm.
- Keep a charged fire extinguisher close to where you cook.

- Consider buying a microwave that beeps to reminds you when you leave cooked food in it.
- Try to cook everything possible in the microwave to avoid the possibility of leaving anything hot on—but remember that there are certain things—such as metal containers—that you can't put in the microwave.
- Have a designated day and time for food shopping to save time and stay on budget.
- The fewer dishes, pots, pans, and utensils you have, the better— there's less to clean and less that can pile up.
- Cook simple foods or meals that take only one or two steps and require little clean up.
- Immediately throw out boxes and wrappers and clean what you can while the food's cooking. (Be earth-friendly: recycle what you can and try to buy products with the least amount of wrapping possible.)
- Be careful if you find yourself ordering out a lot—chances are it's not in your budget and you'll blow through your cash in a hurry.
- Please tip your pizza delivery driver! He's struggling to survive, too. (And some delivery drivers may be fellow students struggling to get through college…like I was!)

Cleaning

It's a dirty eight-letter word. And chances are, unless you have some OCD tendencies to go along with your ADD, your room is somewhere between slovenly and condemned.

> **Info:** You Know It's Time to Clean When:
>
>
> - You can't find the floor.
> - The piles on the floor are higher than your bed.
> - The pile on the bed needs more room to sleep than you do.
> - There's a strange glow from the closet, and you don't dare check it out.

Where to Begin?

When you finally decide to clean your disaster of a room, start with the biggest, easiest tasks. Begin with a few trips around the room to collect different items that are out of place.

Trip one: Collect all garbage, trash, and unidentifiable objects and throw them away.

Trip two: Lump together all loose papers in a bag, small box, or transparent plastic storage box to be sorted later.

Trip three: Put all dirty clothes into your laundry bag or hamper, and immediately hang up or put away any clean ones.

Trip four: Assign a home for anything remaining that seems out of place.

Now that you've made your trips, the Sorting of the Piles can begin.

Attacking the Piles

- Go after the box of papers first, as it might have critical paperwork for class or bills inside.
- Look at each paper and try to discard as many as possible. Ask yourself if it's absolutely essential or totally expendable.
- If it's a bill, put it in a separate bill pile.
- If it's mail you haven't read, throw it in a mail pile.
- Whatever you're left with should be related to school.
- Sort the remaining important papers into these piles by class. You can further divide your papers into piles for those that you'll need in the next week, those that you won't need in the next week, and those that are important but not related to a particular class. Then file each pile according to your color-coded filing system (see Chapter 11 for more about creating a filing system).

- Attack any remaining piles and put things where you'd like them to belong.

Doing the Real Cleaning

Grab a cleaner—such as an organic, enviro-friendly version of 409 or anything with a germ-killing disinfectant—and spray down all surfaces to kill fungi and harmful stuff in the room. Remember, not only can non-enviro products harm the planet, but they can also harm you: you'll also end up ingesting, inhaling, and absorbing whatever you spray or clean with, so choose wisely.

> ## Info: Cleaning Yourself
>
> Buy a plastic bucket or rubber bin with a handle to hold all of your shower toiletries. This way, you can grab this one item (roll up a towel and stuff it in) while half-awake and not start your shower only to realize in a minute that you forgot something.
>
> Oh, yeah...and if you're a guy, try to shower daily. Just because you don't think you smell funky doesn't mean other people agree! Sure, you can wear the same clothes until they stand upright and salute you, but you don't have to be a science experiment yourself.

Well, there you have it: laundry, cooking, and cleaning, all made simple. Well, sort of. Most ADDers (myself included) are not the best at keeping up with these things, and it's when we fall behind that we get into real trouble. So try to build cleaning into your routine and get things put away the first chance you get. And congratulations—the fact you've read this chapter at all means you're likely on a major cleaning campaign as we speak...or, of course, you've burned out and are running for the hills.

Best of luck!

Fraternities and Sororities

"I get by with a little help from my friends." —John Lennon

Many ADD students feel isolated and alone when they get to college. If they're not social butterflies, beginning college can be very over-whelming, and before they know it they're a semester or two down the road and still haven't made any close friends. Getting out, being social, and having a support network are essential elements for survival in school and beyond. Not only that, college life can be a drag without a network of friends. Of course, you could hang out on Facebook 24-7, but we're talking real-life social interaction here!

It's true—fraternities and sororities get a bad rap for heavy drinking, partying, hazing, and an Animal House-like atmosphere. While some of this reputation is honestly earned, there are a lot of good Greek houses that can actually help you in school and afterwards, if you can steer clear of the social dangers.

It's easier than you think to get caught up in the parties and activities and end up drunk and missing class—or missing an entire semester altogether. If willpower isn't your thing, neither is the Greek system! However, if you want a network of friends and a built-in support system, and you're sure you can steer clear of the risks involved, going Greek may be perfect for you.

Fraternities and sororities give you a social outlet and social calendar without having to try too hard to meet other people or impress people. Dating, hanging out, and meeting other students all become easier. And if you choose the right group, you'll meet others with common interests (aside from drinking). You could also make very close friends and business connections for life.

Choose your fraternity or sorority carefully—make sure you find out what they're all about. Before pledging ask:

- What do they really stand for?
- Are they into sports?
- Are they into music?
- Are they into scholastics?
- Do they represent a club or group (marketing, religious, otherwise)?
- What do they like to do on the weekends?
- What do they consider a good time?

Then make a list of all the details you learn. If your needs and interests jive with those on the list, it's probably a good match. But remember, while you get a large group of friends and activities, it tends to pull you away from other competing interests. So ask lots of questions, know what you're getting into, and if you have an addictive personality and they are heavy drinkers, stay away at all costs.

(Be honest with yourself and trust your gut. You're the only one who really knows if you can handle it or not. Honestly, yours truly could have handled it after four years of experience, but as a first year my ship would've been sunk!)

True Story: The Perils of Binge Drinking

Freshman year, my roommate went Greek. He wanted the camaraderie and social life; what he got was a fraternity with heavy hazing. His experience was the reason fraternity stereotypes exist. During pledge week all the pledges were dragged out of bed and across town, stripped naked, and tied to trees. They were forced to consume near coma-inducing quantities of alcohol. His fraternity brothers would bring him home at night and set a trash can next to his bed for the inevitable vomit-fest to follow. Thankfully he survived, though I'm not sure at what cost. I think he became an alcoholic; for the rest of the year, he'd swig two shots of vodka each morning. While his situation was far from the norm, just be careful and make sure you can handle the peer pressure.

In September of 2004, Samantha Spady, a close friend of a former roommate, passed away from alcohol poisoning after binge drinking at a local CSU fraternity house; I mention this so that her tragedy did not occur in vain. For more information see samspadyfoundation.org.

What Is the Time Factor?

Joining a fraternity or sorority has its costs, and the most dangerous is typically not hazing, alcohol, or parties—it's how much time is involved. Picture hanging out with the same friends twenty-four hours a day and trying to get work and studying done. It's hard for anyone to do that, let alone ADDers who are prone to impulsivity, want to make others happy, and have a hard time saying no. Anytime anyone asks us to play a game, watch a show, or have a beer, we forget or drop what we're doing and join in.

If you're already stretched thin with activities or know you'll have a hard time juggling your time commitments (be honest with yourself—this is a big challenge for us, and we often don't estimate time well), you may be setting yourself up for failure. More than a few ADDers have flunked out of school while being the best fraternity brother or sorority sister they could be. Realize that while joining has its benefits in support, social activities, instant friends, and the equivalent of a giant, extended, second family, it's comes at the cost of a serious time commitment.

Greek Life Pros and Cons

The Cons:

- In a fraternity or sorority there'll be social functions and obligations—whether you want them or not.
- If you have a hard time saying no, you'll be in trouble if you live in a Greek house. There'll always be someone walking up and down the halls looking for someone to do something with them.
- Noise in the house can become more than a bit of a problem when you're trying to study.
- Peer pressure can convince you to do things you shouldn't or would rather not do.
- You're so isolated in the house it's often far too late in the game by the time you realize you're bombing classes or too far behind to catch up. When you focus on what's immediately in front of you (as is the case for us) you think life is good and truly believe it, and when you find out it's not, it may be too late!

The Pros:

- There are many fraternities and sororities out there that are far different from anything you'd expect. There are Jewish fraternities, marketing or business major fraternities, drama and music sororities, and perhaps even physics fraternities.
- It's a great way to get an instant social life, make friends, and find others with similar interests.
- You'll never, *ever* have to worry about being lonely…or at least, about being alone. It'll never happen!
- You'll make great connections for life. This can and will open doors for you. As you've heard, it really isn't what you know, but who you know.

Going Greek is a big decision; these are just a few of the considerations to keep in mind. As with any other major decision, be honest with yourself, listen to your gut, and check in with a trusted friend or advisor. Of course, your gut is the most important thing, but a second opinion from someone who knows you well certainly won't hurt. And if you still can't decide, you can always put it off for a year and see how you feel when Pledge Week rolls around again. By then it's a lot more likely to be smooth sailing at school, and it'll be easier to adapt to and overcome the Greek challenges if you do pledge. A year sounds like a long time, but boy, can it give you perspective!

> "We're on double-secret probation, whatever that is."
> —*Animal House*

Love, Relationships, and Sex in College:

> "Put your hand on a hot stove for a minute, and it seems like an hour, sit with a pretty girl for an hour and it seems like a minute. That's relativity."—**Albert Einstein**

Even if you couldn't find a date to save your life in high school, there are plenty of opportunities to meet great people of the opposite sex at college. You don't need to be ultra cool, part of the in-crowd, a super jock, the most beautiful person in the world, or anything like that. Chances are there are people at college who will love you just the way you are.

This can be great for your social and romantic life. And since this is college, you'll have the opportunity for, a serious relationship, or exploring your sexuality. Regardless of what you're looking for, it's a great time to grow, learn about yourself, learn about others, and have a good time. But while the opportunities for dating (and likely sex) abound, you have to be smart about it.

When I wrote this section, I wanted to lay out some of the dangers for my fellow ADDers in this arena without sounding preachy. Believe me, I'm the last person in the world who can or should be preachy here. But perhaps you can benefit from what I've learned (the hard way) from my own experiences and from those of other students to help keep you out of more trouble than you can imagine.

The right relationship and experiences can help you build tremendous self-confidence. A good and loving significant other can give you the courage to come out of your shell and the strength to reach your full potential. In fact, many people have dated and married someone they met at college. You could be one of them.

But if nothing else, you're likely to have a great time—college is much more fun than high school. But—and this is a big but—you have to be smart and you have to be careful.

ADD Challenge: The Power of Love

 Why a challenge? Because with ADD, we can easily go off the deep end.

Sex and relationships can be very addictive, or at the very least, they can short-circuit your ADD brain. If you're not used to the power of emotions when you get involved with the opposite sex, you're in for a surprise. And if you're used to the emotion, but not the accessibility to relationships and hook ups you can find in college, you need to learn how to be choosy and careful.

For all those parents and attorneys out there, I'm not recommending that college students have sex. I'm not even recommending relationships in college. But if we're going to get involved with someone in college— and most of us are—there's a lot to know. When we're in relationships, our ADD minds do funny things that often end up in skewed judgment calls, over-revved relationships, or totally bizarre experiences.

"I have found the paradox, that if you love until it hurts, there can be no more hurt, only more love." —**Mother Teresa**

Dating

College wisdom advises against getting into a relationship in your first year or two. Instead, you should be trying to meet as many people as you can. Your first year is your best opportunity to make strong friendships and lifelong bonds. This doesn't mean you can't do so later on, but it gets more difficult. There's something about the camaraderie you establish in the trenches of your freshman year, struggling along-side each other through the same life experiences, that seems to build the strongest bonds. But you often miss this opportunity if you're in a relationship and fused at the hip with someone, and eventually you may come to regret not taking this awesome chance to meet friends you could have for a lifetime.

You'll also be forever known as the person who dated so-and-so. If you make it for the long haul and get married this will be pretty cool, but chances are, somewhere down the line it will get a bit awkward and grow very old. It'll also limit your opportunities later on when you're ready to meet that right person, but people still think you're dating that other guy or gal.

> "There are four questions of value in life...What is sacred? Of what is the spirit made? What is worth living for, and what is worth dying for? The answer to each is the same. Only love."
> —*Don Juan deMarco* **(1995)**

Relationships

It's an overused cliché, but college really is a time of redefining ourselves and who we are. We've all seen couples glued at the hip, the ones whose names you can only remember as a pair. While they may (or may not) be having a blast, it's hard for them to build their own identities. It's difficult to discover your true talents and what you really want to do with your life when you're so wrapped up in another person. This isn't true for every close couple; the right chemistry helps bring out the best in yourself, and sometimes a college romance is definitely true love. But this is the rare exception rather than the rule.

Whether you're in a relationship or contemplating getting into one, there are some things you should know. First, we ADDers tend to move too fast and lack healthy boundaries. It's quite the combination! I'm sure you've seen "couples" who've been together a day or two and already want to move in together or plan out their entire future. When we begin a relationship, we're often so thrilled to find someone that our brains go into complete shutdown, and it's hard for us to recognize and maintain a healthy balance between dating that person and the rest of our lives.

ADD Challenge: Wait Until You're Ready

I recommend not getting into a serious long-term relationship before figuring out a whole slew of other things. There are some definite advantages to this strategy. Not only will you avoid the problem of missing out on friendships and being linked to someone, but it helps you keep your mind on your studies rather than your full-time relationship.

This isn't just a first-year problem. I've seen some very talented and successful college students fall apart well into their senior year because they got involved with someone and lost perspective. They started skipping class and devoted all their attention to the relationship.

And once we get involved, we have a hard time determining whether it's a healthy relationship or not. Because of our ADD, our self-image starts off a bit skewed and often becomes even more so in a relationship. While throwing ourselves into a relationship with reckless abandon may appear admirable and romantic, it can also lead to disaster. If you haven't looked closely at the reality of the person you're dating or the dynamics between the two of you, it can lead to a long, painful, frequently needy entanglement. We often get so tied up in the relationship—making it better, saving it, whatever the case may be—that we never stop to ask if this is someone we want to be with in the first place.

You see, many ADDers (myself included) have codependent tendencies. We tend to get into rela- tionships in order to "save" or "fix" the other per- son, or vice versa. This can very quickly lead to unhealthy associations, and put- ting someone else's needs, hopes, and dreams well ahead of our own in college means making a lot of sacrifices that can hurt your educa- tion and sabotage your future.

This is not to say that you can't have a healthy relationship in col- lege. A relationship can be a beautiful thing, helping you to excel and be your best. It can give you that boost of self-confidence you need to chase your dreams and achieve greatness. Just be sure not to move too fast or put on blinders, both of which can have dire conse- quences.

"The basic fact is that humanity survives through kindness, love, and compassion. That human beings can develop these qualities is their real blessing." —**The Dalai Lama**

Sex

Again, the caveat: I'm not recommending or suggesting that you have sex. It's a personal decision—yours, not mine. But since you're most likely surrounded by a bunch of horny college students, it's best we get real.

So here's the skinny. First the good news, according to Dr. Edward Hallowell, author of *Driven to Distraction: Recognizing and Coping with Attention Deficit Disorder from Childhood through Adulthood*: sex as a physical activity can be relaxing. Studies at the University of

Wisconsin and John Hopkins University have shown that just thinking about sex can be relaxing (that must mean many, many college students are very, very relaxed). So sex and masturbation can help reduce stress and induce sleep in small doses or with a certain degree of self-control. But do we ADDers do anything in small doses? Often sex becomes a form of self-medication for us, and once it affects our schoolwork, relationships, friendships, or academics, it becomes a problem. Those who jump into something without thinking in the heat of the moment risk getting themselves or their partner into big trouble. It's not too hard to imagine a "little" mistake or error in judgment haunting you for the rest of your life. We are not known for waiting, thinking things through carefully, controlling impulses, and evaluating all the consequences of an action beforehand.

Birth Control and ADDers: Simple Screwups That Can Cost You

- Pulling out is not birth control. It provides zero protection against sexually transmitted diseases (STDs), and no matter how much you think the other person is clean, you never know. If you haven't been tested recently, you can't even be sure about yourself either.
- The rhythm method is also not birth control, let alone STD protection. Don't rely on it.
- Forgetting to take your birth control pill can lead to trouble. Set up an alarm or system to ensure you take it every day at the same time, no matter what. And if you get sick and throw up soon after taking the pill (which may result in decreased protection against pregnancy for that month), talk with your student health center to see if there's a problem with your prescription.
- Keep condoms handy; that way, if the opportunity for sex presents itself, you'll be ready.
- Beware of condom breakage! Follow the directions on the packages, check expiration dates, and keep them out of the heat. If the condom's

used but you're still going, put on another one! We tend to have problems with either not concentrating enough to get the job done, or never wanting to stop. If you're in the latter category, be careful about protection or you could seriously regret it in the morning.

- Think ahead and then talk it over with your partner. Ask your partner about STDs and where he or she thinks the relationship is going. Yes, 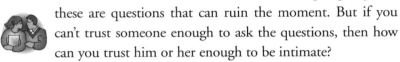 these are questions that can ruin the moment. But if you can't trust someone enough to ask the questions, then how can you trust him or her enough to be intimate?
- If you're a girl and want piece of mind about your birth control—for an ADDer it's just way too easy to forget to take the pill—consider talking to a school doctor about an implant or patch. Just remember that these forms of birth control don't offer STD protection.

> "Sex education may be a good idea in the schools, but I don't believe the kids should be given homework."—**Bill Cosby**

A Few More Things to Look Out For

ADDers have addictive personalities. Like bees to honey, our brains are drawn to what's exciting, interesting, and new. This means we often have a tendency to move to the bedroom too fast, or jump from partner to partner or even rendezvous to rendezvous. It also means we have a tendency to become sex-addicts, either with either one partner or with many. This could get in the way of friendships, grades, and athletics, and at worst lead to an unwanted pregnancy or very serious STD. We often don't know when to say when, so be careful and practice moderation.

Be sure you know the potential consequences of a hookup. Is it a classmate? A group project partner? A close friend of your best friend? (Don't even think about doing anything with a professor, that's playing with real fire!) Will hooking up make things awkward, uncomfortable, or impossible later on?

Realize that things can get out of hand really quickly and that you can easily offend people or start a scandal. The last thing you need is a social crisis to pull you off track in school. So when your judgment is not at its best (such as after a few drinks), try not to act immediately on your impulses. Think about things first and even wait a day/date or two. Trust me—you'll be glad you made the smart, responsible decision.

Relationships can be the most incredible experiences in the world; you could even meet your life partner while in college. Sex, when you're smart and ready, can be another area of great joy. The trick is to tone down your ADD impulsivity and hyper-focus enough to ask yourselves the big questions, both in your relationships and about sex. That's where we occasionally get lost or rush into things (or keep doing things) without thinking them through or thinking ahead. And while our actions often stem from love, they can still get us into trouble.

All that said, don't be afraid to let your hair down a little, to love, be loved, and find love. This is college, after all, and you only experience it once.

> "Your task is not to seek for love, but merely to seek and find all the barriers within yourself that you have built up against it."
> —**Rumi**

Working During School

> "I got the blues thinking of the future, so I left off and made some marmalade. It's amazing how it cheers one up to shred oranges and scrub the floor." —**D.H. Lawrence**

Cash flow is a problem that affects many college students—either college costs more than we can afford, or we spend more money than we have. Either way, we often need a job to survive while we're in school. This can present a nightmarish scenario for an ADD student; since we're often not the best at juggling multiple classes, how in the world will we juggle school and employment?

Working in college can be risky, but if you go into it with your eyes wide open and aware of the risks, there's a good chance you can set yourself up for success. And believe it or not, there are some great advantages of working while in school for those with ADD. For starters, you won't have much time to get into trouble or worry about what to do with the free time you do have.

Advantages of Working

- **Provides spending money.** A part-time job can give you some money to play with or help you pay for school. This always comes in handy.

- **Helps you stay anchored.** Since you can't just skip work and keep your job, work forces you to keep to a schedule. This can be very comforting and stabilizing.
- **Keeps you busy and productive.** A lot of ADDers (myself included) do best when we're busy nearly all of the time. It can push us to be at our best and keep us from falling into complacency or lethargy.
- **Builds self-esteem and gives you a break from school.** Earning money and getting you out of the classroom makes you feel more productive and gives you something to be proud of. Also, no matter what's going on in school, you can separate yourself from it completely while at work: it's a great break from the rigors of college.
- **Teaches skills useful later in life.** In today's economic climate, employers are looking for previous job experience, even from recent graduates. A part-time job or internship can help you get the experience you need, or even help you get your foot in the door of a company that may hire you after you graduate.

Disadvantages of Working

- **Takes up more time.** We already have enough to juggle, and one more thing can put us over the edge.
- **Makes it difficult to prioritize.** We often work in "triage" mode, taking care of the highest-priority emergency first and then moving down the line to put out the other fires. When we have a boss

breathing down our neck, we're a lot more likely to cater to her needs than to the needs of our studies.

- **Burns us out.** When we work too much, we're fried when it comes to our studies, particularly in absorbing information or being creative. Watch out for this one—it's sneaky. You think you're clipping along at 100 percent until you realize your work output has turned into something that smells a little funny.

- **Can cause us to lose sight of who we are and the "big picture."** If we think we are what we do, then we begin to associate ourselves with a minimum wage job, or something that's just a means to an end. Instead of feeling good about ourselves for our productivity and the money we're bringing in, we can start to feel really lousy about ourselves. It's a danger to look out for!

- **Can be the straw that breaks the camel's back.** Whether it's a boss who's demanding, an inability to juggle the workload, coming home fried and being unable to study or sleep, or never getting to see your friends or do what makes you happy anymore, this one more responsibility can often push you too far. However, it's difficult to see this while it's happening, and because there's money involved, we often hold onto the job with all of our might, fearing we'll be flushed down the porcelain receptacle of the world if we dare to quit our job. This can tear us apart, trash our esteem, and take our academics (and friendships) down the tube along with everything else.

- **Compromises financial aid.** Sometimes it looks like the only way to financially survive college is to cut back on classes to keep the money coming in. This may be a losing proposition, however, if you have financial aid or scholarships—both often come with a requirement that you attend so many classes, keep up so many hours a semester, or maintain a certain grade point average to keep the funding. Losing your funding is often much worse than losing a job you may have to quit.

- **Dealing with an unsympathetic boss.** Many students find themselves putting more effort into their jobs than into their school work, because a boss provides a more immediate response to their performance than a professor does—if you're late or doing a bad job, you'll know about it right away, whereas it may take weeks before you find out you've done poorly on a paper. Unfortunately, this can wreak havoc on your studies, leaving you unable to prepare for tests or with assignments incomplete. Keep your focus on your studies.

Info: Signs That It's Time to Quit

- No matter how fast and effective you are, class makes you late for work and work makes you late for class.
- Late at night your stomach starts growling, and you realize you were so busy you forget to eat all day. Again.
- Your cell phone wakes you up in class, and you answer it, "Thank you for calling Vinni's Pizza; how may I take your order?"
- After the day is done, there's little time left for sleep.
- You're forced to sacrifice homework and study time because you're so often stuck at work.
- At work all you can think about is the schoolwork you're not getting done.
- In class all you can think about is how late class is making you for work.
- You feel completely overwhelmed and wish you just had time for a short break.
- You're so tired at work you completely forget how to use a broom.

ADD Challenge: Listen to Your Gut

While it's also possible that things might not be as bad as they appear, it's easy to rationalize your way into a deeper hole when juggling school and work. If you find yourself thinking, "ohhhh, I'll be fine," or "just one more week, then I'll see," when you're under a ton of pressure and your school-work is suffering, stop now and listen to your gut. Your head can talk you into just about anything; your intuition will alert you when you can't keep going at the pace you've established. If you're still in doubt, seek an impartial, outside opinion. Checking with a counselor, the RDS office, a friend, or a coach can help you sort this through and figure out the best way to handle it.

Setting Healthy Boundaries

One of the best ways to manage work and school successfully is to set healthy guidelines at the beginning. Understand when you can and cannot work. Try not to work during your most productive hours for studying. Make sure your work hours don't overlap with a class period. Establishing these rules and schedules is something you'll want to discuss with an ADD coach, a professional at your RDS office, or even a counselor. Knowing yourself and your boundaries is often hard in college, even more so when you have ADD; a professional can help you set reasonable and attainable goals.

Once you decide to take a job you need to be brave. You'll have to talk to your boss before you begin and make sure he understands that there are hours you just can't work no matter what. If he's fine with it, great; if he says there will be times when you'll have to work whether you want to or not, you'll have to find a different job. Also, before you start a job, you should check with your school's financial aid office to make sure the added income won't affect any aid you're receiving.

On-Campus versus Off-Campus Jobs

On-campus jobs often pay less than off-campus jobs, but they are much more understanding about your needs as a student. On-campus jobs are also a good way to make more friends at school.

In addition, there are some cool jobs out there, from jobs that don't require much time and effort (like checking IDs at the gymnasium) to those that can be more stimulating (like working in intramural sports or giving tours to new or potential students).

On-Campus Benefits

I think I got lucky with work-study as an undergrad. I applied to jobs with the intramurals department. I first ran the scoreboard for late-night hockey games and then spent time on the ice as an official. It was great: I got paid to skate around for an hour or two and practice my skills.

Other lucky students have jobs where they basically hold down a desk. Perhaps they check IDs of students going into a building, or they work at a help desk. If it's not busy they can spend their time doing homework, checking email, or playing solitaire. There are many of these jobs available, but you need to start looking early. Talk with older students before you get to campus. If you visit the school, ask in advance. Don't be afraid to talk to people and get a leg up on the competition. You don't want to be stuck in a job you can't do, or one that's too taxing, particularly when there are better ones out there.

Work-Study

Work-study has different meanings at different schools, but it's basically a program where you work for your school in order to cover some of your tuition. At some schools you keep the money you earn; at others, it goes right back to the school. You may get to choose your job or have one assigned to you. Usually, if you sign up for work-study early, you get to choose. Consider something fun (for me, being a hockey ref was pretty cool) or something that allows you to get school work done on the job (such as working at the library, being a dorm desk clerk, or checking IDs at the gym). Since work-study is part of your financial aid package—a percentage of your wages are paid by the government—each school has specific stipulations about it. Check with your financial aid office as soon as you receive your financial aid package to find out whether you're eligible.

Typical College Jobs

On Campus
- Library assistant
- Desk clerk
- Dorm clerk
- Checking IDs in dorms
- Paid escort to help people across campus
- Food service and catering
- Setup and breakdown of on-campus events
- Audio-visual assistant
- Lab assistant
- Teacher's assistant
- Computer lab assistant
- Writing center assistant
- RDS office assistant
- Student radio or TV station help, DJ, or production crew
- Feeding and caring for animals (if there's a veterinary program)

Off Campus
- Pizza delivery
- Waiter, cook, bus boy, host or hostess
- Secretary, receptionist, book-keeper
- Stripper. Yes, I had a friend who did this at college, she made great money, but stripping is definitely not recommended unless you're absolutely sure you're comfortable with it.
- Retail
- Conducting telephone or person-to-person surveys
- Data entry
- Telephone help center
- Medical billing
- Basic computer programming or website design
- Internships (although they may often be deemed "voluntary slavery for experience," internships can be crucial in finding a job after college)

Resident Assistants, or RAs, are hired by the school to supervise a hall of a dorm. The responsibility generally comes with free room and board, a small monthly stipend, and extra privileges, and can be a great opportunity to meet people, make friends, and enjoy shared experiences.

To be an RA, however, you must be sincerely and genuinely interested in helping guide people through their first years of college. It requires patience, compassion, the ability to organize an occasional group function, and a willingness to help people out in the middle of the night. In addition to being available at all hours, plan on being at school a week or two early for training, spending a few extra days there at the end of the year, attending weekly RA meetings, holding monthly hall meetings, and putting on an occasional function for your hall.

You may also have to help out with any emergencies that arise, and if you have a student in crisis (drugs, alcohol, depression, or perhaps nearly burning your building down), you'll need to drop whatever you're doing and help. But that's a rare event, unless you get a truly evil hall or one plagued by an unusual amount of trouble. Other than that, from my experience, the more you put into being an RA, the more you get out of it. I learned much more than I bargained for: compassion, people skills, political savvy, and leadership—all skills that have aided me greatly later in life.

Creative Ways to Make Money

There are lots of very creative ways to make money when you're in school. When I was an undergraduate, other students would bring me their handwritten papers, and I'd type them up for a fee. I also worked as a sort of private writing center, helping students with paper structure, organization, and proofreading. When it snowed, I'd throw on my snowsuit, head to the local neighborhoods, and charge twenty to forty dollars to clear a driveway. Try looking for opportunities to make money on your own time, without a formal job.

Consider another possible way to make money: eBay. If you're a frequent and experienced user of the site, selling items on eBay can be very profitable. I know people who've made a career of going to yard sales, sifting through the junk, finding the gems, and selling them for a ton. If this is your talent, you could make a killing right from your dorm room. But be forewarned—know your strengths. It's easy to lose your shirt if you take insupportable risks.

What are you good at? Making T-shirts or baked goods? Try selling them. Are you proficient in web design? Offer to set up pages for people and companies. Bilingual? Look into tutoring at the English as a second language center. Maybe you could give guitar or piano lessons. Post ads across campus advertising your services or place notices on websites such as craigslist.com or facebook.com and see what happens!

Know Your Limits

The most important thing during college is your schoolwork. Even if you need the money, if you feel that school is suffering because of work, it may be time to quit. However, there are lots of unconventional ways to make money that don't require being tied down to a job. Be creative, only take on as much as you can handle comfortably, and you can successfully juggle work and college.

Info: Textbook Treasure

Throughout the school year, professors are inundated with textbooks they don't need, and they often leave these books outside their office doors for anyone who wants them. It's not unusual to find stacks of books outside a professor's door with a little "free" sign on them. If you've got the time, the motivation, and the inclination, a walk around campus once a week or so (more toward the end of the semester and the school year) can yield dozens upon dozens of books. These books are often very new but have been discarded because they're not part of the current curriculum. As long as the books aren't labeled something like "Not for Resale" or "Sample Only," they can be posted on sites like amazon.com and sold for a pretty penny. I've known students to make a thousand dollars or more in a school year by doing this. (Yes, the author is one of these students!)

"Obstacles are like wild animals. They are cowards but they will bluff you if they can. If they see you are afraid of them...they are liable to spring upon you; but if you look them squarely in the eye, they will slink out of sight." —**Orison Swett Marsden**

Team Sports

"Sweat cleanses from the inside. It comes from places a shower will never reach." —**Dr. George Sheehan**

Want to have fun, get in shape, and do something healthy at the same time? Want to gain focus, a routine, and a social outlet, and perhaps even boost your self-esteem?

Try team sports.

While many of us struggle with team sports (due to problems with focus, concentration, coordination, or social skills) or have little interest in them, they can provide a very positive experience both on and off the field if you give them half a chance. Success in sports can give you the confidence, motivation, and self-esteem to take on the challenges of everyday life; it can be your body armor to carry you over even greater hurdles.

There's a tendency among many of us to stop playing sports that we participated in while in high school when we start college. Either there's pressure from the family to "put school first," or we decide to concentrate all our efforts on studying. What we don't realize is that we're stripping ourselves of one of the most powerful coping mechanisms we have, robbing ourselves of many of the tools we need to succeed in all our endeavors.

Whether we play on the school's Division I team, an intramural beginners' team, or anywhere in between, we often gain more from playing than the time we "lose." For instance, the workouts give us structure and routine, exercise helps us relax and focus, and team sports give us a great sense of pride, belonging, and empowerment. All these benefits, far from an impediment to success, can help you be a better student. Sure, you may have less time to study, but your sport can help you stay more focused, organized, and productive when you are studying. The exercise and teamwork of sports therefore gives you quality, not quantity, studying time.

Choosing Your Sport

While team sports can be great, they're not for everyone. Choose carefully to get the most out of the game, have the most fun, and set yourself up for success. Playing team sports is an amazing opportunity. Evaluate your strengths and weaknesses, decide what team or sport might be the best for your skills, and give it a try. You could be pleasantly surprised by the results.

ADD Advantage: Advantages to ADDers Who Participate in Team Sports

- Fast thinking and reacting
- Willingness to try
- Heightened intuition
- Incredible ability to read other players
- Advanced foresight to see things other players can't or wouldn't see—We're able to think up plays others don't think of, find opportunities that others wouldn't realize (due to our creative, outside-the-box thinking), or perform some of the magic an athlete like Michael Jordan could do, simply because we're able to hyperfocus, which in essence slows down the world around us and gives us the opportunity to find and see things that others can't visualize. Typically, the faster the world moves around us, the better able we are to focus, concentrate, and slow things down. Add an element of extreme creativity to this, and we're in the zone.

ADD Challenge: Disadvantages to ADDers Who Participate in Team Sports:

- May be too distracted to focus on the game
- Could be overwhelmed by stimulus and unable to react quickly
- May forget about others and risk not being a team player
- May appear as though they aren't trying, especially

if they're distracted or thinking of something else (teammates often don't mind if you're not that skilled, as long as you show effort, but if you don't appear to be trying, they're not so forgiving)
- Don't practice or concentrate enough to develop the hand-eye coordination necessary for many team or "ball" sports (this can be improved with practice, but it takes time)

Different Levels

Varsity Sports

If you were a decent athlete in high school, this is worth looking into. Depending on your school's NCAA Division (I is the most competitive and hardest to play for, III is easiest to get involved with), it may or may not be difficult to walk onto a team. If you're very interested in playing a varsity sport in college, check out a school's options and speak to the coaches before you apply. Better to get onto a team and then decide it's not for you than not to take the risk and end up regretting it.

Varsity sports, particularly if you're playing for a Division I school, require a huge time commitment. This doesn't mean steer clear; in fact, many programs and coaches structure your time to enforce specific study blocks, which could be just what you need. However, it does mean your time will not be your own, and it could mean you won't be able to work (i.e., get a job) and your social life may be affected. But the added structure may more than make up for your lack of free time.

Remember—you'll be expected to play well and you won't be able to slack on practices. They'll expect 100 percent commitment from you. In return, you'll get to travel the country, play against some of the best players in the nation, check out new schools, and make good friends. If nothing else, it'll never be boring, and as an ADDer, that's a tremendously good thing!

Info: Don't Be Afraid to Get Help

If you're involved in varsity sports and drowning, seek help, either from support that's in place for your team, from the RDS office, or from an ADD professional. Don't be afraid to ask for help; many student-athletes have ADD, so your coach or other support staff has probably faced these problems before and can help you through. Just remember, as with anything else in college, when you go for help, bring them something to work with, show them how hard you're trying, and they'll typically be more than willing to assist you. They will not give up on you if you don't give up on yourself and if you continue to put in as much effort as possible.

Junior Varsity (JV) Sports

If your school's varsity teams are too competitive and you'd like to play at a lower level, consider trying out for the JV team. It's a great way to make friends, travel, play at a high level (but not too high), and improve your game. Playing JV can have all the benefits of being on the varsity squad with a little less pressure.

Info: The Coach

I've seen many students give up on a sport because of a bad experience with a coach, either in high school or college. It's true that we tend to be sensitive to the motivation, style, and attention of particular professors and coaches. Just as it's important to have the right professor to succeed in class, the same can be said for success in sports. If you're going for a JV or varsity team, and if that's a consideration in choosing schools, meet with the coach in advance and see how you interact. If the coach isn't right for you, and sports are important in your life, consider looking elsewhere or seeing if it's time to move up or down a level. (I don't often recommend moving down since we need a challenge in order to do well; when we're bored or unchallenged we lose focus).

If you hated your high school coach and gave up on a sport as a result, this is a great time to try again. College coaches are often far more professional, dedicated, and motivated, and have worked with a greater variety of learning styles. So check it out before you rule it out.

Also remember the differences in learning styles. If you've got a coach that's always telling you how to do something, rather than showing you, but you're visual, realize you've got a mismatch and that you'll need to either approach the coach about modifying his teaching style, learn things on your own, deal with it, or find a different team. We have to change the way we look at things or change the things we're looking at—or we're in for a world of hurt.

Club Sports

For many students, the opportunity to play at the varsity or junior varsity level doesn't exist. There may not be a team, or there may not be a spot on the team if we're not quite good enough. It's also quite common that we are good enough, but we don't have the time, energy, or desire to devote to the game at that level. For those who are great at a sport, but fall into this category, club sports are an excellent opportunity to have fun and let your talent shine. And for those of us mere mortals who are above the level of intramurals, but not quite good enough for the big leagues (yet), club sports offer a great way to work on our skills and have fun doing what we love!

Generally a club sport is an organization formed by a group of students who are all interested in playing a particular sport regularly but don't want to make the commitment or don't have the skill level to play for the official team. Clubs range from highly competitive to mostly for fun, and there can be huge benefits to finding and playing for one that suits you. As it's mostly a social outlet, you can make great friends, and it still has the advantages of having regularly scheduled games and practices.

Intramurals

If you're not that great at sports or not too experienced at a sport, but you love to play, or if you would like to try out a new sport, intramurals may be your thing. They're a blast, they can introduce you to new friends, and they may lead to some uproariously funny experiences. With intramurals no one's concerned about how well you play or if you win—everyone's just trying to have a good time. (Okay, sometimes the competition heats up, even among beginners, but that's half the fun of it! This is especially the case if you know you don't have skills, and neither do your competitors—for example, beginner's level hockey when you're still working on staying upright!) Your friends or hallmates will often put together a team, or you can put one together yourself. Or just find a flier (try your school rec center or the info desk in your student hall) for a sport you like, sign up, and then show up at the games.

Depending on your school, you may find an amazing amount of intramural teams, including traditional team sports and some incredibly unorthodox "sports":

• Basketball
• Softball
• Baseball
• Football
• Hockey

- Mountain bike polo
- Broomball (picture ice hockey with brooms instead of sticks, a ball instead of a puck, and sneakers instead of skates)
- Ultimate frisbee
- Volleyball
- Water polo
- Field hockey
- Lacrosse

Info: Alternatives to Team Sports

Want to try a sport, stay in shape, or have fun, but aren't into the team sport thing? There's a whole slew of other activities you can try. Typically your school rec center will have a catalog of sports, activities, and classes you can sign up for. They tend to be a lot of fun and another great way to meet people.

If team sports are completely out of the question for you, consider a group workout such as pilates, yoga, aerobics, dance, karate, or one of many other fitness classes. It may take a bit longer to form a core group of friends in classes—they're just less social—but over time they can give you many, if not all, the benefits you'd receive from team sports.

Give It a Try

Team sports have many benefits for us ADDers. They're a great way to blow off steam,; they help us focus, concentrate, and stay relaxed throughout the day; they help regulate our schedule with games and practices; and they're a great way to make friends with people who have similar interests. Even if you never played sports in high school, you may want to give at least intramurals a try—it may do wonders for your focus and self-esteem, and no matter what, you'll have a great time!

Taking Meds: Sports and Meds

I've seen many students fizzle, then fall apart at team sports without apparent rhyme or reason. I know I experienced this in my athletic career as well. Specifically, I was crashing frequently on my bicycle. It turns out that if we're on meds, we get the same benefits of greater focus and concentration in sports as we find in the classroom. This can be essential both for success, and for safety. If you're like me, when you're not concentrating you have two left feet and are always tripping over the ball (in my case, crashing my bicycle as well!). Since I'm not a doctor, I'd encourage you to consult a health professional about this, but I can see valuable reasons to be on your meds for game time as well as for class time (in any case, you'll need your meds for studying later in the day).

Diet fits into the same category here. My dad was a good wrestler growing up. But then he hit a brick wall—and hard. He performed well in practice but then fall apart at the meets. As it turned out, it wasn't nerves, anxiety, or better wrestlers; it was diet. His coach would give him sugar cubes before his matches. His sugar would spike, and then crash, and he'd be weak and dizzy just when he needed his strength. So make sure you're keeping your blood sugar up when you're on the field. Look for sports bars and energy drinks (I'd watch the sugar content of these, though); fuel yourself with a mixture of protein and fat, even during intense efforts (or eaten perhaps thirty minutes before). Bonking (running out of fuel) never leaves you at your best, and in a game, it can make you cranky, aggressive, and impulsive.

"I went to a fight the other night, and a hockey game broke out."—**Rodney Dangerfield**

14

Getting Help

> "**Alone** we can **do so little**; together we can **do so much**."
>
> —**Helen Keller**

While we live in a society that espouses self-reliance and doing it on your own, no man truly is an island, and success with any challenge in life requires looking both inside and outside of ourselves for assistance. It doesn't mean we're weak to look for help, but resourceful; after all, why reinvent the wheel when others have done the work for us?

There are an incredible number of resources and avenues available to get assistance in college, whether we're experiencing run-of-the-mill brain damage in the classroom, a major crisis in school or at home, or complete meltdown. There's assistance for everything you can possibly imagine; you just have to be a bit creative in looking for help, and you'll see it materialize. As the old expression goes: when the student is ready, the teacher will appear.

In this section we'll look at some of the basic avenues you can take to overcome struggles or find assistance for many challenges you'll encounter in college.

The Health Center

> "Health is a state of complete harmony of the body, mind, and spirit. When one is free from physical disabilities and mental distractions, the gates of the soul open." —**B.K.S. Lyengar**

You probably learned about the health center at your school during orientation or when you had to send in your vaccination records. Campus health centers work much like regular medical clinics, though you may want to call ahead to see if they take walk-ins or if you need to set up an appointment. However, since you're a student, if you're dead, dying, or feeling close to death, just drag yourself in, and they'll likely help you out. You may not even have to pay money on the spot. For us ADDers, the health center is particularly notable for being the place where we get our meds.

Taking Meds: Securing Your Meds

Before school starts, determine whether you'll continue getting your meds at home or if you'll start getting them at school. If you'll be getting them at school, set up an appointment ASAP and find out what medical records you'll need to bring. You don't want any confusion or you may miss your meds when you get to college.

Why Go to the Health Center?

While ADD typically manifests itself as challenges of focus and impulsiveness, there are other symptoms that could end up sending you to the health center.

1. The meltdown. If you're feeling completely overwhelmed or suicidal, you can't eat, you can't sleep, or you become inexplicably afraid to leave your room or even come out from under the covers, drag yourself to the student health center immediately. It may be a problem with your meds, it may be something you need to talk with someone about, but whatever it is get yourself some help now.

If you're struggling to make yourself do it, have a friend go with you or ask him or her to drag you there. How you're feeling isn't normal, though it is a common reaction when we push ourselves too hard. Don't judge or look down on yourself for doing this— just get the help you need.

2. **Stomach problems.** Strange stomach conditions including constipation and Irritable Bowel Syndrome are quite common with ADDers. While there are often non-medical options that can help—diet changes (a more natural diet, less junk food, fewer additives, determining allergies to foods like milk or nuts) homeopathy, a healthier routine, meditation and walking in nature for reducing stress—it's best to get things checked out by a health professional first and make sure there's nothing serious that needs to be addressed. Listen to your body. A great way to do this is meditation, which will often tell you if you're abusing your body, if you're pushing it too hard with your mind, if you've disconnected from your inspiration or from the fun in your life, or if you really need to get in and see the doc ASAP. The farther I go along, the more I feel it's a disconnect between what makes us happy and what we're doing, along with an abusive regimen, routine, diet, or lack of sleep and exercise. Conversely, though, we often push too hard in one or several areas, exercise included, which get us into even more trouble with our bodies.

Info: Listen to Your Body

So here's the secret. Hit the pause button, listen to your body, and when in doubt, get it checked out. Then, no matter what, believe you're healthy, know you're healthy, and give thanks for being healthy, even before you're 100 percent. The mind and body are connected. When you give thanks for something that hasn't happened yet, your mind doesn't know it hasn't. Instead, it goes about filling in the blanks to get you where you think you are.

> Try it the next time something negative is going on. You'll be amazed at the results: you may feel better almost immediately. Have fun with this, and you'll see!
>
> (Of course, if you think something's serious, get in and see the doc! 'Nuff said.)

3. **Insomnia.** Having trouble sleeping is also quite common among ADDers. If it's severe enough to affect your school work (or drive you insane), seek help. After anything serious has been ruled out, look into alternative solutions. I've found great help for myself and others from acupuncture, regular exercise routines, and meditation.

4. **Lack of appetite.** This could be caused by feeling overwhelmed or depressed, or it could be a side effect of your medication. Either way, if your "freshman fifteen" is a rapid and unhealthy weight loss, get it checked out.

Info: Research the Reputation

You may have heard that campus health centers aren't all they're cracked up to be. There's some truth to that: sometimes great doctors are passing through, and sometimes the doctors aren't as well trained or as skilled as you would like. However, as college doctors, they tend to have experience with ADD and its effects on students. No matter what you've heard, you should definitely investigate the health center for yourself first.

Now if you're struggling to get a good diagnosis, you don't get along with the doctor, or you're an unusually difficult case, seek outside help. For

the basics—bronchitis, the flu, and ADD meds—
the student health center should be fine, but
trust your intuition. If the place seems subpar,
and you've got another option, don't be afraid of
pursuing it.

And remember, when it comes to ADD,
the most important thing is finding a doctor
you're comfortable with and who knows
what she's doing. If a doctor doesn't believe in
ADD or feels it's overdiagnosed, he makes you feel
dumb, or he doesn't seem experienced (I had one
doctor ask me what medicine I felt I should try), see
someone else. The wrong doc or a bad doc can be
worse than no doctor at all.

Seeing a Doctor

If you need to see a doctor or psychiatrist to help you cope with your
ADD or get your medication, the first thing you should do is get tested,
if you haven't done so recently. Talk to your RDS office to find out if you
need testing and where to go—often there's a testing center at larger
schools or a local place the school would recommend. If there's no
testing facility available nearby, your school psychiatrist can probably
test you for ADD if she has the necessary experience.

Both doctors and psychiatrists can prescribe meds for
ADD, but the trick is finding someone with a lot of experience
in this area. Getting on meds, staying on meds, and finding
the right prescription is often a bit tricky, particularly early on,
so try to find a professional with the most experience possible. If you
have a choice between a doctor or psychiatrist on campus, start with
the "shrink"—chances are they're better trained in ADD treatment
and will be more likely to get you on the right med at the right
dosage quickly.

The Doctor Process

In Advance

- Ask your resources for disabled students office who they'd recommend seeing on campus or at the student health center.
- Make an appointment before the semester even begins. Schedule it for a time you know you'll be at your best and able to focus—for instance, unless you're a morning person, first thing in the morning is likely not the best time.
- Find out what medical records you'll need to bring with you.
- Bring your insurance card, if you have one.
- Write down all the questions you have for the doctor about medications, what seeing the doctor regularly can do for you, and anything else you can think of. Keep these questions in your wallet or purse to make sure you take them with you.
- If you're very quiet or don't like talking to doctors, write down a history of your symptoms and why you're seeing the doctor, or bring a very close friend or relative with you who can describe your symptoms in detail. If you do not give the doctor an accurate history, he or she may not prescribe the right medicine for you. If it helps, when you're writing down your history pretend you're writing a letter to a close friend or confidant, describing your challenges, your experience, where you are now, and what you need help with.

Going to the doctor's office can often be a daunting experience where we feel belittled, unheard, or ill-prepared (no pun intended). That's why following the advice in the list above helps so much, and the info below will get you through the process smoothly. If you're heard and understood, you're far more likely to get the help you need (and with the fewest return visits).

At the Doctor's Office

- Show up to your appointment well rested and prepared. You want to be at your best. While it might be tempting to show your symptoms at their worst, you need to be able to focus, ask questions, and thoroughly discuss your options.
- Arrive early so you're not rushed or flustered.

- Explain your symptoms and what help you think you need as clearly as possible. Be very accurate and open. And if you're very composed and well-behaved with your doctor but a complete mess the rest of the time, let him know this.
- When in doubt, seek a second opinion. If you don't like the doctor you're seeing, don't be afraid to find a different one. Good doctors are hard to come by, and it's very important to have a good relationship with your doctor. Some you'll work great with, while others just may not click with you. If you're not comfortable with your current doctor, look elsewhere. If you're on a health plan where you can only see doctors at your school, however, you may be stuck. So never burn your bridges.
- Don't be belligerent with the doctor, no matter what. Even if you know you're right and he's wrong, arguing will not accomplish anything.
- If you're thinking about trying a new prescription or switching medications, it's important to ask a lot of questions. How long does the medication work (four hours, eight hours, etc.)? What are the side effects? Will it take time to get used to the meds or for them to take full effect? Remember, the goal of meds is for them to help you operate at your best throughout the day. Focusing in class is great, but if you can't get your homework done or are a raving lunatic by the end of the day, is it really serving your best interest?
- Do you have stomach problems, trouble sleeping, medicine sensitivity, rashes, twitches, or anything else out of the ordinary? Make sure you mention this to your doc.

Taking Meds: Dealing with Presciptions

 When the doctor gives you your prescription, put it in a preplanned place. I don't know how many times I've lost my prescription right after it was given to me, and frequent loss of prescriptions may make it harder for you to get medicine in the future, since stimulants are a controlled substance. Also, it's best to pick up your medicine right after your visit, which will both ensure that you do it in a timely manner and help decrease your chances of losing your prescription.

Be Prepared

Like it or not, sooner or later, you'll have to visit your campus health center. But if you're properly prepared, it can be a positive experience that helps you deal with the challenges of ADD. Follow the above tips both before and during the school year to get the help you need to conquer college.

You'll See It When You Believe It

I got injured in April of 2006 while writing this book. I learned a valuable lesson about healing from that experience. For starters, we dwell on unhealth too much. We sense a cold's coming on, and so we know we're going to get sick. Or we twist an ankle and know it's going to take forever to heal.

I tend to look at things from the opposite perspective now. I know my immune system's controlled by my mind, not by that pesky little bug. If I don't want it, I tell it to go away: "Sorry little bug, but you need to find another home; you're not welcome here." If I twist an ankle, I immediately give thanks for it being healed.

Body and mind are connected. We control our bodies not through our intellect but through our feelings and emotions. Feel healthy, and you'll bring your body into health. Feel healed, and your body will find a way to get itself healed (even if that means it walks or drags you to the doctors!). But whatever you do, don't dwell on unhealth, or disease, and do not allow any negative emotions to infil-trate your mind. Our emotions drive our healing. That's why when we know when people are going to pass on; we say they've "given up." So if you give thanks for being healed, feel healthy, and believe you will heal, you will, even if it takes a little time. If you *believe* it, you will *see* it!

"There is no medicine like hope, no incentive so great, and no tonic so powerful as expectation of something better tomorrow."—**Orison Swett Marden**

Working with a Tutor

"When the Student is ready, the Master appears." —**Buddhist proverb**

Simply put, tutors save you unnecessary brain damage. Do you know what Einstein's definition of insanity is? It's doing something twice exactly the same way and expecting different results. As ADDers we're really good at this. And we're particularly good at it when it comes to preparing for tests, difficult classes, and even classes we're required to take over again (ugh). I've seen many ADDers retake classes, thinking that they would somehow, someway, magically do better on a test the second time, just because they'd done it before. If you didn't understand the material the first time, how will you get it now? Avoid the whole mess by getting a tutor the first time around, and getting one early, before you run into problems. As soon as you realize you're struggling to understand the material, find someone who does understand it to help you.

Sure, you can spend hour after hour beating the information into your brain, but sometimes that's still not good enough. For me, no matter how much time I put into Chemistry III, it just did not get any easier. Formulas got all confused in my head, nothing made sense, and I just couldn't see the big picture. For many students, math is their Achilles' heel. It's too easy to refer back to the book, to check the answers when practicing, or to really believe you know something when you actually can't apply it without the book or your notes in front of you. A tutor can help you drill in the information, point out what you don't know, and help you understand—not just memorize— the concepts.

When to Get a Tutor

If you're in a class where things seem like gibberish, get help now. Think of it this way—if you don't understand the reading for a class, chances are good you won't understand the class discussion about it. If you don't get the reading or discussion this time, how will you ever understand the next reading or problem set, then the next class, then…this problem quickly compounds and can spin out of control.

If you're in danger of spinning out of control, if you're already in this situation, or even if you see a test coming up that you know will be tough, put down this book and march on over to (or email) your professor and ask if he knows a good tutor. Better yet, if the class is a common one and you're registered with the resources for disabled student's office, call them up and see if they have a tutor available for you. These tutors are generally free of charge and may also have more experience working with ADDers: they understand how to take the information from the book and help you get it into your mind (and they may have more patience during the process).

Don't think you're stupid or weak because you want to get a tutor; on the contrary, you're being proactive and smart. With ADD it's never a matter of studying harder, but studying smarter. Don't shoot down the idea of a tutor until you've given it a try; it can be the best way to set yourself up for success, keep the stress level low, and give yourself the time and energy to get other stuff done, perhaps even some fun stuff. Don't forget to reward yourself for a job well done—after all, college is not just about hitting the books!

Info: Can't Afford It?

There are many places to find affordable and even free tutors (see list below). However, the big thing to remember is this: If getting a tutor is the difference between staying in school and flunking out, get the tutor. Beg, steal, or borrow—it'll be far less expensive in the long run than dropping out or having to repeat a class. Believe you can afford it, and you'll find a way.

If you're totally desperate, go to your financial aid office and see if there's a small loan you can get to cover tutoring assistance. Perhaps you could even work out a trade with a department member, such as offering to clean the laboratory in return for tutoring assistance. There's always a way.

Where to Find a Tutor

1. First off, check with the professor of the class you're struggling with—he may know a great tutor for his material or even hook you up with his adjunct professor. He'll likely know where to turn.
2. Talk to the department secretary or department chair.
3. Check out postings in the department.
4. Visit your RDS office.
5. Put a posting (or inquiry) online.
6. Know anyone who took the class previously? Maybe she knows of a great tutor or might be a good tutor herself.
7. Still no luck? How about asking a student who's doing really well in the class to tutor you?

- Let the tutor know exactly where you're having difficulties, and show him what you've done and what and how you've been studying. This gives him the best idea of where you're struggling and how to help you get past it. Do not sugar coat things—that's a good way to ensure that you won't get the help you need.

- Try to explain your particular ADD challenges to the tutor. Do you struggle with memorization? Formulas? Confusing facts or mashing them together? Can you only work productively in short blocks of time? Explain your strengths, weaknesses, and peculiarities (regarding studies!) to your tutor so you can both make the best use of the time you're together.

- Tell your tutor where your specific concern lies. Is it a test in three weeks? Is there a project you're just beginning and aren't confident about? Give him due dates and the project or test requirements so you can build a timeline together for success.

- Make sure you mention where and when you work best. This way you won't be trying to meet when you're brain-fried, sugar-starved, or otherwise not concentrating well.

Remember: Working with a tutor is like working with anyone else. We mesh well with some individuals and poorly with others. If the tutor's not to your liking, or his style doesn't gel with yours, don't feel bad about finding another tutor. For me, someone who talks too much without letting me try something drives me insane and I can't work

Working with a Tutor

with him. Know what you want from a tutor and make sure his teaching and communication styles are in sync with your learning style.

Info: Tutor Others to Tutor Yourself!

This is a great, often underutilized option. How does this work? Offer to help another student with the material. I know, I know: it sounds like suicide, particularly if you don't understand the class yourself. But clarity often sets in when we're forced to scrutinize the material and relate it to someone else. This is the same theory behind taking practice tests—when we get it wrong in a practice quiz and then see how it was supposed to be done, we're much more likely to remember how to do it the next time. When you're tutoring, you're forced to try things beforehand and see if they work; whether it does or not, you have to tear the problem apart to figure it out for your pupil, which makes it that much more likely for you to get it right on the exam.

When in Doubt

If I could start school over again, I'd have taken advantage of tutors from the very beginning. From my first class (a disastrous calculus course) to my last, at the first whiff of trouble I should have called in the troops. The right tutor can help you learn in an hour something that might take you eight hours on your own—and that's if you even get it right to begin with! Tutors help you decode confusing material, show you tips and secrets for acing problems, and help you avoid any major complications such as missing key points, not breaking things down into understandable or functional pieces, or realizing that even though your studying's going great, you won't be ready in time for the exam. They are a major shortcut to success and a way to give you more time to do the things you want to do rather than bang your head against a wall, or even worse, have to repeat a class. When in doubt, get a tutor!

"Every act of conscious learning requires the willingness to suffer an injury to one's own self-esteem. That is why young children, before they are aware of their own self-importance, learn so easily." —**Thomas Szasz**

Positive Self-Talk

"To be a great champion, you must believe you are the best. If you're not, pretend you are."—**Muhammad Ali**

Ever done something silly and small, but really wanted to kick yourself for it? Do you tend to blow things out of proportion and get really down on yourself? If so, you're far from alone! Welcome to the world of the hypersensitive mind.

Case in point: My new bicycle frame arrived in the mail today as I came in from a bike ride in the snow. I immediately pulled the frame out of the box to inspect it, and it was beautiful. I carefully placed the frame next to the desk and started taking off my snowy clothes, but as I was wrestling with my jacket I kicked the frame with my metal-cleated cycling shoes and scratched it.

It made my heart sink; I wanted to cry. I know it's not serious, it's just a blemish, but it twists my gut in two. It was the principle of the slip up. It reaffirmed everything I've heard—that I'm careless, sloppy, don't pay attention, and should really watch what I'm doing. I felt sick to my stomach.

Any of this sound familiar?

The quote "to err is human" didn't come about without a reason. Making mistakes doesn't mean you're careless, inadequate, or stupid. We all have strengths and weaknesses, and it's our job to focus on the positives and not sweat the negatives. Life's not perfect. We're not perfect. Now my bike frame isn't perfect. But you know what I say?

Good, I scratched it. Now I don't have to worry about that first scratch. It's already there. It's broken in, and now it's mine.

Accepting your foibles and just letting them go sure beats taking them out on yourself. But yes, it's much easier said than done. The trick is to catch your thoughts in the first instant of negativity, as you're planting that initial seed of the monster that wants to tear you apart from the inside. With practice you can snuff them out, and then you're good to go.

The Power of Positive Thinking

Keeping our brains out of the muck and in a positive place is essential with our high-powered minds. If we don't, our brain power can pull us out of whack quickly. Perhaps it's our greater intuition and sensitivity, but it's so easy for the smallest thing to send our lives into a downward spiral. Therefore we desperately need to laugh at ourselves, practice being positive, learn about ourselves, and cut ourselves a break. After all, we're stuck with ourselves for a lifetime—better to laugh at our shortcomings rather than cry and beat ourselves up for who we are.

Your mind can be your biggest impediment to success, but you can change that—let's instead make it your biggest ally. Here's how you do it.

How Do You Make Your Mind Work for You?

Meditation

The next time you're in a funk or wanting to pick on yourself (perhaps even wanting to grab a two-by-four and get busy), see if you can drop everything (especially the two-by-four) and instead grab a meditation CD or go into a quiet place in your mind and just be with yourself. At these times I like to repeat a phrase or mantra to keep my mind from wallowing in the mire. If that doesn't work, I just start repeating a phrase of thanksgiving, such as "thank you for the day" or anything else I'm thankful for. Quieting the mind or giving thanks is like hitting the reset button on a video game. It stops us in our tracks and resets our thinking. You'll likely stop picking on yourself and start seeing a "big picture" view of what's going on. Even if you're not absolutely beaming, you'll at least come out of this time at peace with yourself and better equipped to handle all of your current challenges!

You Are Not a Failure; You Just Produce Interesting Results!

As ADDers we believe we constantly screw things up and that everyone else is right—that we are doomed to be screw-ups and losers. But we're not, not at all! We're just challenged because others have told us how much we've messed things up—but we haven't; we're just going to the beat of a different drum. The trouble is, we keep playing these wrong and corrupting messages over and over in our heads. And the more we play them, the more we believe them and take actions to reinforce these messages.

Stop it!

Laugh at yourself. Cry. But don't beat on yourself. Because the critics, particularly the ones in your mind, are wrong.

What you believe and think about is truly what you bring about. In essence we create our reality. Think about yourself as the smart, capable person you are, and you'll take actions to make it come true.

Believe in Yourself

This is the biggest challenge for ADDers. Our minds are constantly looking for stimuli, and if we can't find anything fun and exciting, we'll look for something upsetting and exciting. There's always something in our minds or in our pasts we can beat ourselves up about. Even worse, these witch hunts often coincide with our weakest moments. When we need our greatest strength and encouragement, we instead pull out the two-by-fours and go after our own kneecaps. We want so badly to fit in that we believe there's something wrong with us if we don't!

Instead we must be courageous, face our fears, and find ways to believe in ourselves in order to overcome our challenges. We have tremendous gifts, even if we haven't fully realized our potential. We must give ourselves a helping hand and be our own best support—after all, if we don't believe in ourselves, who will?

Appreciate Yourself and the World around You

Appreciating the beauty and energy of the world around you generates amazing creativity and peace of mind. Look at the beauty just on your campus—trees, blue skies, beautiful old buildings. There's beauty all around you, and the more you appreciate other things, the better you feel and the more you'll begin to appreciate yourself. When you're appreciative, you cut off any negative dialogue and replace it with empowering messages and positive self-talk. You draw energy from the things you enjoy.

Be Creative

Allowing our minds to stretch their legs and be creative helps us feel better about ourselves. Our minds were geared for this. And being creative makes us feel productive and therefore useful. Rearrange your room, draw, write, or do whatever it is that makes you feel most creative, and you'll see yourself go from a negative place to a positive place with an energy you can carry forward into all areas of your life, particularly the ones in which you're struggling.

Be Thankful

A great way to get your mind off of negativity and into a positive place is through gratitude. Being grateful and appreciative is the first step toward turning things around in your mind. When you're thankful, there's just no room in your mind for negativity or for trashing yourself.

Especially be thankful for your passions. Do you know what you love to do? Do you know what you want to do in life? Are there things you enjoy more than anything else? This is your passion, and it will be your key to success, as well as what makes your life meaningful. The more you find and do what you love, the more you'll succeed and go on to great things. So whether your passions are big or small, your life's goal or your favorite hobby, be thankful for everything and anything that brings you joy.

Listen to Positive, Energetic, Fun Music

Music has incredible energy, healing potential, and motivational power. For example, I just got a new CD from Eek-A-Mouse, perhaps the craziest singer I've ever heard. With an off-the-wall creative mind, he's one heck of a fun reggae artist. I'm listening to his CD as I'm editing this chapter to keep me in the positive place I need to be to get through it! The right music energizes, makes you feel great, and helps you overcome any challenge that may come your way. Personally, since this chapter has some heavy stuff in it, I need the positive music to keep my mind from whirring off into the negative. Try music yourself—just make sure it's fun and upbeat.

Build Confidence

You're much better than you often give yourself credit for—and this is important, because it gives you the self confidence to take on the day and overcome its inevitable challenges. Sure, you may not test well or be a math whiz or Nobel Prize–winning author—not yet, anyway—but you know you have talent. So tell yourself that, and believe it with all your heart, soul, and might.

"I am a good person." "I am good at math." "I will have a great day." Take a break from reading for a second here and come up with a message right now. Repeat it a few times to yourself. And after you put this book down, repeat it again. When you go to bed tonight, repeat it again. Keep saying it until you believe it, until it gives you the confidence in yourself to go out and make it happen.

Think of a Time You've Helped Someone

One of the best ways to get into a positive state of mind is to think of how helpful you've been to another person. Have you helped someone out recently? Have you gone out of your way to do something nice? Chances are you have. And this means you can't possibly be as bad as you think you are. Make a list of all the characteristics you like about yourself or all the thoughtful things you've done. This doesn't have to include just the big things but the little things, too—like letting someone in front of you in line, making someone smile, giving someone a helping hand, and so on.

Realize That You Don't Have to Earn Happiness

MY STORY

"You can tell a lot about a fellow's character by his way of eating jelly beans."—**Ronald Reagan**

I used to love chocolate ice cream. In high school, with all my internalized, negative messages, I honestly believed I had to earn something as good as chocolate ice cream. I thought that if I didn't earn it, I didn't deserve it. I would make bargains with myself, like, "Since you're training for cycling, this means you need to win a race before you're allowed any ice cream."

Isn't this a messed-up way to think?

Problem was, it didn't end there. At first I had to win a race before I could have chocolate ice cream. When I won a race it changed. It wasn't good enough to win just one race, so I still didn't deserve to eat chocolate ice cream. In fact, I became angry with myself after winning because I had only won one race. What kind of a loser am I? I thought. So then it became "you must win two races," then "you must win a *big* race." And how big was big enough? None were. So not once did I allow myself to eat chocolate ice cream in high school, because I didn't feel I'd earned it or was good enough.

This is totally illogical. Don't do it! If you're doing this right now, go out and get the ice cream; reward yourself. The only way to be the person you want to be is to focus on the positives, to believe in yourself, and then you will see it—not the other way around. Since we bring about in our lives what we think about, the way I was thinking was a guaranteed way to fail, not a reward mechanism designed for success.

Follow Your Passions

To be a happiness magnet, follow your passion and inspiration. Do what you love. The more you're doing what you enjoy and feel passionate about, the more you'll attract the happiness you desire into your life.

Ever wonder why someone has more friends than somebody else? Chances are they're happy and doing what they love—they're supercharged with this positive energy that's palpable. Positive energy's like a magnet, attracting other positive people, events, and things to you. Happiness is contagious; you'll be happy when you're doing something you enjoy, and you'll spread that happiness to others.

Be the magnet.

ADD Advantage: Setting Boundaries

It's one of the hardest things for us to do, but setting boundaries is essential to our growth, and to our very survival! While we want to please others and be good members of the tribe, we need to set boundaries to live our own lives and rise above the influence and judgment of others. Our friends and family care about us and want us to be happy, but they can only make decisions from their perspective—and they aren't us. What would make them happy would not necessarily make us happy. This often means setting boundaries and distancing yourself from these opinions in order to achieve your dreams. Obviously you can't get a new set of parents (trust me, you wouldn't really want to do that anyway), but if you're hanging around friends who aren't going where you're going or don't agree with your goals, you may need a new set of friends. Surround yourself with positive people who support and inspire you to achieve your passions and dreams.

Get Rid of Your Envy

I once watched the most beautiful black Porsche driving by. Wow! I thought. Then I thought, I'll never have something like that. First off, what a great way to bring about what I think about. Bad Michael! What a horrible thing to say to myself! I then looked at the driver, however who was a stressed-out, middle-aged, rather large—dare I say obese?—gentleman. I was out on my bike watching this, and I quickly switched out of envy into compassion. Quite frankly, I don't want the car if that's what it comes with. Maybe the grass isn't always greener on the other side; maybe what I've got really is pretty good. Besides, I'd want electric.

As ADDers we have a tendency to assume everyone else has it easy. And while it's true that most people aren't facing the same struggles, everyone has their problems. Like everything else, this is a matter of perspective. Just remember that someone else might have a better car, house, backpack, snowboard, dress, or whatever, but we have amazing minds and will do things in our lives others can't even imagine or dare to do. Celebrate the positives in your own life, and you won't covet someone else's.

Try Something New

Ever notice how you rarely regret the things you try, but really kick yourself for the things you don't go for? Sure, if you try something new and out of the ordinary like skydiving, BASE jumping, or rock climbing, you may get bruised and battered, but if you keep at it you'll get better and better. (Hmmm, maybe these aren't the best examples …but you get the point!) If you don't try, you'll just give yourself endless grief, and worse, you'll never know if you like something or could have excelled at it. Come up with a list of things you want do but are scared to try. Then go do them. There's nothing to lose!

Don't play life safe…unless you're just waiting for the end. After all, if you're not going to have fun now, when will you? So live life to the fullest, and live life now. Our creative minds demand that we live life large. We're not good at the mundane, the basics, the repetitive, or the desk jobs. We need to dream, find our passion, and follow it, each and every day. Our passion is our compass, leading to even greater happiness. And chasing big dreams is the only way for us to be happy.

Info: Feeling Trapped

Often our angst, anger, or inner turmoil is really an expression of feeling trapped. The next time you're feeling this way, meditate and explore these feelings, and you'll see what I mean.

Feeling trapped is our gut's way of telling us we're heading off track or stuck following a path someone else chose for us. We feel trapped when we're living life too small, when we're living someone else's dreams, or when we're putting off happiness till tomorrow but the tomorrows never come. When we smother our creativity, are heading in the wrong direction (according to our gut), or ignore our passion, we feel stuck, trapped in our bodies, caught living someone else's

> life, trapped seeking someone else's dreams. This feeling just leads us to berate ourselves. We want to scream and yell and break free from this noose. Once you understand this feeling and its cause, a whole world of possibilities opens up to you. Once you see options, you're no longer stuck. When you realize you don't have to live someone else's life and that happiness can be yours, you'll start thinking a lot more positively about things.

Make Positive Thinking a Habit

Practice being positive. It's like anything else: you get better at it when you work at it. Let's start by standing. Stretch, give yourself some room, and do twelve jumping jacks, all the while repeating at top volume, "I am a good person. What I desire is on its way." This should preferably be done in an open doorway, with boxers over your head.

Okay, fine, you caught me—but there are ways to make positive thinking part of your routine without looking like a nutcase.

Start the day with a positive statement. When you wake up, have a positive statement posted somewhere you can't miss it each morning—maybe on the ceiling above your bed, or on the bathroom mirror. Starting your day with the words "Today will be a great day" will start you off on the right foot.

Make a thank you chart. I have a thank you chart in my bathroom to remind me of everything I'm thankful for. Some people like to start the day giving thanks the minute their feet hit the floor. Giving thanks and being in a state of gratitude is a great way to realize that every day you're still here is a great day to be alive.

Meditate when you wake up, before you go to sleep, or both. I like to do a short meditation each morning to remind me of why I'm here, what I'm doing, and how to have a great day. This helps me keep my priorities and passions at the forefront of my mind, and when I'm faced with decisions, it helps me act in alignment with my goals. It also helps me visualize the day I desire, and then bring it into reality.

I also do a short meditation at night to give thanks for an amazing day, unwind, and dream of an incredible future. It helps me fall asleep and have more positive, restful dreams. I often wake up in the morning smiling from the previous night's meditation! (I know this sounds loony, but isn't it better than waking up dreading the day and feeling just awful?)

Repeat a positive mantra each night in bed. Just like meditating before bed, repeating a positive mantra before you sleep can make a huge difference. Somehow it repeats in your head overnight, and you'll find yourself still saying it when you wake up. This helps bring these thoughts into existence. In essence, you're burning a positive message into your brain.

Info: Good Bedtime Mantras

- I am strong, healthy, and happy.
- I am positive, friendly, and outgoing.
- I am good at chemistry, math, and all subjects.
- I am healthy. I am happy. I am loved.
- (If there's a cold coming on) I feel healthy and happy.
- I am thankful for my health.
- (If you're going to bed way past your bedtime) I feel energetic and refreshed.

Stay away from negatives, such as "I will not be sick." Your mind doesn't understand don'ts, can'ts, and won'ts. Don't believe me? Okay, give this a try: don't think of a black cat. Haaaa! Get my point? You immediately thought of a black cat. That's how our minds work. So keep your mantras on what you desire, rather than what you don't! "I will be strong and healthy" will have you waking up energized, healthy, and ready to go!

Put Positive Affirmations around Your Room

Place positive statements and affirmations about things that are happening to you and around you now—they will help you reach your dreams and enjoy each and every moment rather than wait for happiness to fall out of the sky. Looking at your goals all day will keep you striving for them.

Put up pictures that match your goals. Make sure the images in your room match your passions. They should invite that which you desire. Pick out tangible representations of your dreams and visions for the future.

Key point, though: don't put too much up everywhere! This clutters our minds and freaks us out on the inside. Make whatever you have up count, but try not to go too crazy. Too much of a good thing may generate the opposite results!

Brainwash Yourself through Audiobooks!

MY STORY

After I was injured in April 2006, I needed to keep my mind in a positive place, to remind myself what was important and where I was going. I used Dr. Wayne Dyer's book *Inspiration: Your Ultimate Calling* to help. I played it each morning as I headed out for my morning "crutch." By listening over and over again I was programming my mind to react in the way I desired it to when faced with adversity.

You can do this when you're walking to class, studying, taking a break, or stuck in the car—listen anywhere and everywhere. Like nighttime mantras, inspirational audio books can help you reprogram your mind and keep you on track. They will literally help you transform your life and achieve your dreams.

Spend Time in Nature

My best advice for anyone struggling with negative thoughts is to take daily walks in nature (or at least outside), preferably at sunrise and sunset. There's something magical and mystical about nature, particularly at these times. It recharges your batteries, gives you perspective, and energizes you. Walk through an old, dense forest or a beautiful park early in the morning and just try to feel bad. Sometimes it takes forcing ourselves outdoors before we feel any better. But if that's what it takes, do it. Just remember, when you're out there, don't dwell on the negative. Here's a trick: Focus on one tree that's fifty feet in front of you. See the beauty in the tree and say, "What a beautiful tree." When you get close to it, picture yourself touching its bark or branches. Then focus on the next tree and repeat. It clears the mind and helps banish negative thoughts. This is actually a mindfulness meditation exercise, and works like a charm!

Do Something Fun and Creative on a Daily Basis
Creativity helps us find our happy place. Giving ourselves creative activities daily recharges our mind and helps us see the positive side.

Join a Motivational Group
See if there's a motivational or inspirational group near you that meets once a week. These groups can inspire members to reach for their dreams and give them the strength to overcome challenges and keep themselves from falling into the negative. They often meet early in the day to get you moving in the right direction. You'll find once you graduate that many of the top professionals and entrepreneurs in this country belong to such groups and meet once a week in the early morning to set themselves up for success!

Read, Read, Read Positive Books, Then Read Some More
College is an awesome time of self-exploration! We can do so much more than we believe, and we're capable of incredible greatness. Find an exciting topic that'll help you conquer college and the world. Look for authors who spark your interest. Find books and audiobooks on success or books by your favorite athletes, artists, or movie stars, people you admire who have achieved success. Try reading for half an hour before you fall asleep. These positive thoughts will be bouncing around in your psyche as you sleep.

Clean and Declutter

When I'm down or stuck in a rut, one of the first things I'll do is clean my desk and my room. I'm far from a compulsive cleaner, but doing this gets me moving and focused on something positive, and makes me feel productive. When I declutter my room, I'm also removing the junk from my mind. I finish feeling strong and resilient, thankful, and far more positive. And I've got a clean room and desk to work from to boot!

Inspiration: Be a Tinkerer and Supercharge Your Mind!

There are some incredible books out there to turn you into a superstar. There are books to help you improve your memory, attract the perfect relationship, make a million dollars, contact aliens, and who knows what else. The common theme is this: with the author's help you can be, do, and achieve anything you want. All you have to do is see yourself as capable of change. We're really in much greater control of our minds and destinies than we've ever been told. By tinkering with ourselves (sort of like repairing an old car) we can make our minds into whatever we desire them to be.

My latest kick is something called lucid dreaming. It's the idea of being conscious while you're dreaming so that you go where you want, see what you want, do what you want, and even learn what you want, all in your dreams. Sound pretty crazy? Maybe. But if you're like me, you've probably had a dream or two where you've been somewhere in your dream, and then saw it in your daytime world. So who knows, maybe I can visit places in my sleep, or meet with Einstein and discuss relativity. I have no idea!

But it's fun to try, and you have to have a hobby! So far I've found that a lot of my down days are days when I had a particularly bad dream the night before. I didn't realize this until I started reading about dreams and journaling about them. The reading I've done suggests we can actually have fun and explore in our dream world, which would also eliminate the negative dreams that put me in a funk first thing in the morning.

What a way to stretch the limits of our minds and imagination! We really are the creators or cocreators of our existence, so why settle for what we've got? Why not experiment and see what our minds are capable of? After all they say we're only tapping into 10 percent of the brain's potential. Whether it's lucid dreaming, exploring your spirituality, becoming a Zen master, or reading about how to make a million dollars before you're twenty-one, find a topic of interest and stretch the limit of your imagination and abilities to the max. This is an incredible, magical, amazing world if we want it to be!

View the world as a magical place, and you're going to have fun. One topic I've been playing with on audiobooks is quantum mechanics and the mysteries of the universe. I started with movies like *What the Bleep* and then had real fun with audiobooks such as *Dr. Quantum's Presents a User's Guide to the Universe* by physicist Dr. Fred Alan Wolf. If I'm in my room, chances are I'm playing a CD or audiobook that's teaching me about something interesting or something that'll help me improve my life. It's a blast. What a time to live in! In what other time could we learn so much more outside of class and about ourselves than in the classroom? In what other time could we learn such incredible things and feel so empowered about our abilities and our futures? Find an interesting topic and have a blast!

Do things you're good at and enjoy on a regular basis. This can be your body armor for positive self-esteem in everything else you do; it's essential that you don't quit the activities or sports you were good at in high school just so you have more time to "be serious" in college. You'll be much more serious and successful (and happy) when you give yourself the positive strength and energy you get from the activity you love. So don't give up what you love for school—though you might consider the reverse!

Info: Make Your Own Zen Zone

Know how some people's dorm rooms feel totally relaxing, while others make you want to scream? Try to create the coolest, calmest pad you can. You can do it on the cheap through Goodwill, Savers, or another thrift store. Consider buying a small fountain or a natural sounds machine or tapes, go feng shui crazy, add Zen posters, buy potted plants. Put anything and everything in your dorm room that's both an extension of you and makes you feel more calm, tranquil, and relaxed.

The more positive energy in your room, the more positive people you'll attract into your life. And remember that though ADDers struggle with organization, the less cluttered the environment is (both desk and walls), the easier it is for your brain to relax and stay positive. Ditch everything you don't absolutely need. The less stuff you have, the less draining mental energy is associated with it. Everything has energy, but if it makes you want to go on a murderous rampage, perhaps it's not the type of energy you want.

Keeping Life in Perspective

Positive self-talk follows indulging your passions, doing what you love, taking care of yourself, and cutting yourself some slack. Love yourself, be your own best friend, and reward yourself for being here, in college, no matter what. Remember, happiness attracts more happiness. So find joy in something—anything, no matter how small—and your joy will expand, your happiness will grow, and soon you'll be positive without even having to try. Instead of hooting and hollering the next time you stub your toe, you'll laugh out loud, realizing the hilarity of the situation. Laugh, play, enjoy life, and have fun. No luck there? Follow the above advice and shake things up, move around, try something new. ADD has one great thing going for it: Though it's easy to get down on ourselves, it's also easy to incite a quick turn around!

Info: Blocking Negative Thoughts

 Over time, through meditation and practice, you can learn to stop negative thoughts before they get rolling or to replace them immediately with more positive thoughts as soon as things start to go south.

However, if you're not there yet and you can't stop the first thoughts of negativity, then learn to simply observe them. By watching them, without taking ownership of these thoughts, you take back incredible control over your mind and your happiness. I find that if I just recognize negative thoughts rather than dwell on them, it keeps me from heading in the wrong direction. In fact, recognizing them can be empowering—you're taking control of your mind!

To recognize your thoughts, you want to use a technique to see the ideas but not get wrapped up

---

in them. I picture myself in a subway station. As the train comes into the station, I see the idea that's on that train. For instance, instead of thinking "I can't believe I forgot to start my history paper last week," think, "that's a train for my history paper." Then just let it pass on by the station. Resist the urge to hop on board the train. After a few trains pass, you start to feel better, more in control of your thoughts and ideas.

Talk yourself through it. "I see myself stressing over the history paper." "I'm okay seeing myself stressing over the history paper." "Stressing over the history paper isn't that bad." With this example. This inner dialogue allows you to see the fear and separate yourself from it rather than getting stuck in it. Write yourself a reminder about the test on Friday, but let the "freak out about the test" train pass on by. You're a lot more likely to absorb the information better while studying if you're calm (when the material you're studying is not as emotionally laden), and you'll feel more confident and prepared during the test.

"When one door closes, another opens. But we often look so regretfully upon the closed door that we don't see the one who has opened for us." —**Alexander Graham Bell**

Getting Unstuck

"When we feel stuck, going nowhere—even starting to slip backward—we may actually be backing up to get a running start."—**Dan Millman**

It's not uncommon to find ourselves in a funk. Sometimes we label it depression, other times we say we're in a rut, overwhelmed, or just plain inert. Call it what you will, but with ADD, sooner or later you're going to get stuck. No matter what particular emotion you're feeling, be it sadness, frustration, etc., it feels like you're stuck in a terrible spot that you'll never get out of.

Getting stuck isn't necessarily a bad thing: it helps us reevaluate our lives and consider what we might like to be doing differently. It's as if we're forced to squeeze through a narrow passageway, but once we pop out the other side, we've often gained an incredible new perspective. Unfortunately, the squeeze can be pretty painful. To get through, the trick is to maneuver through the loops, twists, and knots of our ADD minds and figure out what's really going on and how to fix it.

MY STORY

Make a Move

Movement of any kind will often help shake us out of a funk. One time when I was feeling absolutely terrible about myself, I flew into a rage, smashing the positive and motivational pictures I had on the wall, breaking their frames into itsy bitsy tiny little pieces. Then I went to bed to cry.

But soon I realized I had to clean up the mess.

That turned out to be a good thing. I cleaned up the mess, then the rest of the room. Cleaning gave me a sense of empowerment; it made me feel more in control of my day and of my life, and this sense of being at the helm rather than being taken for a ride was what I needed to pull myself together.

While I was cleaning I started to feel hungry, and when I'm sad (or almost anytime—I don't need much of an excuse, really), chocolate is the answer. It helped me start to feel even better, and while I was on a roll, I tackled a bit of the work that'd been looming over my head and making me feel completely miserable. I didn't worry about doing it perfectly; I just did as much as I felt comfortable doing and got some of it out of the way.

With those few things accomplished, food in my belly, and a bit of order in my life, I set an alarm and went to sleep. When I woke up the positive momentum continued—I took a short hike, which was meditative and helped me put a routine back into place.

The key to getting unstuck is to do something, anything, to get yourself moving again. Preferably, it's doing something fun, something you're passionate about, or an activity that breathes energy and accomplishment back into your life—but anything, even flossing your teeth, cleaning your desk, or cleaning your room, will do. Once we've overcome inertia, we're rolling!

Ways to Snap out of the Funk

1. **Meditate.** Quieting your mind through meditation is one of the greatest gifts you can give yourself. Not only does meditation give your mind a break from the constant onslaught of thoughts, but it can be the pause you need to step back and understand what's going on. Chances are your body, soul, or mind has the answer inside, but until you stop thinking a thousand things at once, you'll never hear what it is. The minute you go quiet, it may just come to you.

   Not sure what I mean? Ever tried to remember a name, movie, or song that was just driving you silly? I bet it wasn't until you stopped thinking about it that it finally came to you. That's exactly what I'm talking about here—until we stop fighting and wracking our brains, we often can't find what we're looking for.

2. **Listen to music.** Music has energy, and the right energy can be healing and energizing. The next time you're stuck or feeling down, put on some great music. Pick something with energy and a beat that will get you moving. I'm listening to an

oldie but goodie as I write this: *Greatest Hits* by the Police. Sting has helped me through lots of study sessions.

3. **Watch a movie.** Put on a music video or motivational movie. I have to do Pilates every morning for training. I love it and hate it. Left to my own devices, I'd surely never get it done. So I throw on the movie *Stick It*, a fictional account of a rebellious elite gymnast. Watching workouts they say are tougher than those of Navy SEALs combined with an energetic soundtrack, gets me going despite an extreme desire to go back to bed.

4. **Reconnect with nature.** Take a hike, hit the trails, or take a walk in the park. (I'm fond of following deer trails into the woods…it's fun to follow their meandering without worrying about anything else.) Find someplace quiet to just breathe the air and reconnect with nature. Stuck in the city? Try to find a lake, a pond, or another large body of water to walk around. Doing it at sunrise or sunset will just compound the effect. There's a special energy at these times—it may be extremely hard to be up and about when the sun comes up, but I've never seen someone stuck after they come back from a sunrise hike.

5. **Explore.** There's something about seeing new sights that helps shake things up and get us unstuck. Bored of your hikes or the local trails? Go check out someplace new. No trails around? Explore the city. Just get out and look at the world around you.

6. **Listen to an audiobook.** You can use audio books to reprogram your brain. When I was injured and unable to keep up my routine, I started listening to inspirational audiobooks all the time, during "walks" (on crutches), in the car, anywhere I could. They helped remind me of the important things in life and strip away my self-pity. Simply put, they helped me see the positives of my situations, rather than allow my mind to dwell on the negatives.

You can also educate yourself with audiobooks. Learn more about your ADD, the mind, intuition, spirituality, science, quantum mechanics—whatever helps bring you a greater understanding of yourself and the world you live in. It can be quite insightful and motivational, and it may even help you find your life's passion and direction.

7. **Talk to a mentor or professor you trust.** They're not just there for class but also to help you through the tough spots. They have most likely guided many other students with experiences similar to yours and will both understand and know how to help.

8. **Seek professional help.** This is never a bad idea—just make sure it's someone with ADD experience.

9. **Try meds.** The right prescription can help get your ADD under control. Typically meds will "unjumble" your mind and pop you out of the funk. Talk to your doctor about your different medicinal options.

10. **Look at homeopathic solutions.** There are many natural products touted to help those with ADD, and while I don't think they're the most potent way to deal with your symptoms, they're worth considering, particularly if you aren't already on meds.

11. **Change your diet.** Perhaps you're starving your brain of the fuel it needs. Not only will this cause you to become stuck, but you'll feel cranky, lethargic, and depressed to boot. If your diet is really high in carbs, sugars, or fats, try a more balanced diet that's higher in protein and lower in fats and sugars, and see if that helps. If nothing else, it'll get you into better shape, and that alone may help snap you out of your funk. Also, some students overeat when they're depressed; others stop eating altogether. If you tend either way, try to get this back into balance.

12. **Give yourself a new look.** Get a haircut, buy some new clothes, or otherwise change your appearance. How we look often affects how we feel; if we dress up and start looking our best, our thoughts and attitude can start to mirror our outer appearance.

13. **Reshape your environment.** Like changing your appearance, the more you change the look of your surroundings—unclutter (fill your car with old clothes, drive to Goodwill, donate, and then think about what you did), re-organize, and make your environment more soothing and appealing—the better you will typically feel about yourself. I know that it's hard enough to clean when you're upbeat, but try it when you're down just to set yourself in motion. Want something really fun to try? Go grab a book on feng shui and get

busy; you'll be amazed by the difference! (There's even a book out there called *Dorm Room Feng Shui* by Katherine Olaksen).

14. **Cook something.** This option may not be open to you if you live in the dorms, but if it is, bake some brownies, a cake, or some other dessert to reward yourself for just being you. Actually make something—don't just throw it in a microwave. Often a creative act is just what we need to feel productive and good about ourselves, and cooking can do the trick.

15. **Stick with a routine.** The more predictable you make every day, the easier it will be to get things done and the more productive you'll feel. I once heard a student say, "It's hard to get depressed when you're too busy to find the time." If you've filled your day with repeatable activities like work, volunteering, or a club sports team, you'll feel more productive and worry less, and it'll help you gain the stability and foundation to put things back together again.

16. **Pray.** Getting in touch with something greater than yourself or simply quieting the mind with prayer can start to make you feel calmer and more like yourself.

17. **Make a mantra.** A couple years back I faltered while on my bicycle, riding across a desert highway between Reno and Salt Lake City. I had to find the strength and energy to keep going. I began repeating a sentence in my head, a mantra that I use to this day: "Help Me, Guide Me, Give Me Strength." This helped me stop worrying and gave me the strength to continue. Repeating a phrase in your head is a small thing that can make an amazing difference.

18. **Give thanks.** Try thinking about and giving thanks for what you have, all the positives in your life, even if they seem few and far between at the moment. Give it some time and reflection and you'll surely come up with a long list of things, which should make you feel better as well as give you downtime and rest.

19. **Appreciate the beauty around you.** It's hard to be appreciative and lethargic at the same time. Pick things you like around your room (like your computer, television,

favorite book, etc.) and think about what they bring to your life. Though it may feel a little silly, doing this exercise can make you feel more energetic and better about your life.

20. **Start thinking love.** It's really hard to be angry with yourself or down when you're trying to share love, care, and compassion with those around you. Whether we like to admit it or not, we're all part of a collective human race, and it's amazing how a simple, kind thought can make us feel better about ourselves. It's very hard to feel bad about yourself when you're thinking loving thoughts, and it always seems like the amount of love you give to others is returned.

21. **Perform an act of kindness.** Thinking kind and loving thoughts definitely helps, but sometimes the best way to re-energize and to help ourselves is to physically help someone less fortunate. Try it—it can be quite addictive!

22. **Start dreaming.** Write down a wish list of what you'd like in your life. This will get your mind going, get you thinking more clearly, get your adrenaline and endorphins up, bring a smile to your face, and help you see that the world really is still open to you. Make a "dream board." I have one by my desk. There are pictures on it of everything I dream of accomplishing in life.

23. **Make yourself laugh.** Many people with terminal illnesses or those who are recovering from severe injuries employ this strategy. Laughter seems to have healing powers. Rent comedy movies, watch your favorite sitcom, or even just force yourself to laugh, and your brain chemistry will start to change, making you feel better.

24. **Pet an animal.** It's amazing how much energy you can draw from a furry ball of unconditional love. (I have to give a big shout out here to my personal fur balls, Pumpkin and Sawa—they are my love, energy, and inspiration!)

25. **Set a big goal.** Sometimes the biggest dreams can open up our minds, help us focus, and give us the self-confidence we need to get through the daily grind and move ahead.

26. **Think big.** What would you do if you knew you couldn't fail? What would you try? Where would you be? Write it down (no matter how silly) and start working toward it. You'll be amazed at what you can accomplish!

27. **Make plans for tomorrow.** Give yourself something fun to look forward to.

28. **Read a book.** Do you have a favorite book? Find one that interests you, tune out the rest of the world, and jump into it.

29. **Listen to an amazing speaker.** Perhaps it's Tony Robbins, Wayne Dyer, the Dalai Lama, or someone else. Download and listen to an audio speech by one of these guys. It often provides new perspective and makes you feel more upbeat about the world.

30. **Join a club, group, or spiritual or religious organization.** Find a group that helps you focus on something other than commiseration, be it positive energy, a higher power, a club event, sports, intramurals, or anything else that takes the emphasis off being stuck and depressed.

31. **Try aromatherapy.** Scents can trigger thoughts and ideas and give us energy. Ever smell something that takes you right back to your childhood and makes you feel incredibly good? I often have apple cinnamon candles or other fun scents permeating my place. It's soothing and energizing.

32. **Try sound therapy.** I have a sound machine with a choice of sounds, but I personally find the sound of birds chirping to be the most effective in drawing me out of a rut. I also like the rain option; it's soothing and pleasant. Natural and other beautiful background sounds can have an amazing impact on your energy and attitude.

33. **Acupuncture.** The mind and body aren't separate—helping your body feel better helps your mind, too. Acupuncture can relax the body, remove tension, and release depression. You may be surprised by the results.

34. **Treat yourself to a massage.** Perhaps your school has a massage therapy program? If so, you may be able to get an inexpensive (or even free) massage from a student! A massage not only relaxes you but recharges you, giving you greater energy and making

you feel good about yourself. One great way to use massage is to set an appointment for a specific time each week. Use this as your reward for a hard week!

35. **Surround yourself with positive people.** We ADDers are extremely intuitive, and if you're constantly around negative or unhappy people, you may not be able to avoid picking up their vibes. Be careful of the energies around you and work to change them if you feel they're bringing you down.

Finding Your Passion

If I had to offer one foolproof way to get unstuck, it would be passion. That's the key to success with ADD—and perhaps to success for anyone, ADD-sufferer or not. When you're doing what's fun and enjoyable you can't help but open up, feel more energetic, and get things done.

Passion can guide you. Passion can give you purpose. And passion feels good. So when you're stuck, do what you feel passionate and inspired about. Have fun, and you can't help but be successful!

> "Out of clutter, find Simplicity. From discord, find Harmony. In the middle of difficulty lies opportunity."—**Albert Einstein**

Depression

> "When it is dark enough, you can see the stars."—**Charles Beard**

I'm always amazed and distressed at how easy it is to fall into depression when you have ADD. One minute you feel like you're on top of the world, and the next you're wondering how you've ruined your entire life—even before you're twenty-one.

As ADDers we have an incredible ability to see ourselves with a completely skewed self-image—picture a warped mirror at your county fair. Because so many people have beat us up mentally and/or physically for so long, we become convinced that we're worthless and are ready to recount our negative characteristics to everyone we meet. It's as if we feel better about ourselves, more loved, when we can prove that we're no good. With our skewed mirrors, we look like crap, we feel like crap, and by God, we know we're crap. Anyone trying to prove otherwise will only piss us off.

I've been there more times than I care to admit, and I've worked with many other ADDers in the same boat. Let me tell you from experience—it really doesn't have to be this way. You can get through it, and whether you believe it or not, despite the worst of circumstances (and I've seem 'em all) it gets better on the other side.

What's the Difference between Sadness and Depression?

Sure, we all feel miserable at times, but that doesn't mean we're depressed. There are lots of challenges that come with ADD—upsetting, frustrating challenges that can create self-doubt and make us sad. It takes time to get over such challenges. But these temporary funks aren't usually hard-core clinical depression. When I'm talking about depression, I'm talking about not wanting to move, eat, think, breathe, walk, talk, anything. It's a very dark hole that feels impossible to crawl out of. And it lasts—it doesn't show up during an unpleasant phone call and disappear just as quickly.

Individual events such as failing a test or going on a bad date can surely help you start digging yourself into that hole, but if it's just come about, you're more likely sad than depressed. Depression generally isn't something you get over right away; it's something that sticks with you and feels like a dark cloud, even on a sunny day. It's a feeling that nothing's fun or even worth doing, or that you've just lost your enjoyment for life. I've also heard it described as a sense of incredible fatigue, where your energy is so low that it feels almost impossible to get up in the morning, let alone get yourself to class. I know that at times like this, I've felt like hiding under a desk lacking the energy or ability to deal with anyone or anything else. Interruptions, in particular, made me edgy and anxious, feeling as if the sky really were about to fall on my head.

One of my most severe cases of depression came from writing this book. I was pulled away from writing to help a close friend, and I stopped doing my work and began to feel like a failure. Over time, I started to feel more and more like a loser, and I wanted less and less to associate with the real world. I berated myself constantly, and after a while, I felt there was no reason to live anymore. I gave up hope and could see no way things would ever get better. Looking back I know it wasn't just sadness—it was severe depression.

How Do You Beat Depression?

There are many ways to cope with depression. Diet, exercise, meditation, acupuncture, counseling, establishing a routine, and many of the other techniques I've mentioned in this book really can make you feel better. Having a goal, passion, or dream helps, too. In the movie *Riding Giants*, Laird Hamilton, one of the world's greatest surfers, describes the depression that comes with having no waves to ride: "What if you were a dragon slayer and there were just no more dragons; then you wonder, 'Who am I and what am I doing here?'" Something to work for gives you purpose.

There is no clear-cut answer to depression; it often takes looking at the world in a different way. As one of my favorite speakers, Dr. Wayne Dyer, says, "When you change the way you look at things, the things you look at change." This shift in perspective can give you hope, sort of like realizing that the sun really is always shining just above the clouds. When we have hope or direction, we can pull out of almost any tailspin. You just need to believe in yourself.

Turn On the Light

Our ADD minds are like lightbulbs—we light up and come to life only when there's electricity in the air. When things are too simple, too boring, too monotonous, or just don't seem worth doing, the light often goes out, and that's when we're in trouble. Here are some easy ways to get the light shining again:

- **Eat.** Eat something immediately. I'm not talking about self-medicating with food—but when you feel miserable and dizzy and at wit's end, try fueling your mind and stabilizing your blood sugar as the first step.

- **Stop abusing yourself.** Stop beating and berating yourself. Bringing anger and hostility to the situation only escalates the battle and adds fuel to the fire. When I'm most upset with myself, I think of my friend who passed away from suicide. I think, "Do you really want to go down that path, Michael?" This question always shocks me back into reality and helps me slowly step away from the situation, enough to stop being angry with myself and think about fixing the problem.

- **Brainwash yourself.** When I get down, I start listening to inspirational or spiritual audiobooks from one or many of the spiritual mentors in my life. That could be Dr. Wayne Dyer, Deepak Chopra, the Dalai Lama, Pema Chodron, Dr. Andrew Weil, Louise Hay, Cheryl Richardson, or one of many others. I also force myself to crack open a book or two, such as *If the Buddha Got Stuck* by Charlotte Kasl, PhD.

   These books help remind me of what I already know: first, that I'm not alone and that I'm certainly not the only person going through this; and second, that everything in life really does happen for a reason. Once I remember these two things, I can start to put myself back together again.

- **Exercise.** Take action—kick yourself out of the house for a walk, hike, bike ride, anything that gets your blood flowing and your endorphins going. It may be no fun at all, but it starts to shake loose the darkness and lethargy. For me, physical activity helps me stop my negative thoughts and move toward positive solutions.

- **Meditate.** Once I've calmed down a little, I start meditating. Take some quiet time with your mind to sort through the details of your situation (see the meditation section for help in this arena).

- **Do something creative.** Try journaling, drawing, photography, playing a musical instrument, or some other creative activity. When we're being creative, we seem to find inspiration from or tap into an unlimited amount of energy both inside and outside of ourselves. As ADDers we're filled with creativity, and when we start to use a little of it we generally feel much better about ourselves. Things tend to spiral out of control when our creativity's being stifled or we're not able to shoot for our dreams.

- **Restore order.** Start cleaning. Putting some order back into the chaos that your life can become during these times helps unclutter your head. Think of it as cleaning away the bad and welcoming in the good.
- **Force yourself to be around people.** When you're sad, try calling a friend or making yourself go out. You can also attend a religious service or group meeting to be around others. All too often we create our own funks by hibernating. Staying away from people gives us a very skewed perspective of life and takes us away from the energy we gain by connecting with others.
- **Kick-start your routine.** As well as cleaning to put your environment in order, add order to your schedule with a routine. For instance, hiking or walking each morning when you get up or making sure you go to bed at a certain time can ground you, removing feelings of drifting and uselessness.
- **Set a goal.** Give yourself purpose and set a goal—something fun, something challenging, or just something you're interested in. When we're connected to spirituality or our inner strength, it's because we're doing what we want to do instead of what others want us to do. Figure out what you enjoy and use it to come up with a challenging goal for yourself. Even better, try to find a way to use that recent funk to make the goal even more successful.
- **Let go of the result.** This may seem completely contradictory to all the above, but it's like the famous slogan "Let go and let God." If you divest yourself of the outcome, you won't sweat the results. Often as ADDers we take life too seriously. It's what we've been taught to do. But screw it. Really—will you die if you bomb a test, flunk a class, or even get kicked out of college? No, probably not. You've survived so far; the probability is high that you'll make it through this challenge, too. And like it or not, you are the person you are because you've made it through past challenges, and you're better for them. So if you don't sweat the outcome to this problem, no matter how severe, and if you realize

Depression

there's a reason for it that you'll understand later on, it becomes much easier to cope with. Think of every challenge as an opportunity in disguise...or if not an opportunity, at least something you can laugh at.

Info: The Chemical Connection

In *Magical Mind, Magical Body* by Deepak Chopra, MD, I learned about an experiment with mice that changed my perspective. In the experiment, one set of mice was given an injection to stimulate the immune system; these mice were simultaneously exposed to the smell of camphor. Another set of mice was given an injection of cancer-causing agents; they, too, smelled camphor. Over time the injections were stopped, but exposure to the camphor smell continued. The first group went on to develop amazing immune systems. And the second group—well, they didn't fare so well. Sorry.

What's the connection to depression? If we view anything or everything in our world as hostile, we start producing nastiness in our bodies that makes us feel miserable and can even kill us. But if we view each challenge simply as a test to make us stronger, we're better equipped to heal, overcome difficulties, survive, and thrive. Wish we could help the mice.

So it's not just a saying that it's all about perspective; it's a biological fact. And who wants nasty chemicals and carcinogens flowing through his bloodstream just because he's viewing the world as a hostile place? I don't know about you, but I certainly don't want to be attacking myself from the inside—I want to feel better, not worse. When I find myself in a bad place, I remember this

Depression and College

Depression can wreak havoc on us in college. Once we stumble and fall, we really start to spiral out of control— and there's no room for this sort of descent in a college schedule. We may hibernate for extended periods of time, feel completely overwhelmed and unable to move, start sleeping late, skip classes, drink heavily, abuse drugs, wallow in self-loathing or self-pity, quit classes, bomb a semester, lose our financial aid, or even be expelled from school. Depression can lead to some dire consequences, put you in tremendous danger, and cause great harm to your possessions, or worse, yourself.

If you're at school and suspect you may have depression, you must get help! Not later, not tomorrow, but now! In a sense, I'll be there with you—I've gone through it myself. Honestly, that's a big part of the reason I do this work and am writing this book: I don't want you to feel as lousy about yourself as I have about myself. I don't want you banging your head against the wall the way I've banged mine. And I don't want you crying and feeling like your entire life is a waste or that you don't deserve to live simply because you don't know how to overcome your ADD. So let's get through this together. There's a better world on the other side.

Getting Help

It's often hard to know when we should seek help. "Am I really depressed?" "Doesn't everyone go through this?" "I'm too tired to seek help." "I don't want to seek help." Or even, "I don't deserve help." These are common questions and thoughts that arise when it comes to depression.

Remember: You're not clinically depressed if it happens on occasion, if there's a trigger, or if it doesn't last for very long. But if it's affecting your schoolwork, friendships, relationships, ability to eat, or desire to do anything, if you feel like all the fun's gone from living—it's time to seek help.

If you can, recruit a friend, roommate, or someone else to help you. In a moment of temporary clarity about what's going on—and seize these when they happen—explain what's going on and see that someone helps get you the help you need. I know I've done this with friends, roommates, and even my sister. (Thank you all!) It's hard to admit such "weakness," or to feel vulnerable, miserable, or humiliated even though you shouldn't. Depression is real, and it's chemical; it doesn't mean you're weak or lack some kind of moral fiber or fortitude. Let them help you—chances are you can return the favor later on, and it's much better than the alternative of falling painfully and deeply into the abyss.

Getting help when you need it is the key to ADD in college, and perhaps to life itself. No man is an island—don't be afraid to ask for help when you need it, and don't panic, because everything will get better over time (a problem always seems worse than it is while it's happening). Everything, no matter how bad it seems, really does happen for a reason. Step back, don't sweat it, get the help you need, and strap yourself in for a wild and crazy ride!

Where Do You Turn?

Walk yourself over to the student health center, student counseling center, family services center, or even your disabled students office. Better yet, is there a faculty member you can confide in? Professors have seen everything under the sun, including many students in crisis. My guess is that the professor's office is one of the most common places for students to have a meltdown or fall apart. Professors are often much like counselors themselves, and the good ones will make sure you get the help you need. Even (or perhaps especially) if you're in their class now, they can help you out.

There's lots of inexpensive or free help available on campus, but here's one big caveat: you *must*, despite any or all challenges, see a therapist, counselor, or counselor-in-training who has significant experience with ADD. If they aren't experienced, they're likely to inadvertently make you feel worse. Counselors inexperienced in dealing with ADD students can accidentally guilt or shame them into feeling terrible about the fact that their treatment isn't working. If you find someone with the right knowledge, however, they can help you work past the guilt you're already carrying and put your life back in order.

Taking Meds: Misdiagnosis

Misdiagnosis concerning ADD, depression, and bipolarity is common. I've heard of people who didn't get a proper diagnosis until they were in their seventies! Can you imagine going your whole life with a misdiagnosis and improper treatment?

Being treated for the wrong condition is unfortunate. It typically doesn't help, and it leads to extreme frustration and in some cases, a medication for the wrong condition. Doctors commonly hesitate to make a diagnosis of ADD, diagnosing the patient with depression instead, when the depression is the result of struggling with ADD in the first place.

I've actually lived this: I saw a therapist once who told me that I didn't have ADD and that tests showed I was psychotic. Psychotic! After months of visits, being told how messed up I was, trying antidepressant after antidepressant (I think I became the king of Wellbutrin), and just feeling like total crap in general, I spent the next several years denying the existence of ADD. I was even

> preaching that it's just an excuse, and that I was
> simply no good.
>
> You get the picture: Bad help only makes the sit-
> uation worse. So if you feel in your heart that you
> have ADD, and they're trying to tell you you're just
> depressed...well, frankly, that's depressing. So go
> get some help from a professional who knows
> what he's talking about.

Finding a Doctor with the Right Experience

This is a tough task, and it takes some work. Typically, it requires asking around. Here are some good places to start:

• **Your resources for disabled students office.** They may have an
  ADD-specific professional you can ask, or they could refer you to a
  student who's had a positive experience.

• **Your school counseling center or family counseling center.** Do
  they have someone specifically trained in helping those with ADD,
  or do they know where to turn to find such a person?

• **A school or local support group.** Online sources such as chadd.org
  or add.org can point you to contacts, resources, and support groups.

• **Your doctor.** Ask your school doctor if she knows someone.

It may take some networking, but the right help is out
there. If you're in a small town, don't be surprised if you
have to go to a bigger town or city. And if you find a place
that boasts nothing but positive reviews of their treatment
of ADD, don't be scared away by a long wait. It's not fun, but getting
the right help is worth the wait; getting poor help or advice isn't worth
anything and can even be harmful.

Just Do it

So what are you still reading this chapter for? If you need the help,
go get it now! No matter what, force yourself to take small steps forward. As Stuart Wilde, author of *The Journey Beyond Enlightenment*,

puts it, "step forward into adversity, do not retreat." And take care of yourself; trust me, someday soon you'll feel a lot better and start to recognize your self-worth again. It's in there. If you have ADD you have special gifts, and sometimes you just need a little help getting past the negative messages burned into your brain to find these gifts. The sun really is always shining above the clouds—sometimes we just need to find a way to get those clouds to pass on by!

> "I learned that courage was not the absence of fear, but the triumph over it. The brave man is not he who does not feel afraid, but he who conquers that fear."—**Nelson Mandela**

Suicide

> "Promise me you'll always remember: You're braver than you believe, and stronger than you seem, and smarter than you think." —**Christopher Robin**

MY STORY

It was an autumn day just about four years ago. I couldn't believe how far I'd fallen and how fast. I thought I was doing great, and then WHAMMO! Down I went.

I'd been on a spiral into the sewer of depression for just over a month, kick-started by graduating from college and choosing to do something I did not want to do. I'd ignored my gut, and now I was paying the price. I'd become convinced that my life sucked and that I had ruined everything. I put a new screen saver on my computer that said, "DIE LOSER." (I think that was actually an improvement; before that, it had said, "YOU PIECE OF @#$&.")

My self-image was completely skewed. I had everything going for me, but all I saw was the negativity. You couldn't

Michael Sandler • • • 333

convince me of anything else, and the more anyone tried, the more I'd defend the fact that I sucked, that my life sucked, that I was a loser, and that I didn't deserve to live. ADD minds are always looking for the most stimulating thought they can find, and when they're depressed they need an enemy, someone to fight, an action to take. That enemy was me.

I could destroy myself. To me it made perfect sense.

I don't think I understood the seriousness of what was going on. I'd promised myself I wouldn't drive when I felt this way, but here I was driving, blood sugar low, and talking on the cell phone with my girlfriend—whose efforts to help only made me feel worse. I was consumed with a burning rage, a desire to destroy myself at any cost. I had to end this pain. I had to stop this suffering. I howled something incomprehensible into the cell with all the self-hatred, pain, and anger I could summon, then I snapped the phone in two.

It was GO time.

I slammed the gas pedal to the floor, and the car lurched forward, accelerating violently. I was crying and screaming, an incoherent yet distinct sound of torture, anger, and terrifying pain. I punched myself in the face and loosened a tooth, then made the tightest fist I could and pummeled myself in the stomach with the hopes of causing internal bleeding.

I could feel the adrenaline boiling through my veins, rage bubbling to the surface, chemicals coursing through my mind. I was completely out of control, hurtling into the unknown. Pedal mashed to the floor, I grabbed the steering wheel and yanked it to the side as hard as I could, as if rolling the car was my last and only hope.

Then silence.

It had not rolled.

It had not crashed.

The resonating hiss of hot rubber across pavement faded away.

Except for the faint, bloody whimpering from my lips, the cacophony of violence had been replaced by complete silence. Deep silence, and an eerie sense of still and calm. The car was stalled sideways in the oncoming traffic lane, stopped inches before a ditch.

Antilock brakes. Instead of the brakes throwing the car, they'd lurched it to a halt. I sat there in my car, stunned by disbelief. First there was silence, and then the wailing and crying resumed. I punched myself in the gut, slammed my head into the steering wheel, and cried as if my tear ducts were attached to a broken spigot. The tears would not stop.

Fortunately for the rest of the world, this was a lonely road. Aside from myself, I'd only scared a few ducks. I could never bear the thought of hurting someone else. That'd be a suffering I can't even imagine.

I wanted to stay there forever, but I could envision adding insult to injury if an officer happened to drive by and ask what happened. I was sure I'd flip out, and probably start punching myself again, getting myself arrested in the process. (This has happened to many of us ADDers.) With this thought in mind, I put the car into gear, gritted my teeth, and stammered, "I will not hurt myself; I will not hurt myself."

Somewhere in my second repetition I flipped out again, punching myself in the face, almost knocking a tooth out. I wanted to remind myself I deserved to be hurt. Then I repeated again, "I will not hurt myself." My fists pummeled my gut one more time, and then, struggling, I managed to hold it together. I was almost home.

At home I ate something and felt immediately better. I still hated myself, still loathed the very thought of my nauseating existence, but after smacking myself in the face a few more times I managed to stop to catch my breath and to assess the damage to my psyche.

The Causes

I pray you never find yourself in such a situation. For me, it was a gut reaction to the pain. In hindsight, I think it's from having an intuitive mind and trying to ignore my intuition. I'd rationalized why I couldn't or shouldn't do what I wanted to do…and very dramatically, I was paying the price. It's part of the double-edged sword of being highly intuitive.

But I didn't know it at the time; I just felt the pain and wanted it to go away. For others, suicide is a more methodical, rational decision. Either way, it's disturbingly easy for us to give up hope, lose the sense of joy in our lives, and start searching for a way to stop the pain.

Stop the pain. Stop the pain. Stop the pain.

That message keeps playing and playing in our heads.

In a way it's ironic—the same voice that's trying to keep us from pain is a major part of the problem. The thoughts of that day, even the chemical feeling of the adrenaline coursing through my veins, have burned themselves into my memory, like drawings on a cave wall that remain after thousands of years. I'm sure I'll have them with me for the rest of my life, reminding me of how completely I lost control, how much I hated myself and my life, and how much I wanted to end things right there.

Why is it that with ADD we're so quick to attack ourselves? Why do we look in the mirror and see such screw ups, rather than the amazing people we are and the potential we have?

Two summers ago I lost a near and dear friend to suicide. What she went through I'll never be sure; but I know she suffered for years before she reached the end of her rope, put her affairs in order, and then checked out. I still think about her every day. She had everything going for her—career, health, looks, friends—but she couldn't see it. And that's how it is when suicide's on our minds. We can't see our potential; we can't see the hope. We reach the inevitable conclusion that we can't change how things are or who we are, a dire situation that seems to offer only one solution: suicide.

The Real Solution

Let me tell you that inevitable conclusion about being unable to change is completely wrong. We can change who we are every moment of every day. Our bodies and minds physically aren't the same ones we had six months ago, let alone six years ago; we're constantly replacing cells and chemicals. And unless you're already on your deathbed, you can always change the path your life is on. You can be or do anything you want—if you want something badly enough, there's always a way to get there.

As Dr. Wayne Dyer, author of *Manifest Your Destiny*, puts it, "If you change the way you look at things, the things you look at change." This is reality: if you're having a great day, everything looks great, and if you're having an awful day, everything looks terrible. Did the world suddenly change because of the day you're having? No, of course not! It's all about perspective.

So first off, if you're reading this and can't talk your- self out of the abyss (and believe me, I've been there), *get help now*. Call 911, call a friend, eat a quart of ice cream…do anything to snap yourself out of the funk, even if only for a minute. Personally, I'd grab chocolate. I know it sounds silly, but so is the idea of taking yourself out of the game right before your greatest success.

The Light at the End of the Tunnel

Every time I've seen someone at wit's end, it's been just before things fell into place in their lives. One of my greatest successes in coaching came with an ADD client who'd reached the end of her rope—no job, no money, recently evicted, a child just out of the hospital with a serious illness, divorced, no prospects for the future—but she didn't give up. Just days later the phone rang: she was offered her dream job, with an incredible salary and a stipend for travel and relocation expenses, not to mention the chance to start life over again.

This isn't a fairy tale. It's often after our biggest challenges that our greatest triumphs appear. Chances are they're already waiting for us; we just have to hang in there and let things turn around. With this perspective I thank God and the Universe almost every day for what I went through. There are only a few real defining moments in my life. One was that fateful day behind the wheel. The other was the day last spring when I almost lost my life on a bike path. Both of these events changed me for the better.

I know your situation may appear hopeless, but no matter what the situation there's a way to turn it around, flip it on its head, and transform a terrible nightmare into an incredible asset.

Suicide and College

In college it's easy for one seemingly insignificant fall to make things spiral completely out of control. Maybe you won't take out the car like I did, but when the going gets tough and there's no support around, who knows what we're capable of doing? College can be a double-edged sword: we have so much freedom we can bury ourselves in a hole. And with ADD, sometimes that hole is bottomless.

It's easy to lose perspective in college. I know how serious things feel, and there's pressure from our folks, our friends, ourselves, our past, our professors, and every other source imaginable, all of which can make a single semester, class, paper, or even quiz feel like a do-or-die situation. In the world of college it's hard to realize how important or unimportant something actually is. After all, we're told our entire future—friends, careers, everything—depends on what we're doing right now.

Though most professors and parents won't admit it, the reality is that none of it really matters. Can you get a good job with poor grades? Sure. Can you get into grad school, even med school, with poor grades? Yes. Can you survive and thrive with ADD even if you drop out of school (like Steve Jobs, founder and president of Apple)? Absolutely! The ADD path is one of extreme creativity. We have our own way of doing things, and thank God for that! We shouldn't and can't take the cookie-cutter approach, even if we want to. And that's a good thing. We'll find new ways of doing things that others never even thought of.

Your happiness, sanity, inspiration, passion, and health are far more important than your grades. And chances are, if your gut is twisting in half, you're trying to do something you're not supposed to be doing (ignoring your intuition) or in a way you're not supposed to be doing it. College should not be a time of unhappiness and frustration. It's about having fun, making friends, establishing lifelong connections, discovering your passion, developing your strengths, and experiencing life.

And remember this: in life, there are no grades. If you're here, you're doing great, because there's always a chance for happiness. (Realize this, too: whether a doctor has a 4.0 or 2.0 when he graduates, he's still a doctor.) Somewhere along the way, we're made to forget about the ultimate goal of happiness. We lose perspective. If you have to, walk out of class, skip class, skip a semester, take a hike, travel, go on a meditation retreat, or look inward and face your fears to take a step back from college and remember what's really important.

Inspiration: Success Stories

I once saw **Donald Trump** speak in Denver. He talked about a time he was walking in New York City as his business was crumbling all around him. He turned to his then-wife Ivana and said, "What does that homeless man have that I don't?"

"What?" she replied.

"He has two billion dollars more than me. I have more personal debt than anyone else in the world. I would do almost anything to just be bankrupt."

Ever hear of **Nelson Mandela**? He spent twenty-four years in prison and when he got out, he became the president of a nation.

Dr. Victor Frankl was put in Auschwitz, the most dangerous of the Nazi concentration camps during World War II. He was given soup made from a rock or fish head for his daily meal. Everyone around him was dying, but he survived and later told his story to help millions.

Mark Plaatjes, a South African marathoner who moved to the United States seeking political asylum, was unable to run in the 1992 Olympics when his former country was finally allowed to compete. Forced to sit on the sidelines, he continued to train, and only three weeks after being granted U.S. citizenship in 1993, he went on to win the World Championships in the marathon.

Getting through It

If you're feeling depressed or suicidal, the most important thing you should do is get help. Heck, if I could put my home number in here, I would, because I know from experience that you can get through this. But outside of getting professional assistance when you hit bottom, here are a few other things you can try:

- **Meditate. Meditate. And meditate**—This'll be harder than anything at times like this, but the answers are always on the inside. Clear your mind, and you'll begin to see the big picture and how to get yourself out of this mess. It'll bring you peace of mind and tranquility on the stormy seas, give guidance, and help you ride things out. It may even be transformational to go silent and look inside during times of incredible strife. (See the section on meditation.)

- **Believe that everything happens for a reason.** This doesn't mean that you're doomed to suffer; it means that everything you're going through now may help you achieve all your dreams in the future. Unless you resign yourself to failure, your future cannot be ruined.
- **Seek a confidant.** As I've already suggested, seek out a professor or other faculty member you can confide in. I guarantee that these professionals have helped students in similar situations before, and they can likely help you. Ultimately they are there to help. And don't worry about being judged at times like this—we all struggle badly sooner or later.
- **Get your mind on something else.** If I were you, I'd start listening to an audio book right away. (You can pick one out at audible.com.) You could also go get yourself the funniest video you can find, or munch on some chocolate or other junk food. Try calling a friend you know is in need—help them overcome a challenge or fix a problem and you'll be amazed at how much better you feel about yourself. When we're helping others it's impossible to feel like a total loser, because we're doing some good. When in need, find someone in greater need!
- **Try to understand your depression.** Start brainstorming, and write down everything you think is fun. If you could do anything in the world you wanted to, what would it be? Now try to find a way to do it. Half the fun of establishing a goal is plotting different schemes to see if you can make it come true.
- **Remember that you have not screwed up your entire life.** Everyone always has the opportunity to start fresh and to build a great future.

Inspiration: There's Always Time to Overcome

Ever hear of Lance Armstrong, the athlete who won the month-long Tour de France, the world's hardest bike race, seven times in a row? He did it after winning a fight against terminal cancer with no health insurance, facing financial ruin, and losing his job, his health, his livelihood, and so much more. But he came back from it all, because until they close the coffin, it's never too late. And though it's hard to keep this in perspective, we're seriously young. People have gone to med school in their forties and fifties. People who started playing sports in their thirties have won gold medals in the Olympics. John Glenn returned to space at age seventy-seven. You have time, and no matter the problem, there's always a way to overcome it.

• **Flip things on their heads.** Time and time again, I've seen that the day after our lowest low is just when a miracle happens. It's almost as if these miracles are waiting to happen; they just want to see if we'll push through and hang around long enough to see them. So hang in there, no matter what, and you'll be amazed at the results. And if the situation's really as bad as it seems, just think of the book you could write and the millions you'll make by talking about it on Oprah. If life really sucks, turn it into a bestseller!

• **Check your blood sugar.** Each time I blew a fuse, I guarantee you I was running on fumes, pushing and pushing myself at work and in school and not giving myself time to eat. If you're freaking out and ready to do something stupid, force yourself to eat something, anything, then give it a few minutes to see if you feel better.

• **Take your meds.** Do you feel better on meds? Have you stopped taking them? In such situations it can be easy to shrug them off as not working, but take them first, then think about whether they help or not. When we have meds that work, we often spiral out of control only when we're not on them. Meds allow us to see things more clearly and give us the ability to sort out our thoughts and come up with a solution. (Of course, if you've been feeling miserable on meds, see your doctor right away. They should never make you feel worse, and the wrong prescription could be what's putting you in danger.)

- **Stop fighting the world and turn things over to a higher power.**

> God, grant me the serenity
> to accept the things I cannot change;
> the courage to change the things I can;
> and the wisdom to know the difference.

This is a great time to stop fighting the world and flow like water, letting the Universe guide you where it may. There's an expression that God never gives us more to handle than we can. Remember, you're not alone, you're never alone, and you will make it through this.

- **Transform.** Often when we're at our worst, there's a great reason for it. When you're feeling the lousiest, it's often because you're a square peg trying to fit into a round hole, doing the things you least like to do, which often are the things you shouldn't be doing. Unhappiness, dissatisfaction, and getting angry about our lives are all signs that we're heading in the wrong direction. Use these down times as life-transforming moments, as possibilities for change. Be grateful for them. It's said that it takes something incredible or terrible to change our lives, to help us transform, or to live life fully for the first time. Viewed in a positive light, this difficult experience you're going through will trigger the transformation you need.

Remember, squeezing through a tight doorway can be painful, but soon enough you're on the other side and the pain's a distant memory.

The moral of this section (and indeed the entire book)? Don't be afraid to seek help if you need it, and never, ever give up. While it's hard to gain perspective in these times, I promise there are much better days ahead and your challenges can—and will—be overcome.

Now won't that feel good?

> "The period of greatest gain in knowledge and experience is the most difficult period in one's life."—**Dalai Lama**

Spirituality

"All that we are is the result of what we have thought. The mind is everything. What we think we become."—**The Buddha**

MY STORY

Keeping the Faith

What you think about, you will manifest. I was thinking of these words on that fateful day in April 2006, as I in-line skated along Boulder Creek, a scenic bike path that parallels the river headed westward through Boulder, Colorado.

I'd just said a prayer for safety and was skating back from a training session when it happened. I was on the lookout for tourists and proceeded slowly. Suddenly a father teaching his little boy how to walk unknowingly led his teetering toddler onto the bike path, directly in my way.

Hit the deck. Or hit the baby. I thought quickly to myself. I was *not* going to hit the baby.

Instinctively I jumped, twisted, and contorted my body (a move that would've made an Olympic gymnast or high jumper proud) to avoid hitting the infant.

It worked. As I landed I struck the ground with a concussive thud, stopping ten feet shy of the little boy. The boy was alright, but I was badly injured.

I nevertheless remained amazingly calm.

I thought to myself:

Ten fingers.

Ten toes.

Boy's okay.

Sun is shining.

Life is good.

And then, I began to smile.

You see, I've been injured several times before, though I knew this one was the most severe. While racing in Europe (trying to make it to the Tour de France), for example, I once had a safety official wave me through a blind turn into an oncoming car. That hurt. Badly. And it ended my European career. I didn't believe I could ever recover, and though I'd been spiritual up to that point, once I was injured I began to think "God is dead." If there was a God, how could this possibly have happened? Why did I have my career taken away from me because of one terrible oversight?

This chapter section on spirituality isn't meant to convert you or force you to believe in anything you don't want to believe in. But since that first accident my own mind's changed. I've gone through a lot. I've seen a lot. And I've witnessed far too many coincidences to believe they're anything but small miracles or perhaps magical guidance. As I hit the deck, my belief system was unshaken. Perhaps it was even strengthened.

Somewhere along the line I'd gone from "believing" or taking something on "faith" to knowing from experience that spirituality exists and is all around and inside of me (and all of us).

In April, I fractured my hip, severely shattered my femur (one-half inch over and it would have severed my femoral artery), and I'd also broken my arm. They drilled through my knee to put things back together. In fact, the doctors weren't sure they could put it back together at all, and after surgery I required multiple blood transfusions to keep me going.

And yet, as I lay on the path, I smiled.

Life is good.

Everything in life happens for a reason. Only a minute before the accident happened I'd prayed for safety and guidance on my upcoming journey…and now I lay shattered on the ground. Hmmm, maybe this was the guidance I was look-ing for? Honestly, there was a sense of relief. I'd been wrestling with a twinge in my gut, and now I knew it was right on track. I was not supposed to be on this particular journey right now. I didn't know the future, but I knew that in time, I'd know exactly why this occurred. Time not only heals all wounds, it gives clarity and insight.

At the hospital I was told the extent of my injuries. The doctor said my leg might not go back togeth-er right. I told him that I had no worries, that I had every confidence it'd go together better than he ever expected.

When I awoke I could barely move. I was incredibly weak. And yet, I was smiling. Though I was so weak I couldn't raise my head, I knew I'd be fine. Shortly after-ward, the doctor arrived. "I have great news!" he said. "It went together better than I thought it would. I expect you to make a full recovery."

Recovery would be tough. I was given blood transfu-sions for the first twenty-four hours, and it took three days before I could make it out of bed on my own. But I knew I wasn't alone. I knew this had happened for a reason, and that I'd turn this negative into a positive.

I couldn't afford to think otherwise. My belief system and spirituality helped me overcome excruci-ating pain. It helped me defy immense odds. And it gave me purpose and clarity of vision.

Whether you believe in spirituality, in magic, or just in yourself, if you know you're going to make it, you're going to make it.

"Your work is to discover your world and then with all your heart give yourself to it." —**The Buddha**

As I write this, nine months have passed since the accident. More than ever, I know the accident happened for a reason. I feel I'm healthier and happier than ever, that I have more to contribute to society and more compassion to help. I even discovered a new hobby when I was forced to slow down: photography. You see, while I was recovering I couldn't move at Mach 1; instead, I had to go at a much slower pace, and I began to discover the beauty in the world around me. This beauty and discovery alone more than made up for the temporary pain and hardship, which wasn't painful at all...I'd say it was a necessary and beautiful education.

I'm running, hiking, swimming, and cycling again, and whenever I ride pasts the spot where the accident occurred, I stop, say a prayer, and give thanks that it happened. I'm not the same person I was because of this challenge and opportunity, and I thank God and the Universe each and every day.

You, like me, have an opportunity to reinvent yourself, make a great future, and live an inspired life. Personally, I think my prayers before the accident were answered. I was praying for safety and guidance. And then I was knocked flat on the ground. Why? Perhaps because I wasn't supposed to be skating across the country and risking everything.

But this isn't the end of the story; it's just the beginning.

As you'll see below, knowing you're not alone and believing in your inner strength, a sense of spirituality, or just the magic of the world around you can give you incredible strength, power, determination, and courage. It means that you can do anything you want to do and that you can be anything you want to be. When you tap into this inner strength, you can succeed at anything, even—or especially—conquering college. But that's just the beginning. Harness the strength inside of you, and you'll do anything you set your mind to.

Use Your Gifts

Throughout the book I've encouraged you to find your passion, do what's fun, and explore what inspires you. These are your gifts.

I believe our gifts come from a spiritual place. But wherever they come from, I believe they're wrapped around our hearts before we're born. It's our job to discover our gifts and then spend our lives playing instead of working, because when we're living passionately and inspired, working ten, twelve, or fourteen hours a day isn't work. But if we're doing drudgery, an hour or two (or even twenty minutes) can feel like death.

When we find our passion we become inspired and can and will overcome every challenge put in our way to succeed. Challenges stop being brick walls and become opportunities. We're thrilled with everything that comes our way, knowing that we'll tackle every challenge, jump every hurdle, and succeed no matter what.

I believe my life's passion is helping people overcome challenges, discover their own passions, and achieve their dreams. Perhaps it's that I can't live a humdrum life—and want others to live to the fullest as well. That's why I always say that I want to help people overcome challenges and see limitless possibilities. Why aim for anything less?

So it's my passion to help people catch shooting stars. It gives me great joy to do this, and I thank God each and every day for this privilege. Though I still struggle with my own challenges, in particular trying to do too much in too little time, it's not work but a gift or honor that I'm able to do this. I feel very lucky.

I viewed my injury in this light. I was fortunate to have this accident. It was a turning point in my life. Yes, I was going to have to overcome the greatest challenge of my life to heal fully, and live a normal life again. But normal just isn't good enough for anyone with ADD. We have to live life large, chase big dreams, and play with our heart, soul, and mind, each and every day.

> "Happiness is when what you think, what you say, and what you do are in harmony." —**Mahatma Gandhi**

The Meaning and Benefits of Spirituality

Spirituality means different things to different people, and different things to the same person depending on context. Since I'm not trying to sway anybody toward or away from a particular view, I'll call it the loving energy inside of us and around us. Whether you call it spirit, God, the Universe, spirit, Spaciousness, inspiration, or energy, it's that inner strength, the voice that helps you keep going when you need it, helping steer you in the right direction.

The best thing about this inner strength is we can tap into it whenever we need it. As Carlos Santana says about finding your passion, we only need to hit the pause button on our lives or our minds to slow down and listen. This is much easier said than done with our minds, but once we've tried it, this energy or voice within us can help guide us, protect us, pick us up when we fall, and allow us to find happiness no matter how dire the circumstances. It's a challenge, to be sure, with our creative minds, but that's where things like meditation and learning to listen to your intuition or gut come into play.

What Spirituality Means to Me

Perhaps Dr. William Tiller, a renowned physicist, a physics professor for thirty-four years at Stanford, and an author of three books and over 250 scientific papers, put it best: "We are all spirits having a physical experience as we ride the river of life together."

I surely don't claim to be an expert here, but my inner strength has helped me overcome some pretty challenging "opportunities," as I like to put it. What is this inner strength? Simply put, here's what it means for me:

There's no such thing as good or bad—they're just judgment calls in the moment. If we view something as negative, we haven't given the world an opportunity to transform it into a positive. We've closed the door on this possibility. But if we reserve judgment, then viewed from a distance, over time, or from a spiritual perspective, everything happens just as it should. "Challenges" today are merely opportunities in disguise.

Everything happens for a reason. This goes along the same lines. I have to remind myself of this when I "make a mistake," "screw up," or make a "bad decision." If there are no bad decisions, just different paths of learning, I'm free to focus on the positives rather than dwell on whatever's taken place. This gives me freedom; living in the present sets me free. Then I can see the magic come from difficult moments.

In the movie *What the Bleep*, physicists such as Dr. Fred Alan Wolf, discuss how we're all one energy and all connected; he says, "there's really no 'out there' out there." We're simply energy. That's the scientific interpretation, which I interpret to mean we're all one. This helps me from feeling lonely, hopeless, or powerless. I feel I can draw great strength from this connection to everyone and everything around me. I've heard it described as the "God force within us." Whether it's a spiritual energy, a magical energy, or just plain physics, when we tap into it, there's nothing we can't be, do, or achieve. When we truly understand the power within us and the fact that we're never alone, we can cast off fear or the belief we can't do whatever it is we want to do. This is not only liberating, but essential for achieving whatever we desire in life. And of course, it's a lot better than living a conservative life of mediocrity.

Knowing that we're not alone, that we're connected by spiritual or physical energy, has helped me reprioritize my life. Instead of being the Jerry McGuire "show me the money" kind of guy, I've taken a more magical or introspective route. Our creative minds and our intuition gives us the amazing potential to tap into this energy. Simply put, we see, feel, and sense things *way* way outside the box. So to me it only makes sense that we care deeply about everyone and everything around us. We have great strength, compassion, and courage to help our planet and its inhabitants and to go deep inside the mysteries of the universe and unravel its secrets. Doesn't this sound like fun?

If you ever get the chance, download and watch the movie *The Secret* (TheSecret.org). It talks about the power of intention or how we can bring about the things in life that we desire. The movie shows how many of the most trusted and successful people in our world, both past and present (such as Franklin Delano Roosevelt and Henry Ford), believed they could define their lives through thoughts and feelings. For example, if you want to become a physician, you put that desire into your heart. You picture it. You see it clearly. And you feel what it feels like. And then you, your energy, and the world around you unite to bring that dream into reality. In short, whether you think you can or think you can't, you're right.

From the perspective of inner strength, magic, or spirituality, the secret is knowing there's energy inside and outside of all of us that'll help us overcome any challenge. It means knowing I'm part of this universe and that we're all connected as one. There is no you, no me, no in here or out there. Everything and everyone is one, all tied together by a power, source, divinity, or energy. Now I call this energy love. But you could call it a cheeseburger, and it'll still give you great strength. This powerful energy inspires me to do what I love and have tremendous success (which go hand in hand). It's also a reassurance that the bottom's not going to fall out from underneath me. Along the way I've seen incredible miracles that help keep me going, often just in the nick of time. And I believe that if I stay positive and meditate, pray, or visualize myself succeeding, this energy will help line up the factors necessary for me to reach my goal. I may not know how I'll achieve my goal, but if I feel it strongly enough and believe it with all my heart and might, I will achieve it—and so will you.

Believe to Achieve

That's exactly what happened when I rode my bicycle 5,000 miles in forty days, solo, unsupported, from Oregon to Washington, DC, for people with ADD in the summer of 2004. I left without a solid plan, without any support, without nearly enough funds, and I had no idea how I'd make it. In interviews I said, "If a leg stops working, I'll reach down and pedal with my teeth." I didn't have a clue how I'd make it, just an inner sense that no matter what happened, everything would work out and I'd make it.

And that's all it took.

It was incredibly difficult, from a crash on a treacherous bridge on the second day which sprained one ankle and the opposite knee, to breaking two teeth and having the screws in my shoes push into my feet from jarring roads, to a fever and a full-body rash. But somehow I continued to pedal. Yet I firmly believe it wasn't me pedaling; it was my inner strength. I was just cheering on the guy on the bike. Despite the most harrowing challenges, somehow, someway, the planets aligned just right to help me achieve my goal. I just knew I could make it, and the most incredible miracles appeared before me.

By California I kept getting lost, and out of nowhere, someone appeared to donate a Global Positioning System (GPS) that mounted on my handlebars. Struggling through the Nevada desert in the black of night, a highway patrol officer pulled over to donate an ultrabright bicycle lighting system. I narrowly missed a tornado and storm that razed the road before me, because I stopped on a hunch in Grand Island, Nebraska. And when my headlight conked out in Amana, Iowa, I was guided into town by fireflies lighting the way on both sides of the road. Miracle after miracle appeared to keep me going. Donations came in out of nowhere from benevolent benefactors. People materialized just when I needed them. Sprinting, I arrived late to NBC in New York City, missing the ADD interview time only to find out they'd had an emergency guest and had moved my appearance time back. A helicopter appeared to guide me into Scranton, Pennsylvania, where I had a massive tire blowout just before the TV crew helped me get it repaired. And a TV crew I hadn't even asked for turned up in

Washington D.C., after my arrival to get a message out about ADD.

It was insane. And I don't know how to explain it other than to say that whenever we put our beliefs out there, whenever we *know* and *feel* with emotion in our hearts that we can accomplish something or anything, this inner strength, energy, or guidance kicks into high gear and helps us on our way. You don't have to believe in God or magic or spirituality for this to occur—just believe in your heart, and you will see success.

Why do I mention this? Because there's no journey filled with more challenges, ambiguity, and unilluminated roads than your following your heart on your passage through college and on to success.

And now the nitty-gritty: things to think about regarding spirituality and your belief system while you're on this amazing journey.

Examining Your Spirituality in College

College is a great time to learn about ourselves, and it's also a time when we want to shirk off our past identities and to reinvent who we are. It's often a time for us to reexamine the status quo, our belief systems, and anything ritualistic (or otherwise) in our lives. It's an amazing time to begin or continue a fantastic inner voyage toward discovering our spirituality and inner strength. Consider college one stepping stone on your path toward happiness, compassion, and enlightenment. Try the following tactics to help you examine your spirituality:

- Make time every day for quiet walks, meditation, church, prayer, temple, or any other way that allows you to think quietly or in silence, listen to yourself, and block out all external distractions.
- Reexamine your life during college. This is a great and natural process, and in particular you should reexamine all of the negative beliefs you have about yourself. We tend to stand in the way

of our own success by not believing in ourselves or by shooting ourselves down when the going gets good.

- Sit down with yourself and actually listen. (Personally, I know that for years I'd do anything and everything to fill every minute of every day so I did *not* have to listen to what was going on inside of me.) This can help you work through all the negative energy you may not have even known you were carrying around.

- College is a great time to question everything about yourself and the world you live in. For fun, strength, or to satisfy your curiosity, consider looking into things for yourself. Read, learn, listen to audio books, pray, meditate, attend services, join groups or clubs, or hang out in the forest, but if you're interested, look into things for yourself. It's a great time to examine these things and see what that is tugging on our insides. Is it a magical power, a spiritual power, or just our own inner strength? Now is a great time to start down the path toward discovery.

- Speaking about that nagging inner voice, hunch, or gut-feeling that seems to keep us out of trouble (or at least warns us in advance), here are some great reasons to listen to your intuition in college. I know, this can be exceptionally difficult for us — after all, we've been told we "act first and think later" or that we're far too rash or impulsive—but if we learn to quiet our minds just a little, to hit the pause button when necessary and train ourselves to hear that inner voice (rather than override it with other people's voices, opinions, and rationality), then our intuition can be a powerful 'conquering college' tool.

What Are the Benefits of Listening to Your Intuition?

Direction

Listen to your inner self, or your intuition, and it will steer you in the right direction.

Listening to your heart and doing what feels good or fun is your spiritual guidance system. You may veto your gut, but if you truly listen to it, it'll never steer you wrong.

Security

Being inspired or "in spirit" gives a reason for our existence on this planet, and with that comes a great sense of security. If you intuitively know that things will work out and if you know you have gifts, abilities, and purpose, then the universe will take care of you.

Freedom

When you trust your gut and let go of fear and anxiety, you're free to focus your energy on what you truly want. This gives you incredible power, enthusiasm, and happiness, helping you overcome any challenge. It allows you to chase your dreams.

What Are the Benefits of Spirituality?

I feel almost silly for writing this heading, because in my view of the world, we're all spiritual beings who have a human existence. In quantum mechanics, the study of physics at the smallest level, it turns out there's nothing but energy in the world and that thoughts (the non-physical) affect things (the physical). Therefore, we're all spiritual beings, we all have a spiritual existence, and we couldn't be non-spiritual even if we wanted to. So, what are the benefits of spirituality? Spirituality is everywhere, whether we want it or not. With that said, plugging into your spirituality and understanding what it really means to you can give you great strength, power, conviction, peace of mind, health, wealth, happiness, compassion, and whatever it is you desire.

Specifically for college, plugging into or connecting to your spirituality gives you the following:

- **Strength.** When the going gets tough, spirituality gives you the reassurance that you're connected to something greater that will give you strength when you need it.
- **Belief in yourself.** When we think we're all alone, it's easy to see ourselves as a cosmic mistake, an error, something that's not worthy of anything or capable of any good. Once spirituality opens our eyes to the fact that this isn't the case, that we're all born with gifts and a purpose, it becomes much easier to see the positives in our lives.

- **Manifestation of your desires.** There used to be a schism between science and religion—the belief that one or the other was absolutely right, that there was no need for both—but now we live in an amazing and exciting time. We've got quantum mechanics, which shows us that thoughts, emotions, and the very act of observation change our world on the most fundamental level.

- **Knowledge that you're not alone.** I used to get lonely a lot. Inner spirituality helped me realize that I was never alone. No human being truly is. Through the energy that holds us and everything else together, we are connected to everyone and everything around us.
- **Freedom from anxiety and fear.** We tend to be the biggest impediments to our own success: we don't believe in ourselves or

give ourselves credit. We wind up hedging our bets, making bad decisions, or giving up entirely, sometimes right before our greatest triumphs. Spirituality can reassure us of our own abilities and give us the courage and strength to go for it.

What Are the Advantages to Spirituality and Intuition in College?

Spirituality can help you find direction in choosing courses, majors, clubs, extracurricular activities, and even friends. It can be the internal guidance system that keeps you out of trouble—

 remember the last time your gut was screaming at you not to do something and how much you regretted it when you did it anyway?—and it can even help us figure out what to do after college.

It can help you establish confidence in yourself, and can even lead you to take courses or majors that you might not have dared to take because you didn't think you'd succeed.

Tapping into our inner strength can get us through the toughest exams, projects, and late-night study sessions. It can give us a reason to go on and overcome obstacles when we'd much rather throw in the towel.

The decisions we're faced with in college often don't have clear right or wrong answers, and with ADD it's easy to become frozen in inaction or to act impulsively and make poor decisions. Taking the time to get quiet and listen to our gut improves our decision-making ability. At the very least, it gives us time to think about the possible consequences of our actions.

Chances are, at some point in college you'll slip into the abyss of danger or depression. But if you can remember what's in this chapter and stay connected to something greater than yourself, you'll turn this time into a positive experience, something to grow from and learn about, rather than a setback.

Out of the Abyss

I used to say that college is the best time to work through ADD issues: when we're free to fly from the nest, even if we plunge a bit, we start to figure things out and then really take flight. However, I've recently rethought this a bit. Until I plunged on my own, I didn't realize how far or how quickly I could fall. That is one of the reasons staying connected to a source of energy that can pull you through the darkest times is so essential when you're in college with ADD.

I can remember my darkest days. Just after graduating, I went from feeling on top of the world to falling into the deepest abyss of ADD self-misperception: fear, hatred, and self-loathing. Somewhere in the midst of my desperation I caught an infomercial/telethon on PBS with Dr. Wayne Dyer. The spiritual self-help guru said something along these lines: If you believe in an all-intelligent God or source of everything and know this source created everyone and everything, including you, then you can't be a mistake. Therefore, you must be a good person. Because if you think you're a bad person, then you're telling God he was wrong.

That point hit home with me: who was I to tell God or the Universe he was wrong for creating me and that I must know better than the source of everything? And as a creation of God, I vowed to start treating myself better and to stop the verbal and physical self-abuse. Slowly but surely, this helped me start the steady march to where I am today.

Viewed a different way, if God's everywhere and we're anywhere, then spirituality's a part of us as well. Or if we're all energy, and there's really no separation between anyone and anything, then we're all connected and all a tiny little piece of spirit, as Dr. Dyer went on to say (and as I've heard Deepak Chopra, Stuart Wilde, and many, many others say). We're not human beings having a spiritual existence, but spiritual beings having a human experience.

Kind of makes you think, doesn't it? In my case, particularly after learning about how our thoughts, emotions, and actions could bring about changes in our lives, I got *really*, really careful about what I said to myself!

Perhaps the most important thing you'll gain from your spiritual side is a belief in yourself. Spirituality isn't about which religion's beliefs are right or wrong. It's about using a belief system, whatever your beliefs, to help you overcome your ADD challenges and achieve greatness.

Info: Different Types of Spirituality

Our beliefs and religion are both very personal things, but I think religion differs from spirituality in one key way. A religion is a historical and cultural belief with rules, laws, and mandates that by definition sets up a good side and an evil side. Spirituality, however, is just a belief in something bigger than ourselves, a connectedness to an energy or spaciousness in the world around us. There's room in spirituality for any religion.

Viewed yet another way, religion is the politics of God while spirituality is perhaps the language of God.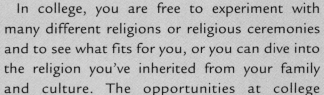

In college, you are free to experiment with many different religions or religious ceremonies and to see what fits for you, or you can dive into the religion you've inherited from your family and culture. The opportunities at college abound. There are often groups for dozens of religions and belief systems, likely some you've never even thought about.

In college I ended up attending dozens of Native American ceremonies. It was incredible! I personally checked out many churches, temples, a sweat lodge (Navajo Hogan), yoga classes, Pilates classes, group prayer sessions, and midnight prayer sessions, and I even went to Rome on a school break to check out Easter Mass with fellow students. I feel as though all of these different activities kept me close to the higher power and energy that connects us all.

Making Your Spirituality Work for You

- **Begin trusting yourself.** This is the hardest thing for us to do. After all, we've been told our whole lives that we're wrong and everyone else is right. But that's not the case. We need to live our own lives, using our own unique gifts. So follow your intuition. If you want to study cinema, take cinema classes or transfer to a film school. Want to study exercise physiology? Take all the classes you can get your hands on. Need time off to figure out what you want to do? Take it. Steve Jobs did, and he never went back—but he did manage to found Apple Computers in the meantime.

- **If it feels good and you're not hurting anyone else, do it.** Take the fun courses and put off the other courses, or just don't take them at all. Terrible at math? See if you can get a reduced number of math requirements or a waiver as a student with a disability. Make sure you take courses with professors who are sympathetic to those with ADD, and take the fun road, not the hard road. You don't have to do it the same way as everyone else. You are not everyone else.

- **Think big.** As ADDers, thinking big and living large is the only way we'll succeed. A belief in God, spirit, energy, spaciousness, the Universe, or something bigger than yourself can help instill the confidence you need to make big dreams a reality.

- **Be altruistic.** This doesn't necessarily mean selling all of your possessions, wearing a robe, shaving your head, and living like a pauper—unless that's what you want to do. (Send me photos!) But since we have incredible gifts, and we're bored and frustrated with the existing paradigms, we might as well help change the world. Instead of just going for the money, find ways to help others, help the planet, make people happy, make people feel better, or make the world a better place. So what if you're not working nine to five or doing the daily grind? Who's to say you can't get rich and help others at the same time?

- **Don't worry about others' opinions.** If God, Source, or spirituality is inside of each and every one of us and we're not mistakes (and we're not), then we are the only ones who can judge us. This gives us the freedom to be who we truly are and were made to be, rather than live our lives according to other people's standards.

- **Don't sweat your mistakes.** Our creative minds ensure we'll make plenty of mistakes, but if we know we're not alone, that we're here for a higher purpose and that we're helping others, what do mistakes matter? Furthermore, if we know that everything happens for a reason, then there's no such thing as a mistake. It's all just part of our path.

- **Manifest your reality.** According to Frank Alan Wolf, PhD, physicist, and author of *Dr. Quantum Presents a User's Guide to Your Universe* (a pretty fun book or audiobook if you get a chance to check it out), science has provided us with physical evidence that our thoughts affect our realities. This means that we can have or be or do anything we want in life. All we have to do is believe it, see it, and feel it in our minds, and we can create it in our existence. We are the creators of our own destinies.

- **Live without fear.** How much more attention could you put into the tasks at hand if you weren't worrying about the mistakes of the past or those that may come tomorrow? Realize that everything happens for a reason.

- **Don't fight against the universe.** You want to be like water flowing downhill: you want to flow with the world, not fight it. You can't be a square peg in a round hole; if doors open and it's easy and fun, that's the spirit's way of showing you the path you should take. If doors keep closing, that's the spirit, too—suggesting that you go another way. As Chevy Chase said in *Caddyshack*: "Be the ball." A sense of spirituality helps us live in the moment.

- **Give up the need to be right.** If we're just part of a whole, a piece of the interconnected universe, then we're all one. Therefore, judging others, getting upset with others, or hurting others only hurts us. When we give up the need to be right, we gain a sense of freedom and lose the negative baggage that builds up in our heads and ruins our days.

- **Forgive yourself.** Forgive yourself. Forgive yourself. Forgive Yourself.

> "Men often become what they believe themselves to be. If I believe I cannot do something, it makes me incapable of doing it. But when I believe I can, then I acquire the ability to do it even if I didn't have it in the beginning"—**Mahatma Gandhi**

Meditation

> "People asked me if I could fly, I said, 'yeah...for a little while.'"—**Michael Jordan**

Did you ever have the chance to watch Michael Jordan or any other of the basketball greats when they were on fire? It was said that they were "in the zone" and could do no wrong. To them, they didn't throw the ball to the net, they brought the net back to the ball.

Ever felt completely calm and relaxed going into a test, unsure why exactly you felt so good, and then couldn't believe how the answers just came to you?

Being "in the zone," finding the answers, and making awesome decisions by trusting your gut are all the result of having your mind in a meditative state. In this state, your mind quiets, answers you think you don't know suddenly appear, instant guidance becomes accessible, and like MJ shooting the ball, you can do no wrong.

You are in the zone.

So, want to get in the zone for college and for life? Want to find the answers to all of life's questions, even the meaning of life? So does everyone else. But I bet you didn't know this: you already have the answers. They're inside of you. You have the power to heal, focus, quiet your mind, direct your life, and be happy in each and every moment, all at your disposal. You just need to learn how to tap into this infinite energy and wisdom inside of you.

Whether you're looking to decrease stress and quiet your mind, gain increased concentration and focus, find incredible peace, determine your life's direction, gain instant happiness, or answer *all* of your life's questions, I don't think it can be overstated: the answers can be found through meditation.

With our creative minds, we're highly intuitive; when we learn to go inside and trust our intuition, it never steers us wrong.

In simplest terms, meditation shuts off the chatter and lets us plug in to our intuition, our bodies, our spiritual nature, the Universe, or the world around us. When I became serious about making this book, I began meditating. It helped me figure out how to get a proposal together, how to get it mailed out, even who to mail it to; and more than that, it helped keep me on track so I'd take it from a pipe dream to a reality.

Since then I've played with meditation a lot, and so have many of the students (and other ADDers and people with creative minds) I work with. When I was injured in the spring, it was meditation that got me through and turned a potential negative into an incredible positive. Meditation has helped students who were failing classes or tests turn things completely around, acing what had been their most difficult classes. And I've seen meditation help me and others go from anxious, overstretched rubber bands ready to snap at any moment to calm, tranquil, almost enlightened individuals whom others turn to in times of great turmoil.

What Is Meditation?

Meditation comes in many forms. I'll break it down to three forms for simplicity.

- **Structured movements.** Some forms, such as Tai Chi, yoga, and Qi Jong, focus on structured movements and poses, flexibility, and balance to strengthen your focus and quiet your mind.
- **Mindfulness through breathing.** Other forms concentrate on breathing exercises you can do while sitting, laying down, walking, doing a repetitive task, or repeating a phrase to yourself.
- **Sounds, mantras, and visualization.** Many meditations involve sitting down, going through a guided journey, visualizing something in your mind, or making specific sounds or chants to help your mind, body, and energy resonate in a specific way for positive results.

Info: Do I Have to Change My Religion to Meditate?

No way! Meditation can be a transcendent or spiritual experience, but it's not about witchcraft, religion, or throwing away your beliefs. In fact, church, temple, and almost any other organized religious gathering is a form of group meditation to connect to God, the source, or spirit. If you've left church or the synagogue feeling energized and revitalized and with incredible clarity of mind, you've just been in a meditative state and plugged into an incredible power. Meditating on your own, like prayer, can plug you in, take you on an inner journey, and help you find a quiet, special place.

Meditation works by slowing the frequency of your mind. Technically, your mind goes from vibrating at something like 14 to 25 megahertz down to perhaps 4 to 7 megahertz. The lower the vibration, the quieter your mind, the greater you can focus and, at the lowest levels, tap into your spiritual, mystic, or intuitive side (depending on your beliefs). Being "in the zone" means changing your brain wave patterns.

There's now music, software, and devices to help change your brain wave states (to a state that helps you either focus or meditate) along with all sorts of other high-tech devices. In fact, high-tech meditation involves listening to specific sounds (frequencies) and patterns to help synchronize the hemispheres of your brain and put you into a specific brain wave pattern. I've been playing with this and think there's a lot of validity to it. It's like taking a mantra (a specific sound or frequency and pattern) to a whole new level. Now there are CDs, software, and even a few portable devices to help you get into this state.

Since I'm into "simple is beautiful," I think one of the coolest things I've found is the theta wave metronome meditation from Stuart Wilde's CD *The Art of Meditation*. A simple, repetitive beeping noise (almost like an alarm clock) helps get your brain vibrating in tune with the frequency of deep meditation. In this state, it's much easier to block out the world around you and go deep into your quiet mind.

Meditation

A key tech point: Wear headphones when you meditate; it helps block out distractions, gets you deeper into the meditation, and won't freak out those who hear what's coming out of your stereo or computer. On that note, you're more likely to find success in the beginning by meditating in a place where others won't hear you. You'll be less anxious and more likely to go into the meditation rather than fret about who's listening or watching or how silly you sound!

What Are the Benefits of Meditation?

Because meditation can help you achieve anything in life, the applications are almost limitless (just like your ADD creativity). However, here are some of the highlights:

- Better concentration
- Greater focus
- A sense of calmness and tranquility, even in the eye of a storm
- A sense of well-being and faith that everything will be all right and work out for the best
- Decreased anxiety and general stress
- A greater ability to follow through and finish projects
- Greater energy
- Easier time sleeping and better quality sleep
- Better performance on tests, papers, and projects
- Better relationships with others and ability to get along with others
- Greater life focus (goal setting, planning, achievement)
- A better sense of the "big picture"—who you are, why you're here, what's important to you, and where you want to go

For an interesting study on mindfulness meditation study for ADD, go to marc.ucla.edu (Mindful Awareness Research Center).

In short, meditation helps you unlock your unlimited potential. Quieting the mind helps you manifest whatever you desire, whether that's a calmer mind, greater happiness, greater achievement at school, a better sense of well-being, saving the planet, helping others, starting your own company, or becoming CEO of a Fortune 500 company.

Finding Your Concentration

It many be impossible for many of us to believe that we could sit quietly and motionlessly for an extended period of time. However, as it turns out, many of the best meditators out there have ADD-like symptoms. Once we find a method of meditation that resonates with us, we engage our hyperfocus and can use it to take meditation to a whole new level. Plus, we're generally just more open to the world of possibilities, and once we get it, we really understand how meditation can make our minds work for us—which can be an amazing advantage.

> ### Info: Decluttering Your Mind
>
>
> According to Dr. Deepak Chopra, an authority on meditation, healing, and medicine and former chief of staff at Boston Regional Medical Center, "The average person has sixty-thousand thoughts going through their minds every day. The problem is you have the same sixty-thousand thoughts each and every day."
>
> We're stuck in an endless loop of worrying about the past and the future: things we can't change or do anything about. This predicament is particularly troubling for the racing ADD or creative mind because I'm betting we have many more than the average number of thoughts. How can we possibly focus on class, work, our relationships, happiness, or even the basics of taking care of ourselves with that many thoughts racing through our heads? It's like putting alphabet soup in a blender and trying

to pull out whole sentences—good luck finding Shakespeare.

Meditation helps us take control of our minds and slow our thoughts. It helps us stop our overload of thoughts. According to the Meditation Society of America, it "leads to a state of consciousness that brings serenity, clarity, and bliss." These are three things we could all do with a little more of.

The Meditative Process

According to the Meditation Society of America, meditation is a three-step process to take us away from the chatter and quiet our brains.

1. The "normal mind" to the concentrating mind.

The "normal mind" has those sixty-thousand or more thoughts. As we begin to meditate we enter the state of the "concentrating mind." In this state we're still interrupted by innumerable thoughts, but we're able to bring our minds back to our meditation.

2. The concentrating mind to the meditating mind.

With practice, we go from the concentrating mind to the meditating mind. In the meditative state, the chatter subsides and we can focus almost entirely on our meditation. The Meditation Society of America describes the difference between the concentrating mind and the meditating mind as the difference between pouring out oil (our focus) from a jar drop by drop and pouring it out in a steady stream. In the meditating mind, our focus becomes the steady stream of our interest; all other thoughts and interruptions fade away.

3. The meditating mind to the contemplating mind.

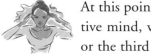 At this point, the really cool stuff begins. In the meditative mind, we find silence. In the contemplative mind, or the third state of meditation, we become the silence.

In short, your ego (the part of you that berates yourself and spews thought after thought) falls away and is replaced by a sense of connectedness, well-being, compassion, love, and knowing. In this state, all things become possible; we shed our fear, our doubt, and any other thoughts that keep us from our goals and happiness. It is also in this place that we're best able to hear our intuition, our gut, or the part of ourselves that's connected to a higher intelligence that helps guide us through life; to find happiness; and to overcome any challenge.

Unsure where you want to go in life or what you want to do? Put that question out there as you enter this state. You'll be amazed at what you find. This is your pure self, the essence of you, the person you were born with and the person you'll take with you to the next life. If you're spiritual, you'll probably call this your soul; if you're not, then it's the inspirational part of you. Either way, it's your higher self, your internal guidance system, and the best feeling in the world.

What Meditation Is Right for You?

If you're like me, you don't want to read any more about meditation—you want to just jump in and try it. Meditation can be a cool new toy. To succeed, we have to become experimenters, figuring out what works best for our minds and bodies, just as we must do with our diet, exercise, routine, and medication. Try all different kinds of meditation techniques to discover which one is a match for you. It's very individual, but no matter which one it is, you'll get incredible results. Ever notice how much better you can think in a clean room, or with an empty desk rather than with clutter and chaos everywhere? That's what meditation does for your mind. You need not be a Buddhist or of any faith at all to enjoy the benefits.

Types of Meditation

I recently did a search online for different types of meditation—the number was staggering! While the basic types include mindfulness, transcendental, Buddhist, Ayurvedic, and perhaps medical, it all comes down to this: many meditation experts of one type or another will say theirs is the best. And they may be right. But for me, I see meditation like choices on the menu of a fine restaurant. All may be great, but some may be more fantastic than others to your tastes. Also, one may be your favorite for special occasions, one you might like as your regular, staple meal, and still others you might like to try from time to time. Just like the restaurant, you're going to have to sample things and find what's best for you.

For us ADDers, I'd suggest starting with a meditation CD, an audio book on meditation, or a class with a guided meditation instructor. (For meditations for ADDers and creative minds, also check out my website, thecreativelearninginstitute.com.)

Guided meditations (in person or on an audiobook or CD) are an excellent way to get into meditation. Without them it's often impossible to maintain your focus, and you'll give up almost before you begin. It gives you the early positive experience you need to stick with it. With ADD, if the first experience is positive, we'll try again, and if not, we'll write it off.

Info: Guided Meditation

 Almost any meditation can be a guided meditation—it just means someone is walking you through the process. Personally, I enjoy meditation CDs. They help me stay focused and bring my attention back if it wanders. There are so many different types of meditation out there, it's great to have someone in person or on CD show you how to do a new one. There are some really cool meditation CDs out there, too: they can help you with focus or with healing or even take you on a fantastical journey toward inner peace, serenity, and discovering your talents and dreams. (After trying too many meditation CDs that had me checking out before they even began, I decided to make a few meditation CDs specifically for the ADD mind. They can be found at thecreative-learninginstitute.com and are led by yours truly!)

What Do Basic Meditations Look Like?

- **Assume the position.** A basic meditation typically involves sitting cross-legged, in a supported position or in a chair, and begins with repetitive deep breathing. (However, you're anything but "typical," so find the position that's most comfortable for you. For me, often that position is laying down on a yoga mat with a pillow under my head and a second pillow supporting my legs.) As you breathe, you may begin counting during inhalation and exhalation, which helps you block out other thoughts.

- **Begin breathing.** Next you may start repeating a sound, called a "mantra," on the exhale, which helps you further block out thoughts and stimulate a particular part of your brain or body (for healing, increased focus, or decreased anxiety). These sounds could be as basic as "ahhh" or "ohmmm" or even specific Indian, Tibetan, or Zen phrases, depending on the meditation and guiding instructor (typically, the voice on your CD).

- **Start making noise.** Typically, you count during the inhalation, then make sounds, repeat a mantra, or focus on a particular goal or objective during the exhalation. For example, count silently as you inhale, one, two, three. Then exhale and say "ahhhhhh," and repeat. It's a very slow and repetitive process, lasting anywhere from five to twenty minutes or so.

  It's often best to start small and work up to longer and deeper meditations. Better to have a positive experience by going slow, perhaps beginning with just a few minutes and working up, than try for everything at once and have a brutal twenty- or thirty-minute experience. That's not the way to build longevity or a healthy new habit!

Go Forth and Meditate!

Meditation helps sort out your thoughts, and gives you some much-needed healing and peaceful silence. It's also perhaps the most important skill that successful people use in their lives. Call it meditation, visualization, quiet time, or reflection, many of the most successful people in sports, acting, business, politics, the arts, and even science credit meditation or visualization with helping them achieve their goals. So go forth and meditate your way to a successful college career!

15

Life after Graduation

> "**Twenty** years from now **you will be** more disappointed **by the things** you didn't do **than by the ones** you did. **Sail away** from the **safe harbor.** Catch the **trade winds** in your sails. **Explore.** Dream. **Discover.**"
>
> —Mark Twain

Wow! If you're reading this section, chances are that sooner or later, you're going to graduate! If you have ADD, do you realize that statistics show that only 5 or 10 percent of students with ADD will ever accomplish this goal?

Congratulations! Even if you're a year or two (or more) away from graduation, if you believe you're going to make it, you will.

So now's the time to begin thinking about your future. Since we tend to triage our lives (focusing on the immediate fires rather than the smoldering coals which later explode), it's best to start thinking about these things early, so we can better steer the ship that is our lives rather than let the ship be steered for us. So let's look at choosing a direction: graduate school and even future employment.

Remember, you can make your future whatever you want it to be; the possibilities are truly endless and limitless, so now's the time to get serious about your dreams. Yes, it's time to get your head back in the clouds, to dare to dream, and then to go for it!

Choose Your Direction

 While many college books ask you to look at life after college just before school ends, I recommend that you choose your direction from the first day you're in school. Don't panic; that doesn't mean you have to figure everything out right away! ADDers tend to bounce around and change their minds frequently, and I'm not suggesting that you tie yourself down today or that you decide what to do with the rest of your life before the week is out…far from it.

And I'm also not suggesting you take the gazillions of "life choices" and "life skills" tests that are out there and treat the results as inalterable truth (though they often are helpful in giving you some ideas). Instead, I'm suggesting you go have some fun.

If you've read the chapter on choosing your major, you already know what I'm talking about. If not, read that too, but here's a refresher: we have brilliant minds—if we're doing what we love. If not, we tend to only get so far before we crash and burn.

You see, as ADDers, our minds open up only when we're using our creativity—we feel good about what we do and we're on task and productive. If we're not using our creativity, we feel trapped and stifled, and it's only a matter of time before we can't take it anymore and stop trying. Whether we quit or get fired, it's not good for our careers.

How do you figure out what career suits you?

• Start writing down what you love to do or would love to do, no matter how outlandish—such as skydiving for a living. Make a list of twenty things you enjoy doing. Come up with another twenty tomorrow morning. Do this for ten days, and see what you come up with. At the beginning it'll be really easy, by the end it'll be really tough, but you'll notice that the best ideas tend to come out when you're really pushing yourself. Don't worry how crazy or out there the ideas seem; this is just a brain-storming activity, and all the ideas are valid.

- Reread your lists—does anything jump out? Is there anything you're dying to do that you could be working on today? We often don't have enough trust or belief in ourselves to really go for it, but for ADDers it's absolutely crucial to pursue what we love, no matter how difficult it seems. If you believe it you can achieve it!

ADD Challenge: Unchallenged ADDers

The Importance of Passion

Here's a good case study of what can happen when we aren't passionate about our jobs. John was the head city inspector for a major metropolis. People looked up to him, even wanted to be him, and he had a large and loyal following. He didn't love what he did, but he was good at it. Unfortunately, tragedy struck his family, and John had to take a lengthy leave of absence.

When he returned, he struggled to perform his duties. On his leave, John had realized he was spending the majority of his waking hours doing something he didn't love. The more he thought about this, the harder it was for him to do his job. Soon, John voluntarily accepted a demotion to get his act together. But the next position wasn't as challenging, and he found it even more difficult to get things done. Over time, John climbed further and further down the ladder of success until he eventually struggled as a part-time city janitor.

This is a true story. John found himself in a position he didn't like, and all it took was one trigger for him to freeze up and get stuck in what he was doing. Once he was stuck, he couldn't do the job

Discover What You Want to Do

If you're totally unsure of what careers would be a good fit for you, relax—you're in the majority. Most people don't know what they want to do for the rest of their lives as they begin college. In fact, when we say "for the rest of our lives," it becomes a big, scary decision and our minds clamp shut. Don't freak yourself out! Chances are you know more about what you want to do and what you are good at than you think you do; you just don't trust yourself.

So, focus on what's fun. Ask yourself whether you'd rather take Advanced Statistics or Human Sexuality, Accounting III or How to Fly a Plane, Scuba Diving or English 101. You get the idea. Right away your gut or intuition tells you which you'd like to do, right? So when you're thinking about choosing direction and selecting courses, listen to your intuition. Go with your immediate snap decision and it'll help you determine what you love. You just have to listen to yourself.

And once you find and take a class you enjoy, it will open the door to more specialized courses in that field and to related classes you can explore. One good course will lead to more opportunities, and soon enough, you'll have figured out where you want to go.

Finding the Fun

- Focus on the fun courses. Chances are, they'll lead to something that will pay the bills, that you're passionate about, and that you'll do well at.
- Get a mentor. Is there a professor or other professional you trust and admire in a field you're interested in? Seek her out, befriend her, and

start talking about career paths and options. As someone with experience in the area, she may be able to help you pinpoint exactly what would suit you best. But be forewarned: everyone has a bias, and if she loves what she does or has been burned chasing her own dreams, she may steer you in a direction that might not be right for you.

- See a career counselor or specialist at your resources for disabled students office. They can help you start to determine direction, to discuss different majors and some of the more creative courses out there, and to find something you're interested in trying.
- Try internships over the summer.
- Try out different jobs over the summer.
- Take independent studies and check out different opportunities. I was thinking of going into law for a while, so I took an independent study course at the county courthouse. Then I took a part-time summer position with a law firm. After both of these experiences I came to the same conclusion: I did not want to go into law.

Do As I Say, Not As I Do

I made an egregious error as an undergrad: I did what was easy, not what was fun. I had always enjoyed studying science, but these classes required extra labs, which meant extra time. So instead I majored in political science, which required only half of the class and lab time. I could also easily write the papers, so this added up to pretty easy As and lots of free time.

But I never thought about what I wanted to do with this degree once I graduated. With a political science degree, the 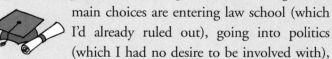 main choices are entering law school (which I'd already ruled out), going into politics (which I had no desire to be involved with), or working for the government (the idea of which I liked even less than law school).

Before college, I worked at a retail ski shop, and after college, I worked at that same shop. It took me five and a half years to get a degree I would never, ever use. If I'd followed the fun instead of skating by in an easier program, I would have saved myself years of misery and the money I've spent paying back student loans from the extra education I needed to make things right.

Getting a Late Start?

Take it from someone who studied political science, business, and computers and now works with people who have ADD: just because your degree isn't in an area you love does not mean you're in big trouble. It just means you need to use your ADD creativity to figure out what you want to do. And this is what you're really good at anyway.

Go back to the drawing board and figure out what's fun—don't worry about your degree at the moment. What have you done for fun on breaks from school? What would you do if you had a million dollars? What would you do if this were your last year on earth? What do you do on Friday nights (besides party)? What TV shows do you watch? What do you like to buy? Where do you like to go? Who do you admire or look up to, and why? Answering these sorts of questions can give you clues as to what it is you love to do.

Start thinking about your answers to these questions. I recommend heading to the meditation chapter and getting in touch with your intuition and quiet mind: chances are all of the answers are inside of you already. While experts and advice can help, the best advice always comes from inside. Go in there and really listen. Remember—and believe—you can do anything you want to do.

Make Your Degree Work for You

Now that you've discovered what you want to do with your life, find a way to make your degree work with it. Want to get paid to ski, but have an accounting degree? Try working for a ski resort as their accountant. Want to hang out on the beach, but have a degree in psychology? Look at an alternative healing program on the Baja Peninsula. Have a business degree, but love to ride your bicycle? Think about starting a new tour company, perhaps one that's more "extreme" or cutting-edge than what's out there already.

Any degree—no matter how worthless you think it is—can be transformed and leveraged to apply to the field of your dreams.

Become an Expert in Your Field

This happens when you're doing what you love. When you jump into a job wholeheartedly, you learn very quickly, and with ADD, there's no other way to jump into a job. In all likelihood you'll move ahead of the pack and open up new and greater opportunities each step of the way.

We all know movie stars who started doing commercials or some other crappy job. We all know CEOs who started in the mailroom and sports stars who started as towel boys. Paul Orfalea started Kinko's with a loan for a single copier and went on to found a two-billion-dollar company. Steven Spielberg purportedly started his career by illegally hanging out at an empty office on a studio lot. When you figure out what you want to do, don't worry if your degree isn't a match. Get yourself in the environment first, then look around, have fun, and see what doors open up.

Remember this, too: what you think about and feel about is what you'll bring about. So get in there and see yourself doing it, feel yourself doing it, and just know it'll happen. Believe in yourself and hold on to your dreams no matter what; you'll make it, even if it takes a couple of years. As long as you're doing what's fun and never give up, you will succeed.

Surround Yourself with Like-Minded People

It's always helpful to hang out with the type of people you want to become: they can help open doors for you and will aid you in seeing yourself as one of them. Want to be in fashion design? Hang out with designers, or join a fashion design industry group. Attend their meetings, go to their functions. Learn from them, and enjoy the first-hand look into your industry of choice.

Get Creative and Make it Happen

Choosing direction is one of the scariest decisions in college, but it need not be. It merely requires listening to your intuition and focusing on the enjoyable things in life. The hardest part is ignoring the naysayers in your head who keep telling you that you can't do it. Instead, listen to your intuition and your gut and have faith in yourself. People you admire have done the same at some point in their lives—they blocked out all the negative voices and just did what they knew they were capable of doing.

The great thing is you can change majors and you can change careers whenever you want to. This is an exciting time to be an ADDer. You're probably best at jumping from project to project, and that's more possible now than it's ever been, no matter what stage of life you are in. Once you discover your passion, go for it—whether your pursuit of it lasts a week, a month, a year, or a lifetime, you'll bring tremendous creativity, energy, and enjoyment to whatever it is you're doing, and that's the key to your happiness and success in life!

Inspiration: You Are Not Who You Were

We often get stuck in the "I'm not good at this" or "I can't do that" mindset. It's a trap. We can do anything we set our minds to, even if we've had a terrible experience at it in the past.

I'm sitting here writing this in one of the most peaceful, quiet, organized rooms I've ever seen. I have more titanium in my left leg than on my bicycle, and I've had a total (including other injuries) of eleven surgeries on my knees. But I now run 10 to 20 miles a day, doing a pain-free, barefoot dance with nature I never expected to be able to do in this lifetime!

So throw out any long-held beliefs about who you are. The past is about who you were, not who you are now.

When someone else tells you what you can or can't do, he or she is also looking at the past.

The past is dead; we have only the present. Each morning you can wake up and redefine who you are, what you're good at, and what you can achieve. Sure, yesterday you were bad at math, but if you want to be good at math, you can be. Wake up tomorrow, tell yourself you're good at math, find a program that sounds like fun and a tutor to match, and go for it. Just keep telling yourself you're good at math, and soon enough, you will be. You can do anything you want if you believe in yourself and who you are. Yes, as the saying goes, where there's a will, there's a way.

"The greater danger lies not in setting our goals too high and falling short, but in setting them too low, and achieving them."—**Michelangelo**

Consider Graduate School

"It's kind of fun to do the impossible." —**Walt Disney**

If you're considering graduate school, congratulations! While grad school isn't for everyone, in today's competitive job market, if you're going into a traditional career, graduate school can be absolutely essential. Difficult as they are to achieve, potential employers often see undergraduate degrees as a dime a dozen. This isn't the case, but good luck convincing a potential employer of that.

Graduate school can be a terrific opportunity for the ADD student who wishes to hone in on a specialty and to get a better job—undergrad degrees in subjects such as an English, psychology, art history, or political science definitely teach you a lot, but they don't prepare you for one particular field of work. You can either go straight from undergrad to grad school or take time off before grad school. Students in medicine and law often try to go straight to grad school while the undergraduate material is still fresh in their minds. But the really important thing is knowing what you want to study before you start, and that's where time off after earning your undergrad degree may help.

Why Graduate School?

In today's job market, you need to have unique qualifications or be an expert in your field to truly get ahead. And as ADDers, we're not good at the grunt work—if we're in boring or low-level positions, we'll likely do worse than if we had greater responsibilities and challenges.

If you know exactly what you want to do and are positive that additional education would help you bypass the competition, you might want to consider going to grad school directly after completing your undergrad degree. For ADDers, momentum is paramount; you might as well continue on while you still have your study skills and school routine in place.

It may also be easier to get into grad school while you're still in school because your professors can write more pertinent letters of recommendation and because you're on top of your game for any aptitude or entrance exams.

If the idea of having a higher-level degree appeals to you but you're not entirely sure what you'd like to study, look at graduate school guide books to see what programs are available and what fields may be of interest to you. Circle in red anything that grabs your attention. Even if it seems like a crazy thing to study, this initial flash of excitement may help you find your true passion—and if you're going to be in school another two, four, or even more years, you're going to need this passion to both survive and be motivated to actually use your degree when you graduate.

Info: Go in with a Plan

For many students, grad school is the right answer, but for others it may not be such a great idea. Grad school is the place to be when you know what's coming next; it's not a place for self-discovery. Many students go to grad school without an end goal in sight and end up drifting, dropping out, or failing out when the going gets tough.

Another few years spent avoiding the real world by staying in school may sound great, but it means additional loans, debt, or time that could be spent working your way up to a high position within a company or building your own. This is your life, and you never know whether you have a day or fifty years left, so make sure this is what you really want to be doing and can see yourself doing for years after you get your degree.

Info: Travel the World

 College can be quite a sheltered environment, and it's often hard to gain an accurate perspective on the world (if there really is such a thing) from there. Before you make the leap back into school and before you've spent any time away from it, consider taking a trip and exploring the world. Time away from school can give you just the perspective you need to know why you want to go back and to motivate you to get back in there and get things going.

In college and grad school, it's very hard to know whether or not you are headed in the right direction. While there may be diversity in race, gender, and nationality at your school, it doesn't change the fact that there are only three types of people there: students, professors, and other faculty. Everyone around you is associated with the college. You may need to get away from this closed environment or even get out of the town, state, or country to truly experience diverse opinions and to see what's out there. Travel is often an exceptionally positive and life-changing experience.

I know it sounds stereotypical, but traveling the world, going to Europe, spending time in the Amazon rainforests, visiting Asia or Africa, looking for the lost continent of Atlantis, or joining the Peace Corps are all great ways to find yourself and your future path before you go back to school. They give you the opportunity to gain a new perspective on life, on yourself, and on what's important to you, and they can help you determine what you want to do and where you want to go next. It's quite possible you'll come back clearer of mind and wanting to do something completely different than what you had planned.

Choosing Your Direction

Deciding whether or not to go to grad school and what to study is basically choosing a career. After all, if graduate school doesn't give you a specific job, such as being a pediatrician, it will at least give you a general field, such as medicine.

Ultimately, this decision is going to come down to a gut or intuitive feeling. But before you decide, you need to have as much information as you can. Below you'll find a list of tools that will help, but perhaps the most important tool is talking with others and then listening to your heart.

• Read books about graduate school. Look at the different programs available, and see what piques your interest. Can you see yourself doing this for the rest of your life? Would it be fun? Are a lot of people already doing this, or is it a new or growing field?

- Read up on the careers that interest you. See which are growing, where skilled people are needed, and what the predicted long-term trends are.
- Talk with mentors, career counselors, and other professionals. In particular, talk with people who know you and see what they would recommend. Of course, faculty members could potentially recommend a degree to keep you at their school, so make sure you seek advisors outside of your college.
- Join professional trade groups. Interested in computer animation? See if there's a computer animation trade group in your area. As a student you can usually join for free or for a fraction of the cost of a full member. Trade groups are great places to make connections for future jobs, to find references, and to help determine which schools to consider.
- See a career coach, life coach, or ADD coach to help you sort through all this information. He or she will look at where you've been successful in life, why, and what would be a match for your passions. Coaches won't give you the answers, but they can help you on your path to self-discovery.

Getting In

Are you sure grad school's your gig? If I haven't scared you away yet, here are some great tips to help you get accepted at the right place.

- When it comes to graduate schools, names do matter. It's not so much a difference in education as in the doors that will be opened for you. These opportunities come from connections made while in school and the reputation of the school or program. Get yourself into the best school you can, even if it means waiting a year or more.
- Choose a school that is well known for your study area. Just because a school is well known for its MBA programs does not mean it's just as good or as reputable in the sciences. So choose based on the program, not just the name of the school. Again, you want to make sure the connections you make and the prestige of the degree will open doors for you once you're out.

- Don't be intimidated by a highly regarded program or school. If you can get in, you'll make it through. We tend to rise to the occasion—it's often easier for us to thrive in a more aggressive program than in an easier one. Perhaps more importantly, the professors at an upper-end institution may be better suited to help get you through the process. So aim high, but apply to some backup programs just in case.
- Get good references. Great references make a huge difference when it comes to getting into graduate school.
- Look for alumni from a particular school or degree program. If any of your professors or other members of the department graduated from there, their recommendations will have greater clout.
- Get a recommendation from the head of the department of the field you wish to study. Do you know the department chair, or have you or can you take a class or do work for this person? His or her recommendation is much more effective than a regular professor's.
- Get a recommendation from an expert in the field in which you wish to study. A recommendation from such an individual (such as someone who frequently writes and is published in your field of interest) makes another great candidate for a letter of recommendation.

  - Consider working for, volunteering for, doing internships or assistantships for, or taking classes from any or all of the sorts of people listed above.

- If you need internships or volunteer positions to qualify for a graduate school program (such as interning in a veterinary clinic before applying to veterinary school), make sure you get these hours in over the summer or immediately after graduating. If you're not vigilant, you may have to hold off on applying until you can finish these.
- Get a creative undergrad degree. If you want to go to med school, don't get a premed or biology degree—everyone else has one, too. Instead, consider something creative, such as art history or political science. Graduate programs often aren't looking for clones but for well-rounded and diversified class members.

- Bring a unique career path. Are you getting a job before graduate school? If grad school's your long-term plan, figure out what will both give you the experience you need and set you apart from the pack.
- Write a creative application essay. While it seems like a risk, a creative essay (both in your application and in your grad school aptitude tests) can really make you stand out, particularly if you're aiming for a less creative discipline like medicine or computer science.
- Take the time to study and to be as prepared as possible for the aptitude test or entrance exam. Take a prep course if possible, and see if accommodations such as extra time are available for students with ADD or other disabilities.
- Make sure you take all of your prerequisites before you graduate, or you'll have to take extra courses after college, potentially before you even apply to grad schools.
- If your undergraduate major is closely related to the field in which you'll be applying, put your greatest time and effort into these classes; while your grades are important in all classes, your performance here will be closely scrutinized as a potential reflection on your future graduate school performance.

Deciding When to Start Looking

If you are still an undergrad and are serious about going to grad school straight out of college, it's never too early to start thinking about it.

First off, you've got to nail down your prerequisite classes. Then there are potential volunteer hours in your field depending on where you want to attend, connections to make with good potential references, and preparation for the entrance exams. All of this typically takes at least a year or two, so you can generally get by with starting in your junior year. However, for some programs, such as human or veterinary medicine, you'll need to start earlier than that. If you know you're going, the key is to plan and strategize early so it's not all crunch time at the end.

Beware of graduate programs where all of the emphasis for professors is on "publish or perish." In these programs, you may find the professors unavailable or disinterested in their teaching. They may see it as a hassle and an inconvenience that takes them away from their "real work" of getting published. At these schools or programs, it's particularly difficult to get the help you need if you're a student struggling with a disability; they're more do-it-yourself or self-service.

In graduate school programs, I've found that the best professors are those who still have a foot grounded in the business world or their particular field outside of campus. These professors are often very concerned about their reputation outside of school. Because of this, they believe each student who passes through their classes represents their stamps of approval in some way, shape, or form. As a result, they're going to make sure you know the information inside and out. This can make for some really tough classes, but these professors are the best in the world for letters of recommendations later on or to work with on a thesis that will get you hired by the best after you graduate. They also make good advisors because they have more real world, hands-on experience.

The biggest challenge with these sorts of professors is just having them around to get the help when you need it, because typically, when they're not in class, they're not at school. They're working or consulting elsewhere for a living. However, this

Graduate School

also means their classes are more relevant, up-to-date, and cutting edge than those of professors who've isolated themselves in academia.

Find What You Love

Grad school has to be about passion. If you're not passionate about what you're studying, why in the world would you get another degree?

Grad school's a great way to gain expertise in almost any field of your choice, to start down a path toward a successful career, and to gain the honor and prestige that goes with the title you'll earn. But watch out: as an ADDer, you might fall into the trap of leaping first and looking second. Make absolutely sure that you're passionate about the career or life direction of your choice before you jump in. If you're not, take some time off and see the world or start a job, but most of all, listen to your heart. Then, when the desire to go back to school is so strong you can't think about anything else, go for the best program you can, jump in with both feet, and swim with all of your might!

> "The problems of the world cannot possibly be solved by skeptics or cynics whose horizons are limited by the obvious realities. we need men who can dream of things that never were."
> **—John F. Kennedy**

16

ADD and Your Career

"**If one** advances confidently **in the direction** of one's dreams, **and endeavors to live** the life **which one** has imagined, **one will meet** with success **unexpected** in common hours."

—Henry David Thoreau

Having a super creative mind or ADD and a career is a funny thing; if your job matches your passion, there's no limit to your potential. But if you're working in a job that doesn't inspire you and keep your interest, not only will you not be happy but you'll run the risk of self-destructing.

Many of the greatest contributors in business, the arts, politics, the sciences, and sports have ADD. They succeeded where others failed because of the match between the passion in their hearts and the career direction they chose. Typically, it wasn't an easy path; it was a path others dissuaded them from taking. But they followed their hearts, worked their tails off, and found incredible success.

Many other ADDers find themselves bouncing from job to job, career to career, or get-rich-quick scheme to get-rich-quick scheme because they weren't in alignment with their passions, interests, and talents. I've seen ADDers like me struggle for years and years until they found what they loved, and the next minute they were earning six-figure incomes—or more. Conversely, I've seen others fight their way to the top, realize it wasn't what they loved, and plummet through the floor after their brains clamped shut.

You have a couple advantages over everyone else. First, you have the opportunity to think about this now, while you're in college, before you're stuck in a role you don't love. Second, you have a mind that is capable of anything as long as you're doing what makes you happy.

In this section we'll look at ways to find and to begin the career that's right for you. Bear this in mind: always trust your intuition. If you're on a path that seems sensible but doesn't really interest you, nine times out of ten it won't work out well. However, if it seems like what you're doing couldn't possibly be a career because it's so much fun, you're probably right on track!

Discovering the ADD Career Challenges

Having ADD can be a double-edged sword; we're easily excited by job possibilities, career directions, or future paths, but unless we take the time to step back and examine things in detail, we often either head in a poor direction or run into a dead end. And once we realize we're not going where we'd like to go, we're likely to freeze up and get stuck. I've seen it in other ADD students and in myself: one minute we're on top of the world as salesman of the month or employee of the year, and the next minute we're being demoted or let go, we're running for the door with a lynch mob in hot pursuit.

It's important not to jump into something out of the pure joy and excitement of having found something to latch onto, something we're good at. We need to make sure it's the right thing first.

External Motivators

We're often talked into pursuing a career because others would like us to, just for the money, or because we're motivated a bit by pride. Of course it feels great when your folks love and approve of what you're doing, but it's a trap—it's not enough to keep you interested in a job that doesn't inspire you. You have to be internally motivated to keep at a career. Even money, that greatest of external motivators, can't keep you going once you lose the passion.

Why Do We Bounce from Job to Job?

- We often jump into things without thinking them through.
- Initial excitement helps us land jobs that are a poor fit for us.
- If a position is not our passion, it's incredibly hard to stay with it.
- We don't weigh our strengths or, more importantly, our weaknesses before putting ourselves into positions we're ill-suited for and incapable of holding onto.

  - We don't necessarily like being stuck behind a desk from nine to five.
  - We often march to the beat of our own drum, which can lead to trouble with authority.
- We often need creativity to feel fulfilled, and that can be hard to find in a traditional job.
- We need to do what we love to succeed, and if we don't, we struggle.
- We tend to see only the "big picture," which makes it hard for us to handle the details, particularly when we constantly look at systems and come up with ways to make them better.
- We often take jobs that other people (such as our parents or friends) want us to take, instead of following our own hearts.
- We often take jobs for the wrong reasons (such as money), and the reasons don't give us enough satisfaction or rewards to stick with it.
- When we realize how long it could take us to succeed and move up in a job, we struggle to hang in there through the hard work, monotony, and low pay, or we give up too quickly.

  - We jump into something because the opportunity arises and not because it's what we want to do, and we realize too late that it can't hold our interest.

In short, finding a job, in many ways, is like dating: you've got to be really careful who you go out with. In this case, you need to make sure it's someone you want to be with for the long run. If you don't, once the initial excitement wears off, you could be in big trouble: you crash and burn, lose your job, or feel completely trapped. Prone to complacency and comfort, if we find ourselves trapped, we could linger in uncomfortable security for years before drowning or jumping ship. You don't want this to happen to you; you've worked too hard to succeed and to be happy in life!

The key to being happy is discovering your passion, living large, and really going for your dreams both in and out of work.

Determining Your Passion

To succeed in college, in life, and in your career, you need to know your personality and your strengths, weaknesses, interests, and values (read the "Academic Success" chapter starting on page 147 for more details). As always, I suggest looking first to your intuition for your passion, but if you're struggling to find what might be right for you, there are other tools that can help you look.

Taking Standardized Tests

Most career counselors or advisors say that standardized tests on "life skills" or "life choices" are the best way to figure what career would be a good fit for you. Personally, I've never seen much success with these, but they can definitely be a good starting point if you're totally stuck.

Where to Take Them

 Your career center or your career counselor or advisor should be your first stop. They'll either have tests there or know where they're available. Your RDS office typically will have many of these tests. Additionally, they're all over the web, though you'll have to pay for many of the advanced ones.

Brainstorming

Another approach is heavy ADD brainstorming. This is where you throw your creativity cap.

Try this exercise. For the next two weeks take ten minutes each day and write down twenty job opportunities of interest to you. It doesn't matter how crazy the jobs are (even moon station commander), put down whatever you come up with anyway. What you'll find is that the first ten or so each day are fairly easy, but then they become increasingly difficult. However, your last thoughts each day and in particular at the end of the two weeks are likely the best career matches for who you are. So keep it up, don't quit, and go for the full two weeks; you'll be amazed by what you learn about yourself!

Ask yourself these three questions:
- What do I love to do?
- What would I do if money was no concern and I could do anything in the world?
- What would I do if I only had six months to live?

This should be the roadmap for your career choices and your future.

Writing Down Your Goals

One study asked Harvard students what their long-term goals were and followed up with the same students ten years later. It turns out that those who had very specific, clear goals had achieved them well over 90 percent of the time. These graduates felt very successful. However, students who didn't have clearly set goals did not feel they had achieved a level of success.

So it's time to pull out your pen or pencil and write down your goals. Where do you dream to be in a year, five years, ten years? Do you know exactly what you want to do, or do you just have ideas? Maybe you know how you'd like to feel—for instance, perhaps you have no idea what you want to do for work, but you know you want to work in nature, help others, feel affluent or surrounded by abundance. Write it all down.

Put your top goals or feelings on an index card. Carry this card around with you every day, and look at it at least once daily. It will help you fine-tune your goals and will serve as a constant reminder of what you're trying to achieve.

Finding a Career That Interests You

If you have a general idea of what field you'd like to be in or know what you're interested in doing but are unsure of what jobs are available, there are some amazing places where you can find out what sorts of careers are out there.

- **Career counselor, advisor, or mentor.** A professor you've connected with in the field you're trying to break into is great for this—he or she will know you and your skills as well as the opportunities available in the profession. Be sure to talk with him or her for ideas.

- **Former graduates from your program.** Check out what jobs former graduates from your major now have; the career center or alumni center at your school may have this information. This is a great way to brainstorm and to learn what's out there, as well as an excellent way to find connections that can open doors for you.

- **The library.** Another great way to find out what jobs exist is a trip to your library. Your librarian can help; ask what books or websites he or she would recommend for specific industries and careers.

- **Books.** There are many books out there that provide a general overview of the workplace. Try *The Dictionary of Occupational Titles*, which is a list of jobs from the U.S. Department of Labor.

- **Career fairs.** Want a lot of free pens, knickknacks, and other junk? Head to a career fair. Typically, schools host one or more of these a year, and you can also find out about them online or in a local newspaper. Decent-sized cities often have a career fair once a month or more, and they're almost always open to the public. A career fair lets you know what sort of local companies there are, and what specific employers are looking for in a new hire. They can give you an idea of what marketable skills you have or should get. However, don't panic if you aren't what these employers are looking for: the majority of employers are never at career fairs, because people come to them on their own. If you can't find anything you like at a fair, there are plenty of other places to look.

- **Industry/business leader talks.** If your school hosts talks by business or industry leaders or successful alumni, attend them. They are a great opportunity for brainstorming and coming up with creative ideas, and they help generate the excitement and passion you need to get you where you want to go. These talks could lead to amazing connections, too.

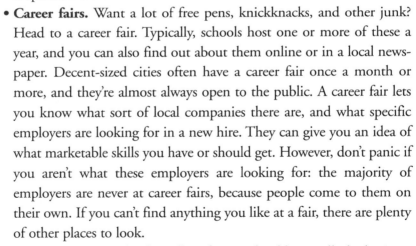

- **Magazines.** To see some creative and interesting options, check out *Fast Company, Entrepreneur*, or other magazines about doing things differently and going big. You should also look at your favorite magazines, such as *Outside, National Geographic, GQ,* or *Elle.* Whatever interests you is a hint to what inspires you and will make you happy and fulfilled and keep your ADD mind satisfied. Even if it seems impossible, look everywhere and see what you find.

- **Successful people.** Use others as a roadmap! Grab books on famous people, successful people, and people you admire (who might be neither famous nor successful) and read up on their lives. Find out how they got where they are and if what they did is something you could see yourself doing. You could even try to contact these people! You'd be surprised at how accessible most people are, and they're often happy to talk about their success. You may be able to get some person-to-person advice.

- **First-hand experience.** If you have a general idea for a career but aren't sure it's an exact fit, check it out for yourself. Look for internships online, in the newspaper, or at your career services office. Or you could go straight to the horse's mouth and visit a company you're interested in working for. Let them know you're thinking about a career in their field, and see if they're willing to bring you on board for a bit. Perhaps there's a project you're qualified to complete, or you could even volunteer or do an internship for course credit.

The Informational Interview

This is perhaps your most important tool in any step of the career process, from soul-searching to landing the perfect position. An informational interview involves contacting people in positions you aspire to be in and asking them if you can meet or talk on the phone about their careers. You are not going in to ask for a job, and you need to be very clear about this if you want their time.

Often they're more than receptive to talking, no matter what level of position they hold. If you share passion and enthusiasm for what they do, they tend to open up and share the real nitty-gritty with you. Perhaps you'll find out this is the perfect career for you when you hear what they really do day-in and day-out. Or perhaps it will have you screaming and running for the hills.

Either way it'll be a valuable lesson, and it will always generate new and exciting ideas. It also tends to generate leads—ask who else in the business you should speak to about this career or field. One meeting tends to lead to more and more, and soon enough, if it's your passion, someone along the way will want to hire you after you're out of school without you even asking for a job!

Starting Your Career

While job search sites like Monster.com and your local want ads might seem like an easy place to begin, these tend to be great places to find a "job" and horrible places to find or begin a "career."

The Hidden Job Market

The best jobs aren't heavily solicited for. If you're in a highly specialized major, such as engineering or architecture, entry-level positions may be

listed on your departmental job board. If not, you'll have to do some serious searching. The majority of jobs are in the "hidden job market": they are unadvertised because they fill quickly and easily, the employer doesn't have time to advertise, or they haven't formally been made available yet. These are the jobs to look for.

I hate to say it, but finding these jobs is all about your connections. It really is whom you know, not what you know. No matter what school you went to, you have as good a chance as anyone to make connections and find that awesome job or career. With your ADD creativity and a bit of pizzazz, it's likely you even have a leg up on the competition.

Sources for Connections

School Contacts

Start with your career center, an advisor, a mentor, a faculty member in your major, or the head of your department; find out whom they know that you can speak with or where graduates similar to you have gone. Once you have a few good names of people in positions you're interested in, set up some informational interviews.

Friends and Family

Still don't have any connections? Ask friends, family members, friends of family members—just start talking to everyone about where you want to go and what you want to do. Finding a job is a lot like a scavenger hunt. One thing (or person) leads to the next and to the next until you finally end up where you want to be.

Info: Spread the Word

If you know what you want to do, think about it, picture it, believe it, and then tell everyone you meet about it. The more people you share your passion and excitement with, the more likely a connection will be made. It's amazing how quickly you might bump into someone who says, "My uncle/father/friend/neighbor/godfather has been struggling to find someone just like you! Mind if I give him your number?" Don't be surprised if this happens.

I've seen students and graduates make their own business cards that give them the title they're looking for—"Future Programmer" or "Next Big Designer"—and that include all their contact info. This way, when you serendipitously bump into someone, he or she will have your info right away.

You should also carry a little notepad with you or use the "memo" function in your PDA or cell phone to quickly get down contact info of any of these potential leads. Ask if it's okay to get their info, and, if you contact them, to use the name of the person who gave it to you. This makes it much more likely you'll actually reach this contact, and it takes the burden off of the other person to deliver your card to the contact.

Clubs, Teams, and Fraternities and Sororities

Don't forget to ask present and former teammates, club mates, and pledge mates if they know anyone who might be able to get you into your chosen field. These connections can be a huge help; particularly in the Greek system, alumni from your house tend to open doors for you or help you on your way. Never overlook this assistance!

Trade Groups

Trade groups can be amazing resources—they're basically PR machines that get the word out about a specific industry, and there's a trade group for just about everything out there. Want to be a professional basket weaver? I'm sure there's a basket-weaving trade group. You can find trade groups online, at the library, or at your career center on campus. Contact the groups and let them know you're a student thinking of going into their field. Typically a membership that costs hundreds of dollars is required, but they'll often let students into events for free or for a token sum. You can attend luncheons, dinners, speaking engagements, and other events where you'll learn about the field, do informational interviews, and make connections, connections, and more connections!

Applying for Jobs

First off, I'll let you in on a little secret: no matter what job you're applying for, no matter how much or how little experience you or the employer has, interviewers don't know exactly what they're looking for in a new hire until they find it. So be creative, use your ADD talents, and convince the company that you are precisely what they need!

Marketing

Getting a job is all about marketing yourself. It's about showing a potential employer who you are, who you're capable of being, and why they'd be making the best decision in the world to hire you. While you don't want to show off what you don't have (do not lie on your résumé or in an interview), be sure to emphasize what you do have to offer.

Make sure that you have an up-to-date, relatively error-free, and professional résumé, that your cover letter is free from mistakes and as compelling as possible, and that you have thoroughly prepared and practiced for the interview.

Résumé

Résumés can be can be extremely hard for an ADDer—we seek perfection, and we're afraid anything less ruins our chances. Here are a few suggestions:

- **Don't sweat it if you fall short of perfection.** Make sure your résumé is as good and as thorough as it needs to be, have a friend or mentor read it for mistakes, and then let it go. Don't get stuck this early in the process.

- **Find a template.** Grab a book or two on résumés and thumb through them, looking for a style or a method of organization you like. You can also find sample résumés and templates online. Base yours on an already successful format.

- **Get help.** See if a career counselor, advisor, or coach can help you decide what information is necessary and check for any mistakes.

- **Think keywords.** Since you likely don't have much job experience yet, look for the résumés that stress skills over work history. These jobs are likely more receptive to a recently graduated hire.

- **Always use strong descriptive words:** Don't write "business major," write "successful business major." Don't write "restaurant manager," write "highly effective restaurant manager."

- **Use their words.** Since computer programs often do the first reading of resumes these days, make sure you use the exact words the employers used in the job description to describe yourself. Make it easy for either a program or a human to see that you have exactly what they're looking for by using the language they've already given you. Be careful not to be too blatant or stretch the truth to make their words apply.

No one may know for sure how to choose the perfect employee, but everyone knows how to eliminate a candidate. Steer clear of any negatives, even if you're filling out an application that asks you to share a previous experience where you had trouble with an employee or management. Remember: Employers are looking for a reason to eliminate you as a candidate. Don't raise red flags and make them unsure about you. Whether on paper or in person, always keep it positive.

Cover Letter

The cover letter is your foot in the door: make it short, sweet, to the point, and catchy! This is your pitch. You have ten to fifteen seconds in the cover letter and/or the résumé to catch a typical employer's eye, and if you don't, it's to the trash with your hard work. Here are the crucial components:

- What position you're applying for
- What they're looking for in a candidate
- Why you fit the bill

As with the résumé, find an online template or an example in a book on which to base your letter and have someone read it and see what he or she thinks. And be charming: this is, in effect, his or her first impression of you.

Interview

The résumé and cover letter serve one purpose: to get you the interview. Now is your chance to dazzle them. Consider attending an interview seminar or practice session with your career center before your interview. The key to success here is confidence, which comes from practice, comfort, knowing the company and what they want, and making your interviewers feel comfortable. Be enthusiastic, share your passion, and have fun!

Accepting an Offer

This is tough, but if you're offered a position, you have to go in ready to play hardball. Research the industry. Research the job. Know how much they may offer as a starting salary, know the market, know what you need, and know what you'd like, and come up with a reasonable figure. Then politely ask for what you want. Don't aim low. Aim a little high. Do this with the complete confidence that you'll do a great job and become invaluable to the company.

And if there's a contract, get legal advice. I guarantee that any money spent on a lawyer now could save you much more money in the future.

Inspiration: How About Saving the World?

 How'd you like a rewarding career that gives you everything you want: money, happiness, a sense of fulfillment and helping others, and a job you'd be proud to tell your grandkids about?

Our brains are often firing at their best (and we're often the happiest) when we're doing things that are unique or original or that we can be exceptionally proud of, such as when we feel we're "making a difference" or helping others. To be happy for life with our creative minds, we also need to express our creativity. Doing the same menial task time after time, without a feeling of satisfaction, of creativity, or of making a difference, can drive us batty.

So how about considering helping the world, saving the planet, tackling global warming, heading in a healing direction or a spiritual direction, or stepping out into the abyss and taking on any one of the toughest challenges facing our people, country, society, planet, or world? Why not work to make this world a better place? Sure, you might not (or might, as

ADD and Your Career

such things are becoming "trendy") make as much money as you would someplace else. But then again, when we're doing what we love, we tend to attract money and success into our lives, and making a difference makes us feel great, which can reduce stress, help us lead happy and healthy lives, and give our children a better place to live! What more could you ask for? Think about it: you'd no longer be "employed" or having a "career," but instead you'd be living your passion and making a difference. As we grow and evolve as a people, society, and planet, more and more opportunities abound: more great ways to make money, earn a great living, or help others. And to save the world we need passion, energy, and amazing, creative minds!

Doing What You Love

We only get one shot at life—why spend all of our hard-earned time, energy, and creativity in a career we don't believe in? If you're donating a third of your life or more to your career, shouldn't it be something that matters to you?

The key to ADD career success comes back to enjoying and being interested in and satisfied by whom we work for and what we're doing. Make sure you're doing what you love and feeling good about it in the process. If you're enjoying your work but find out your company trashes the environment, you may not be able to work for them anymore. We just don't know how to work on something we don't believe in. Trust your intuition and don't compromise your beliefs, even if you're in what you thought was your dream job. You'll find another that doesn't make you uneasy.

Do what you love! Have fun! And save the world! You can do it!

ADD Challenge: The Gray Zone

 For ADDers, myself included, it's sometimes hard to draw the line between okay and not-okay behavior. Is it OK to fudge the books if the boss asks you to? Should you tell them you already mailed the check if you actually haven't? After you enter this moral gray zone once or twice, it will be even harder to determine if what you're doing is the right thing.

So avoid this gray area altogether. If you get the sense that a job might involve gray areas, head elsewhere, no matter how good an opportunity the job seems. Chances are, once you're in the thick of it, you won't be able to say no, it'll be too tempting to do what everyone else is doing or what you're told to do, or the money or rewards involved will seem too good. Don't put yourself in this position—you could be ruining an innocent person's life or finances, and you run a good risk of damaging your future career.

"Don't ask what the world needs. Ask what makes you come alive, and go do it. Because what the world needs is people who have come alive."

—Howard Thurman

"Trust the dreams, for in them is hidden the gate to eternity."

—Khalil Gibran

CONCLUSION:
Be a Student of Your Life

"**Follow your** bliss and the **universe will open** doors for you where there **were only** walls."

—**Joseph Campbell**

Writing the conclusion to this book has been difficult for me. Perhaps it's my ADD tendency to want to either make something perfect or not do it at all. I've gotten better at this, but it's something I'm still working on. Just like you, I'm going through this same process and am on the same journey you're on, maybe just a little farther down the road.

In one sense, we're partners or classmates on this journey, and in other ways, I feel like college students are my children. I sincerely hope I've helped you learn, grown, explore, and perhaps even mature along your own path to wonder, excitement, and success in this world.

As I end this, I feel like I'm setting my children free to fly from the nest, and with no safety net. I want to tell you anything and everything one more time before you go, but there's not enough room here—and that would be insane anyway.

Always Keep Learning

You are not your body, and you are not your mind. You are the one who controls these things. So keep feeding your mind: teach it, nurture it, and help it continue to grow, expand, and gain new strengths. Make learning a part of your routine, make it habitual, and keep learning for your entire lifetime. College shouldn't be the end of your education, but just the beginning.

Systematize the Process

When you find things that aren't working or that are bothering you, step back and look at what's going on. Perhaps you have unrealistic expecta-

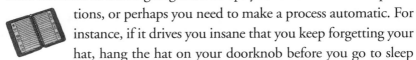

tions, or perhaps you need to make a process automatic. For instance, if it drives you insane that you keep forgetting your hat, hang the hat on your doorknob before you go to sleep each night. No matter what the challenge, the more automatic (and out of your brain) it is, the more likely it'll get done. So tinker with things, figure out what works for you, and then make it part of your lifestyle or routine. Then you won't have to worry about it again!

Express Your Creativity

When we're not creative, we feel like we're trapped or withering away. Never forget to express your creativity in whatever you do. Whether it's cleaning your room or the house, making signs, writing, programming, or whatever, express your cre- ativity to keep yourself happy, healthy, and stress free. Yes, exercise also can be an amazing form of creativity, and something you'll need to keep up for life to keep your mind working at its best!

Relax and Enjoy Yourself

And don't freak out when things don't go your way. Chances are, the events are unfolding just as they should be. If you didn't get the job you wanted, the scholarship you applied for, or acceptance into your preferred grad school, there's probably a reason that you'll eventually be thankful for. If you trust the universe and let go of negative events it's amazing how many doors will open for you.

So don't sweat it. And don't take life so darn seriously. You're only here once—shouldn't you have fun? (And if you're here more than once, shouldn't this be the time you get it right and give yourself some fun?) College is supposed to prepare you for an amazing life, not an early grave. If you feel you're hitting a wall or you're anxious all the time, pause for reflection and ask yourself if you're taking things too seriously or heading in the wrong direction.

Take Your Chances

And don't play life safe. What's the point? We are wired to play hard or go home—we might as well go for it, make a splash, and make a difference (for the better) in the world while we're here. Playing it safe in life is like waiting around for the end.

Do What You Love

Find a job where you can make a difference. Choose a career where you can change lives or save the planet. Go for it all, and do it with all of your heart, soul, spirit, and might. But above all else, do what you love, in passion, in spirit, and inspired. Lead an inspired life. It's the key to happiness.

If you do what you love, you'll become good at it, then great at it, and maybe one day even the best. Because we can't do something halfway, doing what you love allows you to become an expert in your field. And experts always have job opportunities. Do what you love, and over time (sooner than you can possibly imagine) there'll be more jobs for you than you can take, there'll be more people to help than you can reach in a lifetime, and there will be limitless opportunities.

Don't take a nine-to-five job or enter that cubicle just to play it safe.

Soar Like an Eagle

We ADDers can be eagles in a world of flightless birds: we have the ability to soar above the rest. We shouldn't clip our wings to fit in with everyone else, even if there are easy breadcrumbs to be had on the ground. Do you want to live that way?

Keep learning, keep studying, and keep pushing yourself. Try to be the best at whatever it is you want to do. Fly higher, fly farther, fly with more passion, and fly with more heart. We all know we can change our bodies through training. We can become stronger, faster, more agile, and more able than ever before. And we can do the same things with our minds.

ADD doesn't just mean Attention Deficit Disorder; it means "add," as in addition. We have minds that have something extra, something special, something uncommon that others don't have. This isn't a good thing: it's a great thing. This ADD or "ADDition" can lead us to greatness. The farther I go in life, the more I'm discovering that the "ADDed" thing may be our creativity. I'm even starting to think of us as hyper creative, which would explain many of the challenges all of us with creative minds face. It all comes back to living with that Ferrari mind in a school bus world. But when we can express our creativity, boy do we fly!

We can mold and shape ourselves into anything we want. We can increase our focus and attention. We can learn to control our impulsivity. We can become Zen masters, shaping our minds to do whatever we want them to do. It takes practice, time, and knowledge, but we are not limited by our minds, whether we have "ADD" or "XYZ"; we are unlimited because of our unique minds and our creativity, intuition, energy, enthusiasm, and passion.

Believing anything less is selling yourself short. You are here for a purpose, and you have amazing talents and gifts. Your job is simply to discover your passion and watch your talents unfold before you. Live your passions and your dreams and you'll find your purpose, live an amazing life, and help others in the process.

Now go forth and conquer with confidence. You can do it, and I know you will!

"All our dreams can come true, if we have the courage to pursue them."

—Walt Disney

Index

B

beliefs 131, 161, 350, 353, 355-356,
  359-360, 364-365, 375, 380,
  404
  cultural 359
  negative 353
bibliography 197
bilingual 273
bills 141, 143, 252, 376, 402
Birth Control
  and ADDers 263
  pill 263
  problem 75
brain
  chemistry 321
  exercises 29
  patterns 365
  states 365
  vibrating 124, 365
  wave training 24
brainstorm 61, 109, 396
brainstorming 9, 394, 396
budget 3, 38, 41, 128, 130-131,
  196, 198, 227, 249-251

C

caffeine 24, 26, 115, 120
calendar 79, 150, 197
  program 122
    software 33, 83-84, 168
camera, digital 39, 154
career 21, 44, 46, 68, 108, 232,
  273, 337-338, 345, 374, 384,
  403, 409
  academic 91, 240
  athletic 106, 282
  center 394, 396, 398, 400, 402
  coach 385
  counselor 377, 385, 394, 396,
  401
  guidance 231

cell phone 27, 33, 41, 60, 129, 141,
  143, 145, 154, 168, 334, 399
Churchill, Winston 6
class
  material 166, 216
  notes 149, 163, 190
  participation 152, 156
  periods 82, 148, 269
classes
  videotaped 154
classroom
  success 148, 216
  techniques 149
codependent tendencies 262
college
  applications 61
  costs 265
  courses 60, 147
  credit 60, 227
  exams 176
  placement 49
  schedule 329
community colleges 56, 69, 227
computer
  animation 385
  calendars 84
  degree 9
  functionality 163
concentration
  increased 363
  introspective 104
core curriculum
  courses 230
  requirements 89
Cosby, Bill 264
counseling 240, 325
  center 241
counselor 62, 71, 74, 75, 79, 80,
  132-133, 231-232, 269, 330-
  331
counselor-in-training 331
courses
  accelerated 228
  creative 377

modified placement 89
multiple-choice 188
oral 89
exercise
breathing 364
relaxes 97
routine, daily 97
routines, regular 288

F

Facebook 101
faculty members 114, 153, 330, 341, 385, 398
failure 8, 48, 83, 88, 90, 107, 256, 300, 325, 341
family counseling center 332
fatigue 103, 324
fatty acids 114
financial records 73
flashcards 153, 170, 175, 178
colored 139, 178
re-reviewing 153
Ford, Henry 220, 351
Frank Alan Wolf 361
Frankl, Victor 340
Franklin Delano Roosevelt 351
fraternities 254-257, 400
fraternity brothers 256
freshman 98, 115

G

gadgets 37-38, 42
Glenn, John 342
Global Positioning System (GPS) 352
glycemic index 154
high 111
GMAT 9
goal setting 366

goals 76, 221, 235, 269, 291, 305, 307, 309, 321, 325, 327, 341, 351-352, 369, 371-373, 395
Google 200-201
government 271, 377
government, federal 51
GPA 89, 224
cumulative 138
graduate programs 386, 388
graduate school 203, 373, 381-382, 384-387
guide books 382
grammar 40, 186
Gray Zone 405
guidance
counselor 43, 59, 62, 70
system 357, 369
guided meditations 124, 370

H

Hallowell, Edward 97, 262
Hay, Louise 326
health
benefits 102-103
center 75, 113, 125, 285-286, 288
insurance 341
plan 291
healthy habits 108, 112
Henry David Thoreau 17, 135, 374, 391
high school transcript 56
homeopathic solutions 319

I

IBS (Irritable Bowel Syndrome) 113
Illegal drugs 26
immune system 98, 292, 328
impulsive 19, 162, 283, 354
impulsiveness 286

Index

repetition 101, 335
repetitive task 364
résumés 400-401
    professional 401
Ritalin 7, 26
room
    private 47, 177
    quiet 92
    single 47
roommate
    difficulties 138
    distractions 47

S

SAT 61, 92, 335
    scores 56, 61
scheduling softwares 145
scholarships 128, 227, 267, 408
scholastic performance 106
school
    choices 46
    counseling center 332
    counselor 74
    doctor 264, 332
    psychiatrist 289
school, transferring 108
self
    advocacy 69-70, 80
    confident 77
    control 106, 263
    defense 105
    destructing 391
    discovery 383, 385
    esteem 7, 66, 99, 106-109, 266, 275, 282, 298
    examination 170
    knowledge 70
    medication 112, 263
sex education 264
skills
    athletic 108
    marketable 396

negotiation 88
social 7, 275
time-management 18-19
sleep
    deprivation 118
    habits 120
    time, regular 165
social life 135, 138, 242, 255, 257, 277
    healthy 242
software
    dictation 94
    interactive 174
    mind-mapping
    reading 39, 211
    text-to-speech 39, 89, 163, 208, 220
Sophomore Year 60
spell-checker 89
sports
    competitive 106
    endurance 117
    intramural 270
    varsity 227, 277-278
stimulants 24, 26-27, 112, 292
stipend 338
    monthly 272
student health center 75, 263, 286, 289-290, 330
study
    habits 24, 176
    routine 165-166
    skills 382
support
    groups 133, 332
    network 3, 9, 254
symptoms, dyslexia 114
Szasz, Thomas 298

T

teacher ratios 47
teaching style 279